Street-Level Governments

Street-Level Governments

Assessing Decentralization and Urban Services

Robert K. Yin
Douglas Yates

Lexington Books
D.C. Heath and Company
Lexington, Massachusetts
Toronto   London

76274

Library of Congress Cataloging in Publication Data

Yin, Robert K., 1941
   Street-level governments.

   Includes bibliographies.
   1. Decentralization in government—United States. 2. Municipal
government—United States. 3. Political participation—United
States. 4. Community power. I. Yates, Douglas, 1944- joint author.
II. Title.
JS341.Y56   352'.008'0973   75-17644
ISBN 0-669-00076-0

Copyright © 1975 by The Rand Corporation

Published simultaneously in Canada

Printed in the United States of America

International Standard Book Number: 0-669-00076-0

Library of Congress Catalog Card Number: 75-17644

To Barbara and Doris

Contents

List of Figures

List of Tables

Preface

In the 1960s, decentralization suddenly became a major and much debated innovation in urban administration. Advocates claimed that decentralization would dramatically revitalize the urban scene, while critics believed that decentralization would do great damage to the orderly process of government. In most cases, the goal of decentralization was either to improve services or to provide the recipients of services with a greater measure of control over service delivery. Where government was unresponsive or did not provide a needed service, decentralization also included the call for new neighborhood institutions to serve public needs—institutions that did not necessarily have to be built within the municipal bureaucracy. But whatever the form of decentralization, the central theme was to bring government closer to the people being served, and the consequent focus of decentralization was on a social relationship—the relationship between those providing urban services and those receiving them.

This view of urban decentralization—that it is chiefly influenced by and at the same time involves a structuring of the relationship between those who govern and those who are governed—is based on the notion that urban services are the product of policymaking at its point of contact. Urban services operate at the street level and deal with tangible problems and individual residents. Our appreciation for this view has evolved from our experiences in New York City, where during the Lindsay years local government attempted a variety of decentralization innovations: local school boards, urban action task forces, operation better block, and multiservice neighborhood government. Our insights have been particularly augmented by the research environment at the New York City-Rand Institute and our field research in specific New York City neighborhoods: Brownsville, Bushwick, East Harlem, Harlem, Highbridge, the Lower East Side, and Morrisania in 1970; and Fordham, Washington Heights, the West Side, Williamsbridge, and Williamsburg in 1972. At the neighborhood level, urban services mean dealing with the problems of daily life, whether reflected by the diffuse but real need for a continued sense of public safety or by the actions involved in the registering of specific complaints.

The street-level view of urban government also leads to the observation that the different urban services are indeed differently constituted—that the server-served relationship has somewhat different traditions and ground rules in such services as police protection, education, and health—and that the problems of service delivery at the street level are thus not the problems of a single governmental structure but are those of different *street-level governments*. These street-level governments differ in their decisionmaking processes; their internal relations of authority; their ethnic, age, and sex composition of employment; and most important in their openness to the participation and demands of the governed in influencing service policies. In effect, this means that the police service, for instance, is a separate entity that operates independently of and in a different manner from the school system or the health care system.

The street-level view has thus influenced our study of urban decentralization. Our purpose in this study has been to assess the evidence on the decentralization innovations that have occurred over the last decade. We have made little attempt to elucidate decentralization as a political process or to extend our findings on citizen participation to broader questions of democratic theory. Similarly, we have not presented a plea for or against decentralization, nor have we devised a formula for its application in the future. All of these functions seem to be well served by the existing literature. Rather, our study simply sets the decentralization experience in its service context, reports on the findings of our evaluation, and concludes by attempting to explain the experience in light of differences in decentralization strategies and services. To evaluate decentralization, we have gathered over 250 existing case studies of various innovations and have made use of a new case survey method in order to aggregate the lessons from these case studies. We hope that this summary account will stand as a lasting contribution in the continuing effort to understand the problem of urban governance.

Acknowledgments

Many persons have contributed directly and indirectly to the development of our ideas on decentralization. Our colleagues at the New York City-Rand Institute, especially Peter Szanton, Rae Archibald, and Edward Blum, were responsible for initiating many of our interests in urban services. Similarly, members of the New York City government during the years 1969-1972 sensitized us to the politics and management of neighborhood service problems. Lewis Feldstein and John Mudd of the Office of Neighborhood Government were particularly helpful in this regard.

In completing the present study, we most of all must express our gratitude to the investigators whose case studies we have summarized. However, the conclusions from the aggregate findings must not be attributed to any of these investigators but must be considered a unique blending of the existing literature, and we alone are responsible for these conclusions and their shortcomings.

Our study also benefited from the constructive advice of Herbert Kaufman (Brookings Institution), Lance Liebman (Harvard Law School), Bruce Vladeck (New York City-Rand Institute), and Aaron Wildavsky (University of California), who were all generous with their comments on earlier drafts. Their suggestions made revision and further analysis harder but far more rewarding, and for this we shall be always in their debt.

We are also indebted to Robert Hearn (New School for Social Research), who helped to conceptualize the issues of decentralization. He, along with Eveleen Bingham (M.I.T.) and Karen Heald, a member of the research staff at Rand's Washington office where this study was carried out, gathered much of the material contained in the three chapters on education, health, and economic development. In addition, Karen helped to maintain order and levity during the final stages when the crush of time and the crash of ideas threatened the sanity of all. Others who made helpful comments on various portions of the manuscript include Howard Hallman and George Washnis (Center for Governmental Studies), Robert Weinberg, Paula Shapiro, and William Lucas. Finally, Kim Morrissey and Sally Maitland of the Rand-Washington Library, and Judith Fair, Carol Pyke, Vicky Agee, and Julie Casamajor of the Urban Institute Library enthusiastically helped to locate the relevant literature on decentralization.

As with all collaborative efforts, however, the silent collaborators have been the most important. Among those closest to us, Beth Hunt Gorewitz, Karen Brown, Luetta Stephens, and Marilyn Satterthwaite worked with us through our worst days; Doris, Barbara, Susan, and Robby lived with us through our worst days, nights, and weekends. What follows can only be partial recompense for their contributions.

Thus study was prepared with the support of National Science Foundation Contract No. NSF-C817. The Rand Corporation also provided financial support for the book. The views expressed herein are those of the authors and do not necessarily reflect the views of the National Science Foundation. An executive summary of the study appeared separately in *Nation's Cities* magazine, November 1974.

Street-Level Governments

1

Neighborhood Service Delivery: Historical Development and the Crisis of the 1960s

Neighborhood Service Problems

The basic task of urban government is to provide police and fire protection, operate schools and hospitals, and clean the streets.[a] Presidents may focus on and be judged by their breakthroughs in foreign policy, and governors may emphasize their new highways and community colleges, but the men in city hall are the custodians of the sidewalks; they are the "dirtyworkers" of American government (Rainwater, 1967) who must deal with the most ordinary and intimate needs of their constituents. Moreover, the success or failure of service delivery is judged on a neighborhood basis, with different neighborhoods having different reputations for police protection, schools, sanitation, and housing.

Some urban governments try to improve street conditions by redeploying police, sanitation men, or repair crews. Other urban administrators try to improve the reading skills of poor children by adopting one or more of a bewildering array of new educational techniques and technologies. Municipal executives in general try to increase the responsiveness and accountability of their "street-level bureaucrats"[b] by adopting new personnel procedures and by trying out a variety of organizational strategies: sometimes centralization of control and reliance on "professional" bureaucrats; sometimes decentralization and citizen participation; and sometimes the extensive use of new planning, budgeting, and evaluation techniques. In short, urban governments are constantly looking for better answers to the historical problem of how to organize and deliver urban services.

In searching for answers to service delivery problems, urban administrators are, in fact, dealing with the full range of social policy issues—not at the level of lofty debate but at the point where those broad policies impinge on specific individuals in specific neighborhoods. Criminal justice policy is

[a] Urban services are distinctive because they are highly visible, tangible, and direct. They may also be allocated differentially by government to serve the needs of different individuals, local blocks, and communities. For these reasons, the realm of urban service delivery constitutes a natural political battleground. For a discussion of the distinctive characteristics and implications of urban service delivery, see Yates (1973, ch.1).

[b] The concept of "street-level bureaucracy" is usefully developed in Michael Lipsky's "Toward a Theory of Street-Level Bureaucracy," paper presented at the annual meeting of the American Political Science Association, New York, 1969. A short version of the paper has appeared as "Street-Level Bureaucracy and the Analysis of Urban Reform" (1971) and a revised longer version will appear in Hawley and Lipsky (forthcoming).

ultimately about the way policemen behave on the beat and how judges operate in night court; educational policy reflects what is being done in a particular classroom; housing policy is what is built and torn down in a given neighborhood; and welfare policy often reduces to the relationship between social workers and their clients.

In observing the cities of yesterday and today, recent critics have focused on such service problems as the rigidity of bureacracy, the insensitivity of police and teachers, or the inefficiency of garbage collection. (Rogers, 1968; Wasserman, 1970; Kotler, 1969; Fantini, Gittell, and Magat, 1970; Nordlinger, 1973; and Farr, Liebman, and Wood, 1972.) In particular, the critics have seen low-income minority neighborhoods as lacking adequate services and bearing the brunt of an incompetent or inequitable (or both) system of urban service delivery (Marris and Rein, 1967; the *Report of the National Advisory Commission on Civil Disorders*, 1968; the report of the National Commission on Urban Problems, 1968; Altshuler, 1970; Lipsky, 1970; Bellush and David, 1971; and Greenberg, 1974.) Such criticism of city government reached its height in the 1960s when the "urban crisis" was rediscovered. In part, this discovery was stimulated by such books as Michael Harrington's (1962) *The Other America*; but, more important, it was brought home by the sounds of civil rights marches and the anger of black protest in the city. For a brief time when the Great Society's social programs were first being developed and implemented, fear that our large cities were collapsing was matched by hope that creative public interventions could "solve" urban problems. But soon this optimism gave way to what Aaron Wildavsky (1968) has aptly called the "empty-headed blues": the result of desperately wanting to "do something" about the cities while not having the slightest idea what to do and suspecting at the same time that nothing would work anyway.

The dominant public theme for dealing with the service crisis of the 1960s was *decentralization*. Although new technology and the use of the computer were producing managerial reforms of a centrist nature, the greater attention—and greater hopes—were invested in a myriad of urban decentralization programs. Many of these programs aimed for ultimate decentralization by attempting to involve neighborhood residents in governmental affairs. Whatever the program, decentralization meant an attempt to place more decisionmaking functions at the lowest level of service delivery, or at the point of contact between citizens and government. Often it did not seem to matter that these programs did not have attainable goals, for decentralization represented first and foremost the attempt to "do something" about cities.

Decentralization did not suddenly appear as a gimmick in the urban world of the 1960s. Rather, its roots are deeply imbedded in the history of service delivery; and, in fact, decentralization has special prominence today because of the way the historical tensions between bureaucratic-professional control and citizen involvement have worked out in the development of city services. To understand decentralization in the context of this relationship between the "servers and served" (Reiss, 1970) requires a brief examination of the historical evolution of urban services.

The Evolution of Neighborhood Services

Nineteenth-Century Foundations

In the eighteenth and early nineteenth centuries, the typical American city had only the most primitive public facilities and services.[c] The streets of these early cities—many of which were unpaved—were the domain of pigs, dogs, cows, horses, and pedestrians. Rubbish collected on the streets along with manure and human waste, and the job of garbage collection was left to itinerant scavengers and to the pigs. With few exceptions, there was no public water supply, and sellers of "tea water" from the few fresh water wells did a brisk business by peddling their precious commodity from door to door (Duffy, 1968, pp. 30, 48-49). Firefighting was the preserve of volunteer companies who often competed with one another more than they fought fires and, in any case, were effective only when they could find sufficient water. With the development of crude wooden water mains, firefighting improved as firemen were able to tap into the mains through wooden "fire plugs."

In the mid-nineteenth century, police protection was equally haphazard since it was still emerging from the era of the night watch and the rattle. Public schooling was a halting experiment in New York's free schools and merely an idea in most cities (Lazerson, 1971; Kaestle, 1973; and Ravitch, 1974). Various epidemics often swept through the typical city, and the only organized health and hospital care took place in the almshouses (Duffy, 1968, p.232). The almshouses themselves were beginning to replace "home care" and the alleys and cellars where the poor and mentally ill were sequestered. Public transportation was limited to the omnibus—a kind of

---

[c] For an account of these urban services in the eighteenth century, see Bridenbaugh (1955, ch. 1) and Griffith (1936). For nineteenth-century perspectives on the rise of police, fire, sanitation, health, educational, and related social services, see Zeublin (1919); Griffith (1927); Griffith (1933); Schlesinger (1933); and Bellan (1971). The character, development, and changing patterns of urban public administration and service delivery are treated in vivid detail in a number of textbooks on municipal administration that were generally published after 1900 but survey changing management practices in the city during the last part of the nineteenth century. The following such textbooks are particularly helpful in illuminating the origins of urban services: Fairlie (1939); Conkling (1904); Wilcox (1904); Howe (1915); Upson (1929); and Hodges (1939).

horse drawn jitney—and later to the horse drawn streetcar. There were almost no parks and recreation areas in the city (Conkling, 1904, p. 52).

In short, at the beginning of the great immigrations, American cities had hardly achieved a high standard of urban amenities and service delivery. An undeveloped, disorganized urban system was forced to respond to the enormous pressures created by immigration. Put another way, urban problems were running far ahead of the capacity of city government to deal with them even before the modern city began to rise. Even in a simpler urban past, the service delivery problem was already out of control.

Bargaining for Services in the Immigrant City

One does not have to read Jacob Riis or Lincoln Steffens at great length to get a flavor of the poverty and chaotic growth of the larger cities in the 1900s. Edward Banfield (1970, p. 19) would like to point out that present urban conditions—however bad they may be thought to be—simply cannot compare to conditions in immigrant neighborhoods at the turn of the century. In terms of comparative levels and quality of service delivery, Banfield's view is certainly correct, but his view begs many far more important questions about urban service delivery.

Specifically, Banfield's view misses the point that for the past 100 years certain fundamental urban service problems have persisted in an apparently intractable way. Then as now, widespread police corruption was a constant embarrassment, if not a disgrace, to city governments. This pattern of corruption would be of interest only to crusading journalists and an occasionally aroused public if it did not reveal the intrinsic difficulty of establishing tight central control over the footsoldiers of city government: policemen, teachers, social workers, and garbage collectors. Since these public employees work on their own (or in small teams) out on the streets (or in classrooms) and must react rapidly to uncertain and ambiguous situations, it has always been hard for top-level urban administrators to supervise the actual delivery of service and thus enforce uniform standards of behavior. The police, in particular, present a vivid example of the tenuous control that administrators hold over footsoldiers. When city police were first established, policemen on the beat communicated with superior officers only in "face-to-face meetings or by messengers" (Rubenstein, 1973, p. 15). In later years, according to Rubenstein:

Once the men were dismissed from roll call, their supervisors had no certain way of controlling what they did during their tour of work. The sergeants, who were called roundsmen in Philadelphia and Brooklyn during the early nineteenth century, frequently assigned men "meets," prearranged times and places where the supervisors could visually check on them. The only way a roundsman had of discovering what his men were doing was to follow them around and make inquiries among the people who lived and worked on the beats. If he wanted to watch a man at work, he could, and frequently did, accompany him, but this obliged him to neglect other duties. The men were also isolated from each other, and their only way of attracting attention in moments of distress was by swinging the large rattles which city policemen had been carrying since the sixteenth century [p. 15].

Even with new communications technology, the problem of police supervision persisted and indeed made widespread corruption possible. Call boxes followed telegraph networks, and radio cars followed both. Various "pulling" systems have been adopted; and horns, colored lights, and bells have been used to "attract a patrolman to his box for special messages" (Rubenstein, p. 17). But no amount of communications could place the policemen under direct, constant supervision. So policemen have continued to "coop," take bribes, react to dangerous situations, beat up suspects, and occasionally be assaulted; and police officials can still do precious little to regulate these encounters.

It is not only because of their inherent freedom and discretion that the mayor's footsoldiers are so hard to supervise and control. The footsoldiers have also always had strong incentives to treat the relationship between the servers and the served as a form of free market exchange. In a classical bureaucracy, employees are supposed to follow and apply simple rules and procedures about which there is little disagreement. But the street-level world of urban footsoldiers provides little clarity or agreement about the nature of the service "problem" or its appropriate solution. What is an intolerable vice to one segment of the community may be a pleasurable pastime or a means of employment for others. And so policemen have to deal with numbers runners, prostitutes, and owners of after-hours bars, with the knowledge that citizen demands and preferences are sharply divided and that the practitioners of "vice" are willing to pay a great deal for a covert police license to do business.

Similarly, what may seem to be a serviceable if shabby home to a landlord and his tenants may seem a dangerous firetrap to neighbors or merchants on the block. Whose subjective appraisal should the inspector listen to in deciding whether or not to issue code violations? Consider, too, the local neighborhood candy store or bar. What may seem a valued hangout to teenagers and unemployed men may be an unacceptable public nuisance to other residents of the neighborhood. In these cases, as in so many others, the policemen must mediate conflicting interests and apply an ambiguous law in deciding how to act or, for that matter, whether to act at all.

Given the complexity and ambiguity of these service problems, the lack of clear rules for dealing with them, and the absence of a controlling hierarchy that removes his discretion, the urban footsoldier deals with many service demands by means of *mutual adjustment and bargaining* (Lindblom, 1965). Instead of arresting the drunk or the rowdy adolescents, the policeman tells them to move on. Instead of reporting the delinquent student to the principal, the teacher extracts a promise of good behavior. Instead of closing down a "dirty" restaurant or a deteriorating house, the health or housing inspector issues only minor complaints on the promise that improvements will be made. Add the element of cynicism and greed on the part of public employees, and the willingness of offending citizens to buy indulgences, and one can easily see how a full-scale exchange system developed in American cities. Thus, in the history of American cities, services have often not been *delivered* so much as they have been *bought*, *sold*, and *negotiated*. This system of mutual adjustment and bargaining over services was an effective method of coordinating the supply and demand for services and an ingenious adaptation to the conflicting demands and chaotic circumstances of urban service delivery.

In the immigrant city, certain critical factors help to explain why the delicate social relationship between the servers and the served could work. Before the advent of the automobile, police walked the beat, and teachers and urban employees were likely to live near where they worked. Thus, although it is hard to demonstrate, urban footsoldiers at the turn of the century were almost certainly more visible, better known, and more rooted in the neighborhoods they served than their successors today. The living conditions of citizens and public employees tended to be roughly similar. That is, teachers, policemen, and garbagemen were likely to understand from their own living experiences what was going on in urban neighborhoods. The streets, housing, and people of the neighborhood were in this sense recognizable and familiar. Moreover, the urban footsoldiers often had ethnic ties with the people they served. This is manifestly true of the Irish policeman working in a predominantly Irish neighborhood; but if the demand for new urban employees was filled generally by recent immigrants, it must have been true for other ethnic groups as well.

What emerges from this depiction of the immigrant city is a kind of *social symmetry* in service delivery. The relationship between servers and the served was roughly symmetrical when the former shared the same neighborhood, living conditions, and ethnic ties with the latter. This social symmetry was obviously supportive of the personal, even intimate role that existed between citizens and urban service deliverers. With the emphasis on bargaining for services, *trust* became a central ingredient in effective service delivery. If urban footsoldiers were to operate effectively in a close, personal relationship with clients, they could not be distrusted. And they were more likely to be distrusted if they were seen as alien, prejudiced, and ignorant of their client's living conditions.

One other point about service delivery in the immigrant city is worth mentioning — that is, the city was so fragmented and control over service delivery so dispersed that one commentator on New York (Parton, 1866) was led to note:

Perhaps the best way of beginning an investigation of the city government would be to go down to the City Hall and look at it. It proved not to be there. . . . It has been gradually cut to pieces and scattered over the island. . . . Was there ever such a hodge podge of government before in the world?

This "scattering" had the important effect of making urban neighborhoods the only cohesive political and social unit in the city. Service delivery was based in precincts, firehouses, and neighborhood districts. The political organization of the great machines was also based on the small neighborhood unit assigned to the wardheeler (Banfield and Wilson, 1965, pp. 115-27). Finally, ethnic and racial groups built their own small enclaves around neighborhood churches, and the social structures and their elements—the streets, alleys, buildings, stores, churches, families, and civic organizations—were highlighted. If the image of the fast-growing city was blurred in the minds of urban residents, the image of the block and the neighborhood was sharply focused. New Yorkers lived not so much in New York as in Greenwich Village or on the Lower East Side, and Bostonians lived not so much in Boston as in Dorchester or in Southie. What is most important is that in a city of neighborhoods of this sort, information about local needs was widespread, and both the residents and the urban footsoldiers possessed a subtle understanding of who did what to whom, of what needed fixing on the block, and of how a particular officer or teacher behaved—on or off the beat, in or outside the classroom.

The Trend toward Centralization

It should be obvious that there are dramatic differences between this picture of service delivery in the immigrant city and the currently held picture of rigid, racist bureaucracies and deteriorating or nonexistent service delivery. The most widely favored explanations of these differences emphasize (1) the poverty of present-day urban immigrants; (2) the sudden deluge of new demands for service; (3) racial prejudice against nonwhites; (4) inadequate fiscal resources; and (5) at least, in Banfield's view, the social pathology of the new urban poor. However, if we submit these familiar explanations to close scrutiny, they turn out to be highly arguable.

In the first place, it is by no means clear that today's urban poor are worse off than their predecessors. Comparisons are difficult at best, but given rising levels of affluence, it seems likely that today's poor are considerably better off than their nineteenth-century counterparts (Banfield,

1970, pp. 19,117). Second, it is even less clear that the scale of current immigration will impose a new order of magnitude of burden on city services. In fact, the growth rate in most large central cities began to decline in the second or third decade of this century, and the sharpest rates of growth (and hence of new demands) had already taken place by the 1960s. It can be argued in reply that although urban growth has slowed, the combination of middle-class outmigration and low-class immigration produces a net effect of service-demanding residents that is historically unique. While we would be foolish to dismiss the scale and importance of this influx, it is hard to see how it compares to the net effect of immigration during the decades in the nineteenth century when the size of some cities doubled. Third, although it is clear that prejudice against blacks is deeply rooted, it is not obviously of a sufficiently different order of magnitude from Yankee prejudice against the Irish to explain large differences in service delivery. Fourth, cities obviously find themselves in serious fiscal straits today, but it is instructive to note that cities have frequently been on the verge of financial collapse ever since colonial times. For example, the tax drain caused by educational improvement and the resistance to that fiscal burden is noted by Lazerson (1971, p. 242); that new services caused severe financial strains and drove cities close to bankruptcy is documented by Bridenbaugh (1955, p. 9) and Wade (1964, p. 77).

Finally, the argument that the present urban poor are, through various forms of antisocial behavior, destroying their cities and their services is simply untenable. On this point, Banfield's account of criminality, immorality, violence, and drunkenness of the nineteenth-century urban populace serves as a stark reminder that in many ways, the nineteenth-century city was a much rougher and nastier place than the city we know today. Historical accounts of the nineteenth-century city indeed bring to light many kinds of urban poverty and squalor: for an account of infant mortality and outbreaks of epidemics, see Duffy (1968, pp. 119, 259); for a description of streets that were open sewers and littered with dead horses and cats, also see Duffy (1968, pp. 117, 191); for early incidents of rioting and racial discrimination, see Bridenbaugh (1955, pp. 299, 305); for drug addiction, see Musto (1973, p. 5); for air pollution due to chimney smoke and the absence of parks and other recreational facilities, see Hodges (1939, pp. 333, 363); and for the absence of garbage collection (and the use of hogs and vultures as scavengers), see Bellan (1971, p. 215).

If the familiar explanations for present-day urban problems are at least mildly suspect, where do we look to find a more satisfactory set of answers? Our contention is that given the bargaining nature of urban services, three interrelated forces can account for the development of service delivery to its present state: the search for power and control in the city, the professionalization of urban service employees, and the rise of new technology. Each of these forces led to the increased *centralization* of service delivery, which in turn threatened to destroy the street-level relationship between the servers and the served.

The first factor involved the search for power and control in the city. The evolution of urban power and control throughout the last one hundred years has been of a centrist nature. For instance, in establishing a new political order in cities, the great machines sharply centralized power and control of service delivery (Merton, 1957, p. 72; Mandelbaum, 1971, pp. 364-5; and Scott, 1973). In most successful machines, even though neighborhood-based political organizations remained crucial, the focus of political attention moved away from the neighborhood to city hall—following the path of power. Later, reform mayors further centralized power by building larger bureaucracies, often with mandates from newly passed revisions of the city charter. The power changes have occurred at different rates in different cities, but the trend, up until the 1960s, had always been in the same direction—toward city hall.

The second factor that led to centralization was the growth in urban services of a professional ethos—emphasizing scientific management, training, specialization, and meritocratic criteria of recruitment and promotion. The rise of professionalism among teachers, social workers, or policemen can be understood in part as a strategy for increasing the status of these occupations. But, even more important, professionalism implies that service delivery should not be based on exchange or mutual adjustment with citizens but on the authority and expertise of those who deliver services. This means that the system of service delivery should be governed hierarchically and not be left to the vagaries of joint determination with citizens. And so public managers, preaching professionalism, reached for methods that worked in industry and sought to replicate the beguiling system of strong hierarchical administration through the progressive centralization of power and control (Katz, 1973, pp. 56-104). That police departments and schools were not simply factories with clear cut production functions, technologies, and divisions of labor did not deter the prophets of scientific management.

Three other aspects of the professional ethos had important effects in shaping the structure of urban service delivery. First, at the core of professionalism lay the notion of standards. While amateur administrators may be content to make ad hoc, pragmatic policies, the professional wishes to establish explicit and uniform rules of conduct that dictate how a trained policeman, teacher, or fireman *should* behave in delivering their services. To set uniform standards in this way is to rise above ad hoc, haphazard judgments; it is also to impose inflexible rules and to threaten the discretionary powers of the urban footsoldiers. Second, the professional ethos entailed the belief that professionals possessed some special sort of trained discipline or expertise that would permit them to do their job better than amateurs. The fact that such expertise might not actually exist again did not deter the emerging service professionals. They latched on to what they could find in the way of "scientific" theory and proclaimed their expertise on the basis of adherence to scientific methods. Nowhere was this dynamic more vivid than in the rise of the social work profession (Lubove, 1969, p. 55; and Levine and Levine, 1970). When social work operated as a volunteer service, with "untrained" personnel working in settlement houses and making home visits, it had a strong missionary flavor and stressed empathy, personal contact, informal "helping" techniques, and, of course, moral uplift. By contrast, social workers as professionals, with psychoanalytic and administrative theory as their credo, emphasized the "treatment" of the poor and the meticulous reporting and regulation of services, and produced a more impersonal and aloof professional-client relationship. This kind of professionalism worked strongly against the bargaining for services that gave the earlier system of service delivery its flexibility and its strong personal linkages between citizens and public employees. Third, professionalism also carried with it a strong impetus toward specialization of tasks in service delivery. In particular, specialization meant the rise in police departments of large detective bureaus, and within the bureau, vice detectives, narcotics detectives, and so forth. In education, it meant the rise of department chairmen, assistant principals, assistant superintendents for curriculm development, and the like (Katz, 1973; Kaestle, 1973, pp. 159-84; Rogers, 1968; and Wasserman, 1970). This division of labor might simply have been a curiosity of administrative organization if it had not substantially affected the role and status of the footsoldiers at the street level. With increased specialization, the patrolman and classroom teacher were no longer the central figures in service delivery; rather, they were lower-level bureaucrats in a hierarchical system that created strong incentives for the most able to leave such work for detective bureau or the central board of education. For these reasons, specialization implied a different sort of centralization—one that drew talent away from the street level by conferring benefits and status, not for skillful daily work with citizens but for technical, administrative, and investigative expertise.

The third major factor leading toward centralization involved the rise of new technology. The earliest urban services, such as police and fire protection, water supply and garbage collection, road paving and street lighting, had originally developed in an ad hoc, disconnected way. In many cases, services were provided privately with each resident taking care of his own service needs. Even when city government began to provide services directly, service delivery was loosely organized and often chaotic as city government tried to keep up with the demands of a fast-growing urban population. One reason for this fragmentation, as we have seen, was the simple weakness of governmental organization. But, more fundamentally, the poor technology involved in early services reinforced the centrifugal pattern of service delivery—that is, when policemen lacked devices for communicating with central headquarters, when the streets were cleaned by wandering public scavengers, and when fire companies had limited mobility and limited communications, it was intrinsically difficult to establish centralized control of municipal operations.

As service technology developed, so did the extent of centralized bureaucratic control. Basic technological improvements like the telephone increased the possibility of central surveillance; similarly, the introduction of public reservoirs, almshouses, and hospitals all served to consolidate previously atomized services. The development of recordkeeping technologies, culminating in the computer, gave central managers extensive control over their bureaucratic systems. Finally, nowhere was the centripetal effect of technology more evident than in the nineteenth-century development of urban transportation (Holt, 1972). The first transportation "system" was, of course, completely private and decentralized. People walked or drove their own horse and buggies. The first "public" conveyances, the omnibus and the horse drawn streetcar, replaced self-service with a consolidated service but only to a slight extent. The omnibuses still wandered around the city along highly erratic routes, were run by a great number of different small companies, and attracted only a few riders. Thereafter, with each advance in transportation technology (before the automobile), services were consolidated further until private or public monopolies arose to run centralized traction systems. In transportation, technology tied the city together and gave rise to a highly centralized system of operation.

What makes the evolution of service delivery so interesting is that from the turn of the century to the 1960s, these centralizing forces were working indirectly to destroy the social symmetry of the older street-level structure. In addition, other changes brought about by the reformers and the rise of a national social welfare system worked directly to attack the street-level system.

The reformers sought to dismantle the neighborhood-based political patronage and exchange system, which they viewed as the cornerstone of machine politics and thus of political corruption. The reformers believed that the way to rescue service delivery from the depredations of political self-interest and especially from venal bosses was to create a centralized civil service and to place political power in the hands of a small number of "neutral" administrators serving on boards and commissions that were insulated from street-level politicals (Lubove, 1969, pp. 2-6). Whether or not the reform tradition achieved its positive goals of good government, it did in many cities achieve its negative purpose of taking authority and autonomy away from neighborhood-level service administrators, and the result was to further weaken (but not destroy) the system of local allocation and adjustment in service delivery. Finally, the growth of federal social programs, which began before 1932 but was powered by the large-scale interventions of the New Deal, further centralized the design and fiscal control of service delivery. This was especially true of the urban renewal and public housing programs begun by federal initiatives. Service arrangements that were once negotiated by street-level employees and citizens were now often redefined by directives from Washington and were expanded, reorganized, or superseded by new service delivery mechanisms as a result of more distant bargaining processes among federal, state, and local officials.

In the face of changes in the urban power structure, professionalism, centralizing technologies, reform movements, and federal intervention, the street-level world of service delivery was largely transformed. Some street-level arrangements continued to slip through the new central controls. The persistence of police corruption, erratic garbage collection, and highly differentiated teaching methods and welfare regulation is proof of this point, with the widely reported police corruption scandals in New York (which led to the Knapp Commission), Philadelphia, and Chicago only the most recent examples. What bureaucratic centralization could and did do, however, was to make the service delivery system more cumbersome, rigid, and remote. Put another way, centralization could insure that service delivery was not intentionally hand-tailored to varied neighborhood interests and not explicitly based on ad hoc exchanges and accommodations. Professionalism tended to increase the distance between footsoldiers and citizens by making policemen and teachers less members of the neighborhoods they served and more members of a separate, professional guild. Bureaucratization increased the complexity and formality of procedures and of communication channels between city governments and its citizens (see Martin, 1965).

The Neighborhood Service Crisis of the 1960s

The service crisis of the 1960s emerged at a time when urban bureaucracies were overly centralized, inflexible, and removed from the neighborhoods. The crisis consisted of a sharp rise in the demand for services that was reflected by runaway crime and fire alarm rates, overloaded sanitation systems, and schools that produced large numbers of dropouts and failures. The crisis also consisted, it should be remembered, of entirely new types of tensions: harassment of service employees by residents, vandalism of public property, and complete disrespect for city government's bureaucracy. And the crisis was neighborhood-based: Poor and "transition" neighborhoods suffered the most, while residents of upper-middle-class, white neighborhoods often remained oblivious of conditions in the rest of the city.

The Loss of Social Symmetry

Over and above the debilitating effects of centralization on the server-served relationship, the population turnover in most cities by the 1960s threatened destruction of the street-level bargaining, mutual trust, and social symmetry that characterized the immigrant city. Policemen, teachers, firemen, and other public employees tended to be white and working class, and not to be residents of the port-of-entry neighborhoods where the new immigrants arrived. The social bond between the servers and served was thus to a large extent broken, and it is no surprise that feelings of mistrust, hostility, and alienation grew rapidly among nonwhite urban residents. From another point of view, the city's footsoldiers also suddenly were forced to live in an unfamiliar, hostile, and threatening urban world. Policemen and teachers who knew their way around the old white neighborhoods because they grew up in them (or ones like them) were now faced with angry demands and protests and with the loss of neighborhood support and approval. They often became "dirtyworkers" to their families and sympathetic observers—and "pigs" to their bitter clients (Wilson, 1968). The incipient movement toward public service unionization, begun in the early 1960s for valid economic and occupational reasons, now gained an emotional, almost paranoid source of support from these changed social conditions (Cole, 1969; Connery and Farr, 1970; Wellington and Winter, 1971; and Stanley, 1972).

The decline in social symmetry also took more subtle forms. The accounts in urban textbooks about the policemen, teachers, or social workers who could tell a "good" kid from a "bad" one presumed an intimate understanding on the part of the footsoldier, not only of particular individual residents but also of the appearances, life styles, and attitudes of residents. But when residents became unfamiliar, even alien to the deliverers of services, the capacity of policemen and teachers to make careful distinctions on the basis of subtle cues was vastly reduced. In the extreme case, all sixteen-year-old black males wearing apple hats come to look like "probable assailants" to policemen unfamiliar with a neighborhood and the people in it. Equally, with increased social distance, residents are less able to interpret the behavior and attitudes of public employees. What the footsoldiers may think of as tough but fair conduct may appear to be blatant racism to nonwhite residents. Indeed, charges of police brutality do not primarily involve physical force, but rather stem from the residents' perception that police behave in an insulting way, make implicit racial slurs, or fail to treat nonwhites with due respect. On the other hand, policemen, teachers, and other footsoldiers easily take strongly expressed demands, grievances, and protests about services to be hostile acts and direct personal attacks on them and their institutions.

Renewal Problems and Social Problems

At the same time, it is important not to try to explain too much by the loss of social symmetry and the resulting breakdown of social communication, for clearly there were other aspects of the service crisis. For one thing, many cities were no longer young or fast-growing, nor were they mounting large-scale services for the first time. Rather, the cities were old, their physical plant was deteriorating, and they were suffering an increasing rate of decay. Although urban governments had been successful in laying out new services as their cities grew, few governments have been very successful in renewing or restructuring old services. In part, this is because it is less costly to produce new goods and services than to rehabilitate old ones. With new construction or the creation of new programs, one does not have to worry about clearing away outdated equipment or methods of operation; one does not have to worry about dealing with intricate interdependencies (between services or programs); and one does not have to worry about challenging entrenched interests and disrupting established patterns of behavior. On this logic, it was clearly easier to build a new service system in response to the demands of the immigrant city than it was to restructure and reform an established service system. Thus, the institutionalization of services was an administrative triumph coming as a reaction to the nineteenth-century growth of the city. But, in the 1960s, the same phenomenon of institutionalization took on a very different meaning: It was a source of persistence and inflexibility and therefore an obstacle to responsiveness and adaption to new demands.

Second, urban government was grappling with a different and more difficult class of services in the 1960s than it had been 50 years earlier. Then, the main task of government was to build the physical city: street paving, street lighting, water and sewage systems, parks, and large-scale capital projects such as bridges and public works. Absent debilitating graft, cities had little trouble in actually delivering these goods.

By contrast, the services demanded in the 1960s were intrinsically difficult to deliver. The typical urban "problems" were crime in the streets, drug addiction, unemployment, and delinquency. No one knew the solutions to these "social" problems. (For more on the difficulty of the social problems approach in urban research, see Yin, 1972, pp. ix-xvii.) Even trivial problems, such as the sending of false fire alarms, baffled administrators. The array of potential solutions which remained similar to those tried for decades, included:

[A] siren to attract attention to the firealarm box and provide for apprehension of the false alarmist. Another patent contains a camera which takes a snapshot of the individual setting off the alarm. The best idea, from the human-interest standpoint, includes a pair of handcuffs which manacle the "culprit" the instant he sets off the firealarm [Hodges, 1939, p. 501].

More important, urban administrators had simply never known how to prevent widespread family breakdown in poor neighborhoods, ensure that health and housing regulations were enforced,[d] prevent high rates of welfare dependency among new immigrant groups (black or white), or educate low-income children (Greer, 1972, p. 108).

Reactions to the Crisis: Centralization and
Decentralization

When faced with the service crisis of the 1960s, urban administrators came up with many remedies; some called for further centralization but others espoused a new theme—decentralization. The centrist strategies were extensions of what had occurred in the past, now packaged under such labels as program budgeting, operations research, and service efficiency. Mayors moved to increase central bureaucratic control by creating "super" agencies, strong budget bureaus or city planning agencies, and specialized staff functions at the very top. Cities turned desperately to new applications of space-age technology for other potential solutions. The evaluation of the success of these centrist strategies, however, must be left for another occasion.

Our prime attention in this study is directed toward the wide array of decentralization strategies that were tried. The move to decentralize is potentially of great significance in the continuing evolution of neighborhood service delivery. For the first time, in the late 1960s and early 1970s, cities tried at last to turn the tide and to reform the point of contact of service delivery; for decentralization, above all else, has meant the enhancement of the functions of both the servers and the served. The innova-

---

[d] Arthur Schlesinger (1933, p. 110), notes that the first tenement housing laws were enforced sporadically, if at all; Constance Green (1965, p. 116), adds more generally that most of the early tenement and plumbing laws and building codes were all but unenforceable.

tions that were attempted are by now well known: police-community relations and team policing programs, districtwide and citywide decentralization of schools, new neighborhood health and mental health centers, neighborhood councils or little city hall facilities for multiservice programs, and community development corporations (Schmandt, 1972).

The purpose of the present study is to assess these various decentralization efforts as they occurred in different services and in different cities. The study reviews the record that decentralization has amassed and attempts to explain the outcomes of these decentralization efforts in terms of the inherent differences among urban services and the decentralization strategies tried in each service.

References

Altshuler, Alan. 1970. *Community Control*. Pegasus, New York.

Banfield, Edward. 1970. *The Unheavenly City*. Little, Brown & Co., Boston.

Banfield, Edward and James Wilson. 1965. *City Politics*. Harvard University Press, Cambridge, Mass.

Bellan, Ruben C. 1971. *The Evolving City*. Copp Clark Publishing Co., Toronto.

Bellush, Jewel and Stephen David, eds. 1971. *Race and Politics in New York City*. Praeger, New York.

Bridenbaugh, Carl. 1955. *Cities in Revolt: Urban Life in America 1743-1776*. Oxford University Press, New York.

Cole, Stephen. 1969. *The Unionization of Teachers*. Praeger, New York.

Conkling, Alfred. 1904. *City Government in the United States*. The Century Co., New York.

Connery, Robert H. and William V. Farr, eds. 1970. *Unionization of Municipal Employees*. Academy of Political Science, Columbia University, New York.

Duffy, John. 1968. *A History of Public Health in New York City, 1925-1866*. Russell Sage Foundation, New York.

Fairlie, John. 1939. *City Management*. Crofts and Co., New York.

Fantini, Mario, Marilyn Gittell, and Richard Magat. 1970. *Community Control and the Urban School*. Praeger, New York.

Farr, Walter, Lance Liebman, and Jeffrey Wood. 1972. *Decentralizing City Government*. Praeger, New York.

Green, Constance McLaughlin. 1965. *The Rise of Urban America*. Harper and Row, New York.

Greenberg, Stanley. 1964. *Politics and Poverty*. Wiley, New York.

Greer, Colin. 1972. *The Great School Legend*. Basic Books, New York.

Griffith, Ernest S. 1933. *Current Municipal Problems*. The Riverside Press, Cambridge, Mass.

———. 1936. *History of American City Government: The Colonial Period*. Oxford University Press, New York.

———. 1927. *Modern Development of City Government*. Oxford University Press, London.

Harrington, Michael. 1962. *The Other America*. Macmillan, New York.

Hawley, Willis and Michael Lipsky. forthcoming. *Theoretical Perspectives on Urban Politics*. Prentice-Hall, Englewood Cliffs, N.J.

Hodges, Henry. 1939. *City Management*. Crofts and Co., New York.

Holt, Glen. 1972. "The Changing Perception of Urban Pathology," in Kenneth Jackson and Stanley Schultz, eds., *Cities in American History*. Knopf, New York.

Howe, Frederic. 1915. *The Modern City and Its Problems*. Scribner's, New York.

Kaestle, Carl F. 1973. *The Evolution of an Urban School System*. Harvard University Press, Cambridge, Mass.

Katz, Michael. 1973. *Class, Bureaucracy, and Schools*. Praeger, New York.

Kotler, Milton. 1969. *Neighborhood Government*. Bobbs-Merrill, New York.

Lazerson, Marvin. 1971. *Origins of the Urban School*. Harvard University Press, Cambridge, Mass.

Levine, Murray and Adeline Levine. 1970. *A Social History of Helping Services: Clinic, Court, School, and Community*. Appleton-Century-Crofts, New York.

Lindblom, Charles E. 1965. *The Intelligence of Democracy*. The Free Press, New York.

Lipsky, Michael. 1971. *Protest in City Politics*. Rand-McNally, Chicago.

———. 1971. "Street-Level Bureaucracy and the Analysis of Urban Reform." *Urban Affairs Quarterly* 6 (June), pp. 391-409.

Lubove, Roy. 1969. *The Professional Altruist*. Atheneum, New York.

Mandelbaum, Seymour. 1965. *Boss Tweed's New York*. Wiley, New York.

Marris, Peter and Martin Rein. 1967. *Dilemmas of Social Reform*. Atherton Press, New York.

Martin, Roscoe. 1965. *The City in the Federal System*. Atherton Press, New York.

Merton, Robert K. 1957. "The Latent Functions of the Machine," in R.K.

Merton, ed., *Social Theory and Social Structure*, rev. ed. The Free Press, New York.

Mushkat, Jerome. 1971. *Tammany*. Syracuse University Press, New York.

Musto, David. 1973. *The American Disease*. Yale University Press, New Haven, Conn.

National Commission on Urban Problems. 1968. *Building the American City*. U.S. Government Printing Office, Washington, D.C.

Nordlinger, Eric. 1973. *Decentralizing the City*. M.I.T. Press, Cambridge, Mass.

Parton, James. 1866. "The Government of the City of New York." *North American Review* 102, pp. 455-6.

Rainwater, Lee. 1967. "The Revolt of the Dirtyworkers." *Trans-Action* 4, (November), pp. 35-40.

Ravitch, Diane. 1974. *The Great School Wars*. Basic Books, New York.

Reiss, Albert, Jr. 1970. "Servers and Served in Service," in John P. Crecine, ed., *Financing the Metropolis*. Sage Publications, Beverly Hills, Calif.

Report of the National Advisory Commission on Civil Disorders. 1968. Bantam Books, New York.

Rogers, David. 1968. *111 Livingston Street*, Random House, New York.

Rubinstein, Jonathan. 1973. *City Police*. Farrar, Straus, and Giroux, New York.

Schlesinger, Arthur M. 1933. *The Rise of the City*. Macmillan, New York.

Schmandt, Henry J. 1972. "Municipal Decentralization: An Overview." *Public Administration Review* 32 (October), pp. 571-88.

Scott, James. 1973. *Comparative Political Corruption*. Prentice-Hall, Englewood Cliffs, N.J.

Stanley, David T. 1972. *Managing Local Government under Union Pressure*. Brookings Institution, Washington, D.C.

Upson, Kent D. 1929. *Practice of Municipal Administration*. The Century Co., New York.

Wade, Richard. 1964. *The Urban Frontier*. University of Chicago Press, Chicago.

Wasserman, Miriam. 1970. *The School Fix*. Outerbridge and Dienstfrey, New York.

Wellington, Harry H. and Ralph K. Winter, Jr. 1971. *The Unions and the Cities*. Brookings Institution, Washington, D.C.

Wilcox, Delos. 1904. *The American City: A Problem in Democracy*. Macmillan, New York.

Wildavsky, Aaron. 1968. "The Empty-Headed Blues: Black Rebellion and White Reaction." *The Public Interest* 11 (Spring), pp. 3-16.

Wilson, James Q. 1968. "The Urban Unease." *The Public Interest* 12 (Summer), pp. 25-39.

Yates, Douglas. 1973. *Neighborhood Democracy*. Lexington Books, D.C. Heath, Lexington, Mass.

Yin, Robert K., ed. 1972. *The City in the Seventies*. Peacock, Itasca, Ill.

Zeublin, Charles. 1919. *American Municipal Progress*. Macmillan, New York.

2

Decentralizing Urban Government: An Evaluative Framework

Federal Precursors to Decentralization

The development of urban decentralization strategies had an accidental quality. The federal government may well have provided both the critical policy initiatives and the main impetus to urban decentralization, but Washington did not start out with this purpose in mind (see Farkas, 1971). Rather, the federal government began in the early 1960s to consider new strategies for dealing with the old problem of juvenile delinquency. In the Juvenile Deliquency Demonstration program, begun in 1962, the stated purpose of federal policy was to encourage the "coming together" of neighborhood residents to discuss delinquency problems (see Marris and Rein, 1967, for early juvenile delinquency efforts). In so doing, citizens were typically engaged in what could at best be called an advisory role in policymaking. Equally, in the far more extensive urban renewal program of the late 1950s and early 1960s (Godschalk, 1967; Wilson, 1966; Abrahamson, 1959; Rossi and Dentler, 1961; Keyes, 1969; and Davies 1966), citizen participation was a sidelight; some would say an afterthought or a cosmetic feature to smooth the acceptance in the neighborhoods of decisions made in Washington and city hall. Thus, in the development of federal policy before 1964, citizen participation was no more than a slogan (and an aspiration) of radical community organizers like Saul Alinsky (1946; 1971), and decentralization and community control were ideas whose time quite clearly had not come.

The Community Action Program

The War on Poverty is widely believed to have been the critical turning point in the development of decentralization strategies. But again, in the planning and initial development of the poverty program, decentralization was more an accidental product than the explicit purpose of national policy. After all, the War on Poverty was designed to alleviate poverty and, in so doing, to improve the education, health care, and employment opportunities of the poor. As the various chroniclers of the War on Poverty have reported, citizen participation, as it was expressed in the Community Action Program, was an inspiration of unknown origin; the insertion of the

21

term "maximum feasible participation" in the original legislation occurred without widespread debate or attention (Ferman, 1969).

Whatever judgment one wishes to make about the Community Action Program, it only served as a *partial* impetus for decentralization. The Program, for instance, did not clearly entail neighborhood-based community control, nor did it operate to increase the power or authority of district-level service administrators. The Community Action Program did, however, attempt to increase the power and influence of the poor so that they could make their voices heard more effectively in city hall, and the tactics pursued are perhaps best described as those of shaking up and challenging city governments. But citizen participation took place in citywide organizations, not neighborhood-based ones, and citywide boards determined policy. Moreover, the poor often did not do very well in these centralized community action agencies. Recognizing this fact, Congress in 1966 passed the Quie Amendment, which required that at least one-third of the members of community action boards be representatives of the poor.

Nevertheless, the Community Action Program did play an important indirect role in creating the foundations for urban decentralization. Even though community action groups might be drawn to the center of urban government in the course of fighting city hall, they did constitute a new neighborhood-based infrastructure of storefront organizations and street-level leaders. More precisely, the main theme of the Community Action Program was to provide a legitimate role for the clients or recipients of services in program administration and decisionmaking. Responsibility for program management, in other words, was decentralized to the lowest possible echelon in the bureaucratic hierarchy (for an excellent discussion of the design and implications of both the Community Action Program and Model Cities, see Sundquist, 1969). Thus, even though the clients participated on a citywide and non-neighborhood basis, the Community Action Program provided opportunities for a new group of participants to gain first-hand experiences with social problems and public policy. Later, when various kinds of decentralization experiments were launched by city governments, the veterans of community action programs were heavily represented on the citizen boards of the new experiments.[a]

At the same time, the War on Poverty did develop a range of less dramatic and controversial programs concerned with service delivery, and these programs had the effect of creating new institutions in the community and of increasing the capacity of street-level institutions to provide services for specific neighborhoods. In particular, the antipoverty program pro-

---

[a]There have been numerous assessments of the CAP experience. In addition to the many reports on single cases, the following major studies are all based on multiple cases: Daniel Yankelovich, Inc. (1967); Kramer (1969); Greenstone and Peterson (1973); Barss, Reitzel and Associates, Inc. (1970); and Staff and Consultants' Reports (1967). Other major reviews include Ferman (1969) and Strange (1972).

moted the organization of neighborhood service centers staffed by state and local officials responsible for code enforcement, public health, public welfare, and other functions. By 1968, about 800 such centers were in operation. A prominent aspect of this service strategy was the establishment of neighborhood health centers that from the outset were to involve residents extensively in decisionmaking and administration (Hollister et al., 1974). These service centers were certainly not the most publicized and most controversial part of the War on Poverty, but they were the most enduring part, and they constituted another bridge to later decentralization strategies.

The Model Cities Program

It took only three years for the federal government to react to its own Community Action Program and to try to end the intense conflict between city hall and the neighborhoods that had become the hallmark of community action. In late 1967, Congress, under pressure from many big city mayors, passed the Green Amendment, which removed the "maximum feasible participation" clause from the community action legislation and stipulated that a "local government could either become the CAA (Community Action Agency) or designate an organization to fill the role." Thus, the majority of Congress decided that it had accidentally created the embarrassing political "mess" and, by implication, that citizen participation was not the bright idea that it had seemed to be earlier but was rather a possible menace to the orderly workings of government.

In this context, it is not at all surprising that the Model Cities Program, begun in 1966, reflected a tepid and chastened federal attitude toward client participation. In sharp contrast to the ambitious theme of maximum feasible participation, the Model Cities Program was merely intended to develop a "means of introducing the views of area residents in policymaking," with ultimate authority and control over programs and expenditures vested in city hall. At the same time, the Model Cities Program had a strong neighborhood focus—in which resources and services were applied to specific territorially defined entities—that the Community Action Program lacked. In this respect, the Model Cities Program provided a complementary impetus for decentralization—that is, whereas the Community Action Program had emphasized client participation but was not strongly neighborhood based, the Model Cities Program had the reverse characteristics (Sundquist, 1969).

Like the Community Action Program, the Model Cities Program also produced some surprises for federal policymakers and some unintended consequences. For one thing, in some Model Cities programs, neighborhood residents managed to gain more power and control over programs than the federal government had bargained for. Before the Nixon Administration moved to tighten city hall control over neighborhood programs, there was some evidence that residents in certain "model neighborhoods" had come to dominate policymaking boards and had achieved veto power over program expenditure (U.S. Department of Housing and Urban Development, 1973c). Second, the Model Cities Program also produced an odd-lot assortment of new neighborhood organizations that expanded and reinforced the organizational and leadership infrastructure in the neighborhood and so also increased the range and capacity of street-level institutions concerned with service delivery. In short, Model Cities enhanced the effect of the Community Action Program in developing an increasingly elaborate and well articulated demand structure for services. Finally, since the use of Model Cities funds as fiscal bonuses for city bureaucracies and as resources for programs in the "model neighborhood" could occur only if both bureaucratic and neighborhood components were coordinated with each other, service officials and some local residents had a strong economic incentive to cooperate.[b]

Two Dimensions of Decentralization

The net effect of the Community Action and Model Cities Programs was to prepare the groundwork for urban decentralization. Besides the obvious contributions made by these programs to political consciousness-raising and the training of new neighborhood leaders, what is most important is that these two programs each emphasized one of the two critical dimensions in the development of urban decentralization.

The first dimension of decentralization, coming mainly from the Community Action Program, involves a *client* imperative. Decentralization thus focuses on the status, rights, responsibilities, and powers of client groups served by public programs, regardless of residential location. *Decentralization here has meant the transference of responsibility and power to those very people who are affected by the program or innovation in question.* The theme is based to a large extent on the citizen participation efforts instigated by the federal government as carried to its logical extreme under the Community Action Program where low-income residents, who in the past had been excluded from participating because of their powerless

[b] As with CAP, there have been numerous assessments of the Model Cities experience. See for example, U.S. Department of Housing and Urban Development (1970) and (1973a), which are studies that were carried out by Marshall Kaplan, Gans, and Kahn, Inc.; Booz, Allen Public Administration Services, Inc. (1971); Warren et al. (1974); Washnis (1974); and U.S. Department of Housing and Urban Development (1973b), which report is by Neil Gilbert and Harry Specht. A controversial evaluation of the Model Cities program was carried out by the President's Task Force on Model Cities (1969), headed by Edward C. Banfield.

position, were deliberately engaged in program administration. The client dimension of decentralization, then, has led to a general association between any decentralization attempt and the increase in responsibility and power of those being served, especially low-income and disadvantaged groups. (The literature on citizen participation is simply too voluminous to be enumerated; Selznick, 1949, and Davis and Dolbeare, 1968, note that citizen participation had been the subject of public programs before the 1960s, and Cole, 1974, presents a comprehensive survey of citizen participation in more contemporary programs.)

The client dimension, however, has not been the only aspect of decentralization. A second, equally important dimension that comes more from the Model Cities experience invokes a *territorial* imperative—that is, the target of decentralization is thus also a particular neighborhood, its physical assets, and its resident population. *Decentralization here has meant the expenditure of new resources and efforts, from whatever outside agent or level of government, to a small, geographic area.* In this sense, neighborhoods had only infrequently been the overt targets of public policies before the 1950s. Since then, the urban renewal and Gray Areas programs were among the first to focus on particular neighborhoods and were in a way designed to cope with the worst neighborhoods (the former program promoted physical rehabilitiation and the latter program, with its emphasis on juvenile delinquency, promoted social rehabilitation). The later Model Cities Program, of course, which was conceived as being more comprehensive, included both physical and social rehabilitation. The territorial dimension of decentralization has led to a general association between any decentralization attempt and improvement in the physical and social conditions of specific neighborhoods, and decentralization has come to be associated with specific neighborhoods such as Harlem, the Lower East Side, Hough, Watts, Hyde Park-Kenwood, Roxbury, and the like.

Both of these dimensions of decentralization can be found in varying degrees in a given project or innovation. In some cases, when we speak for instance of neighborhood government, both the territorial and client dimensions are maximally decentralized, and the innovations should produce both increases in client control and improvements for the neighborhood. In other cases, as in a citywide grievance procedure that gives a larger role to clients or in the strict physical redeployment of services or facilities, decentralization is really occurring along one dimension but not the other. The fact that these two dimensions have generally not been explicitly contrasted in the past may account for some of the confusion over the term "decentralization," since for some observers decentralization automatically connotes the client dimension and thus raises one set of expectations regarding the transference of political power, whereas for other observers decentralization automatically connotes the territorial dimension and raises another set of expectations regarding neighborhood issues. This confusion is certainly easy to document among advocates of decentralization; however, among its critics, Etzioni (1969) and Kristol (1968) also confuse the issue, since one emphasizes territory and the other emphasizes clients.

Decentralization Strategies

These two dimensions can facilitate the placement of various decentralization *strategies*, or the ways that public organizations implement and pursue decentralization, into a common framework. For instance, one of the most common distinction is between administrative decentralization and political decentralization (Altshuler, 1970, p. 64; Hallman, 1973; and Kaufman, 1969). Both strategies call for the increase of administrative discretion and power for district officials, but the latter also implies an increased formal accountability to client groups (regardless of whether the client group is defined by residential, income, or even political eligibility rules). These two strategies, then, would be regarded as falling at equal points on the territorial dimension, but on different points on the client dimension. In fact, we can identify and place all the major decentralization strategies within a matrix that is defined by the interactions between these two dimensions. If, for simplicity's sake, the territorial dimension is defined by either a citywide or a neighborhood focus and the client dimension is defined by three degrees of client involvement—negligible (where clients have no formal role in policymaking), informed (where clients have an indirect role), and dominant (where clients have some formal role)—then a simple 2×3 cell matrix emerges.

The different cells make it possible to contrast seven distinct decentralization strategies that have been used, sometimes in isolation and sometimes in combination with each other, in nearly every decentralization innovation:

1. *Community Relations*: The attempt by a service agency to build informal relationships between service officials and clients. These innovations are generally organized on a citywide basis and clients have only a negligible role in administering the services. Many police-youth programs fall into this category.

2. *Physical Redeployment*: The attempt by a service agency to relocate facilities and staff to serve the needs of specific neighborhoods directly. These innovations are organized on a neighborhood basis, but clients still have a negligible role. The opening of a storefront office would be an example.

3. *Administrative Decentralization*: The attempt by a service agency to grant its own district officials greater discretionary authority to be more responsive to neighborhood needs. These innovations are also organized on a neighborhood basis with clients having a negligible role. Innovations allowing district officials to set priorities and control their own budgets would fit in here.

4. *Grievance Mechanisms*: The attempt by a service organization to establish new procedures for receiving complaints directly from clients and for disposing of such complaints by modifying services where necessary. These innovations are generally organized on a citywide basis, but clients do play an indirect role in influencing services. A new city hall complaint office is an example of this innovation.

5. *Employment of Neighborhood Residents*: The employment of residents who are client eligibles or represent client interests in the service delivery organization, usually in paraprofessional positions. The projects are generally neighborhood-based, and clients again have an indirect role in relation to service administration. The hiring of teacher aides to help teach students is an example.

6. *New Neighborhood Institutions*: The development of separate institutions outside the existing service bureaucracy to fulfill neighborhood needs. The innovations are organized on a neighborhood basis and clients have at least an informed role. Neighborhood health centers or community development corporations are the most common examples.

7. *Political Decentralization*: The attempt to give clients direct governing control over a service being delivered to a specific neighborhood. The control may be exercised through the traditional election process, special elections, or some other selection procedure whereby client representatives serve on a governing board over the service. These innovations are both neighborhood-based and intend a dominant client control over service administration. New York's new local school boards in each school district are examples.

In all, these seven strategies, which can be arrayed in the 2 × 3 matrix as shown in Table 2-1, clearly display important similarities as well as significant differences. In the first place, the strategies have in common the fact that except for administration decentralization, *they all make some direct attempt to affect the relationship between the servers and the served*. Community relations programs make an attempt to broaden the informal social bond between the two. Physical redeployment is an attempt to bring the two literally closer together. The grievance, employment, and political decentralization strategies attempt to influence function relationships, and new neighborhood institutions attempt to develop totally new relationships between a new group of servers and the served. However, the strategies differ in their treatment of this relationship between servers and served and fall into three separate categories: (1) those that are *weak* forms of decentralization because significant decentralization is not intended on either territorial or client dimensions (physical redeployment, administrative decentralization, and grievance mechanisms would be the weaker forms, with community relations being the weakest of all); (2) those that are *moderate* forms because some decentralization along both dimensions is intended (employment and new neighborhood institutions would be the moderate forms); (3) and those that are *strong* forms because substantial decentralization along both dimensions is intended (political decentralization). The terms "weak," "moderate," and "strong" are thus applied throughout the present study as descriptions of the intended degree of decentralization, and are unrelated to the outcomes or effects of decentralization.

The weak strategies of community relations, grievance mechanisms, physical redeployment, and administrative decentralization exhibit a common underlying approach that emphasizes service responsiveness. Here, the thrust of decentralization is to increase the communication between citizens and public employees—for example, by working to make public employees more involved with and responsive to residents and to make residents more involved with and trustful of public employees. However, the weak strategies often involve unilateral actions where government often moves with new programs on its own to increase accessibility and responsiveness. In these actions, citizens play a consumer role and may actually be only passive participants rather than equals in forming new service policies and procedures. Moreover, the weak strategies can take place on a citywide basis, so that the territorial element need not be neighborhood-based.

The moderate strategies—the development of new neighborhood institutions and the employment of neighborhood residents—reflect a different underlying approach that emphasizes capacity building. Here, the primary thrust is not on increased communications between servers and served and does not require a delicate effort to stimulate a reciprocal learning process between the two. Rather, the thrust is on the improvement of neighborhood and resident capabilities for delivering services. The improvement is supposed to follow the creation of new resources that can have a direct, immediate effect on service problems. For instance, rather than restructuring hospitals so that they might address previously unmet needs for health services, the capacity-building strategy assumes that new institutions can meet these needs directly without the need to "rewire" the existing service systems. Similarly, rather than retraining teachers to be more responsive to neighborhood needs, hiring paraprofessionals from the

Table 2-1
Decentralization Strategies Placed Along Territorial and Client-Oriented Dimensions

	Client Role in Administration of Service		
Territorial Focus	*Negligible*	*Informed*	*Dominant*
Citywide	Community Relations	Grievance Mechanisms	
Neighborhood	Physical Redeployment	Employment	Political Decentralization
	Administrative Decentralization	New Neighborhood Institutions	

community will have the same effect but will act directly on the problem and simultaneously increase the ability of the residents to respond to their problems by providing training opportunities. In sum, the logic of capacity building is that services can be improved without having to improve server-served communications on policy matters.

Finally, the strong strategy of political decentralization reflects a third underlying approach to decentralization that emphasizes control. Here, the thrust is not on improving the street-level partnership (as in weak strategies) or on increasing neighborhood or resident capabilities (as in moderate strategies); it is on the increased political control of service delivery by neighborhood residents. Thus, in contrast to capacity building, the control approach does not skirt the existing structure of service delivery but seeks to confront it and fundamentally restructure power relations within it. The assumption is that the conduct of public employees in specific neighborhoods or districts will improve if the employees are made to follow client-determined policies and procedures. Since this control is exercised in the neighborhood setting, the immediacy of interpersonal relations and of feedback about specific service problems will make citizen control more effective than if similar changes occurred on a citywide basis.

Citizen Participation

Not to be confused with the decentralization strategies, but overlapping heavily with some of them, are the formal mechanisms for citizen participation that can exist—that is, the relationship between citizens and government may be reflected in the *electoral* process (voting for members of both the executive and legislative branches at federal, state, and local levels), in the *judiciary* process (bringing individual suit against government action), or in the *administrative* process (establishing a citizen board to advise or govern a specific project). Of these three, the federal programs of the last decade have had their greatest effect on the administrative relationship, with the Community Action Program and the notion of "maximum feasible participation" setting the tone for subsequent social programs.

In general, three different administrative mechanisms for citizen participation are available: the use of volunteers or participants with informal roles, a formal paraprofessional program, and a citizen board structure. Although such strategies as political decentralization almost always involve certain types of participation—for example, the use of boards—the opposite is not always true. A board can be the instrument in applying the grievance strategy—for instance, a civilian review board—and weak advisory boards may even exist with a project that calls for a community relations or physical redeployment strategy. Similarly, although in most cases the employment strategy and paraprofessional type of citizen participation coincide, it is nevertheless important to compare the effects of the various mechanisms and combinations of citizen participation separately from the effects of the decentralization strategies.

Decentralization Outcomes

As with strategies and citizen participation, decentralization can also have several different outcomes. The possible outcomes have often not been clearly defined and hence have also fed the confusion over the expectations from decentralization. Previous discussions have often suggested that decentralization can have economic, administrative, political, and psychological impacts, but then they have failed to describe the specific outcomes that are implied (Shalala and Merget, 1973). In other situations, the outcomes may only have been implicitly assumed, thereby leading to substantial differences in the use of criteria for judging success or failure—for example, judging decentralization by the criterion of the development of community control and a radical redistribution of power in urban society, as opposed to judging decentralization according to the increase of service effectiveness.

There appear to be five specific outcomes that decentralization can have, and although some strategies are designed to produce some outcomes but not others, it is worth assessing each decentralization experience in terms of these five outcomes:

1. *Increase in Flow of Information between Servers and Served.* Decentralization often produces more information and communications, so that those providing services know more about service needs and those using services know more about services provided. The calling of frequent meetings and distribution of printed materials between servers

and served would be examples. However, in the long run, this outcome actually becomes a means for achieving the next four and hence is not considered as important as the next four.

2. *Improvements in Service Officials' Attitudes.* Decentralization can lead to service officials having a more positive view of their own role and of the service being provided, or of the client group and its needs. An increase in sensitivity to client needs might be an example.

3. *Improvements in Client Attitudes.* Decentralization can similarly lead to clients having a more positive view of their role, of the services being provided, or of the service group and its problems. A reduction in hostility toward the police might be an example.

4. *Improvements in Services Delivered.* Decentralization has been associated with expectations of better services, as judged by output (e.g., higher reading scores) or by input (e.g., more teachers per student).

5. *Increase in Client Control.* Finally, decentralization can result in clients having the power to implement their own ideas in service delivery. For example, a local school board can be client-dominated and act as a governing body for the school district.

If these five outcomes are taken as the potential outcomes from any decentralization innovation, then it is a fairly easy matter for the observation of these outcomes to be associated with the seven strategies and with other exogenous conditions, to determine the circumstances under which decentralization appears to succeed or fail.

Street-Level Governments: The Service Hypothesis

This strategy and outcome approach to the study of decentralization allows for the testing of several hypotheses about urban decentralization. These hypotheses include:

1. The five decentralization outcomes may not occur as a result of the same innovation, and there may be tradeoffs among them. In particular, increases in client control may occur at the expense of service improvements.

2. In general, the strong forms of decentralization will be associated with more client control than will the weak forms of decentralization, but the latter will be associated with more success in increased flow of information.

3. Citizen boards and certain board functions will be more highly associated with increased client control than will the other types of citizen participation.

4. Certain exogenous factors, such as the availability of federal funds, the avoidance of pre-implementation conflict, and the active support of the municipal executive, will be associated with higher rates of all outcomes.

We believe that the findings for these and other important hypotheses about urban decentralization are best explained by an overriding characteristic of street-level services. This is that *the server-served relationship varies in different services, and the decentralization experiences will thus best be explained in terms of the inherent differences among services*. In other words, urban decentralization can occur only within the context of a specific municipal service—for example, police or fire protection, education, or social services. The different services involve slightly different relationships by which the servers govern the served. The street-level governments for each service will thus operate somewhat differently, and this will affect any decentralization innovation attempted in that service. Even though the success of urban decentralization innovations, as gauged by the five outcomes, may be associated with the occurrence of weak, moderate, or strong decentralization strategies and with certain types of citizen participation, the service hypothesis is that only some of the decentralization strategies and types of participation will tend to occur in the first place in a given service. For this reason, our study of decentralization principally covers five different service areas: public safety, education, health, multiservice programs, and economic development. Chapter 3 will describe the salient differences among these five services. First, however, we describe the methods used in our study.

Evaluating Decentralization

Research Approach: The Case Survey Method

Our approach to the decentralization experience has been to examine the existing literature on decentralization. The richness of the literature, as well as the fact that some innovations that were begun no longer exist, suggested that this approach might be more fruitful than an original field study. A field study, in addition, could not cover the variety of decentralization experiences without incurring great costs and research time. Our findings are obviously limited to those topics that previous investigators have chosen to emphasize, and just as obviously, they cannot touch upon the topics that previous investigators have ignored.

In general, three methods may be used to review existing research and to deduce overall lessons from the literature:

1. *Propositional Method*, which assumes that research is well organized along similar experimental paradigms, so that the reviewer's main task is to compare the original investigators' final propositions or conclusions;
2. *Cluster Method*, which assumes that previous studies have produced large amounts of original quantitative data that are capable of being aggregated and then analyzed;
3. *Case Survey Method*,[c] which assumes that previous studies are a heterogeneous collection of case studies, so that the reviewer's main task is to aggregate the characteristics (and not necessarily just the conclusions) of these cases.

The propositional method typifies traditional reviews of laboratory research. In psychology, for instance, the experimental paradigm is so consistently applied that an analysis of the proposition or conclusions presented by previous studies can be fruitfully carried out.[d] The cluster method has been made popular recently by the increasing availability of various sources of survey data that deal with similar issues, so that a clustering and then reanalysis of the results of several surveys can be carried out (Hyman, 1972; and Light and Smith, 1971).

The case survey method, in contrast, is only in its formative stage of development. Yet, for reviewing the decentralization literature, it is the most appropriate of the three approaches because, to the extent that it is empirical, the decentralization literature consists mainly of case studies of individual innovations. These case studies do not follow a similar research paradigm, and therefore the propositional method is inapplicable. To weigh one investigator's conclusions against those of another, when both investigators have used entirely different research (or nonresearch) logics to arrive at their conclusions, would simply be foolish. Further, the case studies do not provide the rich sources of quantitative evidence that would be needed in order to justify using the cluster method.

In fact, the case survey method was devised specifically to deal with the problem of reviewing as disparate a literature as is found on decentralization. The first and somewhat cruder application of the case survey approach was made in Yin, Lucas, Szanton, and Spindler (1973). In that

---

[c] The authors are deeply indebted to William Lucas of The Rand Corporation for his assistance in elaborating the case survey approach and its alternatives, and for his advice on the specific application of the approach in the present study on decentralization.

[d] The propositional approach is so common in psychology that a research journal with considerable history and esteem, the *Psychological Bulletin*, is devoted to reviews of the literature. Except until recently, none of the other traditional social sicence disciplines (e.g., sociology, political science, and economics) had a journal just for literature reviews. Our own supposition, naturally, would be that the uniform use of the experimental paradigm puts psychology on a different level from the other social sciences, in terms of both the scientific nature of the evidence and the ability to draw conclusions based on more than a single study.

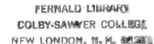

study, the literature being reviewed was on citizen participation. However, the study did not call for a rigorous assessment of the literature, but rather the identification of factors associated with the exercise of citizen power. Thus, the present study on decentralization may be considered the first important test of the case survey approach. The method may be said to have its roots mainly in the use of ethnographic case materials for cross-cultural research (Whiting, 1968). The Human Relations Area Files, for instance, provide materials on over 200 societies that can serve as case studies from which investigators may aggregate lessons about human society in general. The use of content analysis for communications research also provides some parallels, although content analysis is primarily concerned with the relationship between the manifest and latent content of messages and not so much with the aggregation of the messages (Holsti, 1968).

The case survey method as applied to policy studies enables the reviewer to enumerate various experiences found in each case study and then allows the frequency of occurrence of these experiences to be aggregated in a reliable manner. The aggregations form the basis for simple statements of association and nonassociation of different types of experiences. In this manner, the case survey method gives the reviewer a chance to "survey" various case studies. In general, for the review and analysis of most of the public policy literature, the case survey method is more useful than the other two methods. This is because the public policy literature, including the decentralization literature, is based primarily on an uneven set of case studies. Until recently, the main shortcoming of case study literatures was that they could not be aggregated in any sense. The case survey method thus carries the classic case study method, as applied in business or public administration, one significant step forward, for aggregate reviews of individual case studies can now be undertaken with some scientific rigor.

Basic Techniques of the Case Survey Method

The case survey calls for a reader-analyst to answer the same set of questions, or checklist, for each case study of decentralization.[e] Moreover, the questions are closed-ended, so that the answers can be aggregated for further analysis.

In the present study, a case study was defined as *any description of a*

---

[e] The reader-analyst, it should be noted, is a scientific observer. His role is like that of the innovative participant-observer as described by Reiss (1971a; and 1971b). Since the observations become the source of data for the study, the reader-analyst or participant-observer is in a way both the experimenter and the subject in the study. The prime virtue of the reader-analyst is that he is a trained observer and can codify more difficult judgments than can the ordinary respondent.

site-specific organizational change in an urban area; in total, 269 such case studies were found. The checklist questions covered the major characteristics of decentralization, divided into four sections. (1) the *nature of the case study* itself (e.g., the author's background, the source of financial support for the study, and the research design and methods used); (2) the *background characteristics* for the innovation (e.g., the size of city, the source of financial support for the innovation, and the degree of pre-implementation conflict); (3) the *characteristics of the decentralization innovation* (e.g., type of citizen participation, type of services included, and type of decentralization strategy followed); and (4) the *outcomes* of the decentralization innovation (e.g., increased flow of information, changes in attitudes on the part of citizens or service officials, and degree to which citizens had control over the innovation). For all four sections, there were a total of 118 questions that the reader-analyst had to answer. The checklist data then served as the basic body of evidence resulting from our review of the decentralization literature.

In addition to the ability to aggregate various characteristics of individual case studies, the case survey has three other features that address major methodological problems in a systematic review of research literature. These features are the establishment of the *reliability* of the approach, the ability to differentiate *weak and strong responses* on the part of the reader-analyst, and the use of *explicit rejection criteria* for excluding some studies from the review.

Reliability. First, the case survey allows the reviewer to measure the reliability of his methods. The measurement of reliability, and thus the establishment of replicability, is a minimum step for developing any scientific method. In this case, "reviewing the literature" has always been more of an art than a science, and except in rare instances (usually using the cluster approach) there has been no attempt to assess the reliability of the method of review. The capability of the case survey in this regard is very straightforward: Given a fixed set of closed-ended questions, the reliability of the reader analyst's responses can be measured by having more than one analyst respond to each question for a single case study. The amount of interanalyst agreement is then the measure of reliability.[f]

Weak and Strong Responses. A second common problem often faced by those reviewing research literatures is that some judgments are easier to make than others. Certain characteristics of a case study may be so well

[f]Naturally, this is a measure of the reliability of the case survey instrument and does not address the issue of the accuracy of the original case study. Other than examining the case for its research quality, only a replication of the field experience would provide a way of measuring the relationship between events as they occurred and as they were reported in the case study.

described that the reader-analyst feels quite confident of his response to a given checklist question; other characteristics may only be poorly described, which perhaps requires the reader-analyst to draw an inference in order to respond to the checklist question. For a research literature of a highly diverse nature, a reviewer would not want to set his standards of confidence so high that only the most well-documented characteristics were enumerated. In the decentralization literature, for instance, this might involve disregarding many important issues where the type of description rarely makes the reader-analyst fully confident of his responses. At the same time, the reviewer would not want to set his standards of confidence so low that well-documented characteristics could not be distinguished from poorly-documented ones.

The case survey attempts to deal with this problem simply by allowing the reader-analyst to indicate, for each question answered, his level of confidence. Such a procedure is well known in traditional psychological research, where an observer gives levels of confidence, for instance, along with his judgments of some perceptual phenomenon, such as the loudness of a tone. Levels of confidence have not been used as frequently in traditional survey research, however, since the respondent (usually the head of a household) may have neither the training nor the time to provide this answer. In the case survey, however, the respondent is a reader-analyst who is not simply a member of the public at large. The reader-analyst can learn rules for distinguishing among levels of confidence, at least to the degree that he can indicate whether he is "sure" or "not sure" of each answer.

Explicit Rejection Criteria. Finally, exhaustive searches of a given literature will inevitably uncover some studies that the reviewer will not use. In some instances, the reviewer chooses to ignore studies that are only marginally relevant to his topic. In other instances, he may ignore studies because they are of poor quality. In nearly every traditional review of the literature, even those using the propositional and cluster approaches, reviewers have failed to make their rejection criteria explicit. This is a serious shortcoming in any situation; in those situations where a reviewer presents only a small handful of the available studies and notes that the remainder were not of acceptable quality (see, for example, Averch et al., 1972), the lack of explicit rejection criteria is an unacceptable flaw.

The case survey deals directly with this problem in the following way. All case studies found in the literature, or some systematic sample of them, are reviewed by a reader-analyst who responds to a complete checklist for each case. The checklist contains several questions that have been specifically designed to serve as exclusion criteria. After all the case studies have been analyzed, the final caseload may be divided into those that have met the exclusion criteria and those that have failed. In this way, not only are the exclusion criteria explicit, but subsequent analysis that compares excluded with included studies is possible; in short, the actual effects of the exclusion procedure may also be examined.

Applying the Case Survey to Decentralization Studies

The case survey thus involved the uniform application of a 118-question checklist to the case studies of decentralization. Since many case studies covered the same innovation, our findings actually pertain to the *literature* on decentralization and our generalizations therefore only bear indirectly on the actual decentralization experience. The key questions on the checklist were those dealing with the seven major strategies and the five possible outcomes:

Strategies:
Community Relations (Q. 75);
Physical Redeployment (Q. 74);
Grievance Mechanisms (Q. 78);
Administrative Decentralization (Q.76);
Employment (Q. 77);
New Neighborhood Institution (Q. 50);
Political Decentralization (Q. 73).

Outcomes:
Change in Flow of Information (Q. 98);
Change in Disposition of Officials toward the Clients or the Service (Q. 103);
Change in Disposition of Clients toward the Officials or the Service (Q. 102);
Change in Service Effectiveness (Q. 104);
Change in Client Control over Services (Q. 89).

Before presenting the results for these questions, we shall describe the procedures used for assessing reliability and validity and the effects of discarding studies that did not meet the standard for validity.

The search for studies of decentralization involved extensive use of libraries in Washington, D.C., New York City, and Cambridge, Massachusetts; citations from bibliographic sources; and consultations with officials and researchers in the five service areas: public safety, education, health, multiservice programs, and economic development. An attempt was made to include all studies that could be found in a published or unpublished source dated no earlier than 1960. With few exceptions, however, doctoral dissertations were ignored. (Appendix A contains lists of the sources searched and the case studies found.)

Reliability of the Decentralization Case Survey. Since the case survey involved the reading of an individual case study and then the translation of the case study's information into the form of responses to the checklist, the first task was to assess the *reliability* of the method. (See Appendix B for the responses to the entire checklist.) The reliability was tested by having two reader-analysts answer separate checklists for the same case study. For 14 of the case studies, the average amount of agreement between the two reader-analysts was 82.4 percent for answers with a "sure" level of confidence, and 60.8 percent for answers with a "not sure" level of confidence.[g] The percentage of agreement for the "sure" answers may be considered moderately high, since most of the questions on the checklist involved multiple response categories, and hence the level of agreement expected through random guessing was well below 50 percent. (The procedures for precisely testing the significance of agreement levels, however, are not well established. Appendix C presents the percentage of agreement for each question and also contains a discussion of the possible statistical measures that might be used.)

The lower reliability of the "not sure" answers, however, pointed to the need for a separate analysis of all answers according to the two different levels of confidence. To recapitulate the mechanics of the checklist for a moment, every question on the checklist had required the reader-analyst to express his level of confidence by asking him to indicate, along with his substantive answer to the question, whether he was "sure" or "not sure" of his answer. An expression of "not sure" was made every time the reader-analyst could not cite the specific phrase or portion of the case study that contained the answer to the given question. The subsequent analysis of the answers according to the two different levels of confidence revealed two patterns. First, the percentage of "sure" responses for most questions was quite high, thereby making less critical the analysis of the separate answers according to level of confidence. The lowest levels of confidence were found in questions having to do with the outcomes of the decentralization innovations. Table 2-2 shows the levels of confidence for all answers on the five most important outcomes. (The number of case studies in Tables 2-2 and 2-3 is 215 because the analysis was carried out after 54 cases were

---

[g] Before the reliability measurement was made, eight of the original 118 questions were excluded from subsequent analysis. This was done on the basis of a felt dissatisfaction with the eight questions among the original reader-analysts. The questions tended either to call for a relatively nonoperational judgment (Qs. 14, 15, 53, 117, and 118) or for information that most cases lacked (Qs. 52, 83, and 84). Of these questions, Q. 14 dealt with research methods, and it would have been desirable to retain the question. However, the question revealed the difficulty in identifying such research flaws as "Hawthorne" effects, "creaming," and the like; only further original experimentation may be appropriate for adequately dealing with the question.

rejected on quality grounds; see the discussion below.) Second, where the level of confidence was low, the distribution of answers according to "sure" and "not sure" responses was quite similar. Table 2-3 gives the distribution of responses for the three questions out of the five that had the lowest levels of confidence. These two patterns meant that for most of the questions in the decentralization study, separate analysis of the "sure" and "not sure" categories was not necessary. However, future applications of the case survey may require such a dual analysis.

Case Validity and Cases Rejected. A second procedural task was to assess the *validity* of the case study results and to reject any case study not meeting the criteria for validity. Several questions on the checklist were intended to serve as criteria for excluding case studies from further analysis. The criteria were meant to fall under either *internal* or *external validity*. These categories derive from traditional concerns for experimental design, typically as applied to laboratory studies (Campbell and Stanley, 1966; Campbell, 1969; Campbell, 1957; Suchman, 1967; Williams, 1972; and Caporaso and Roos, 1973).

Internal validity raises the question of whether a study's research design is adequate to support the study's conclusions. A poor research design may lead an investigator to mistake a spurious effect—for example, regression to the mean—for an effect attributable to a change in the independent variable. Campbell (1969) has enumerated nine such effects, which he calls "threats" to internal validity: history, maturation, effects of a pretest on the posttest, instrumentation, regression to the mean, self-selection of subjects, subject mortality, interaction between subject selection and maturation, and measurement instability.

External validity raises the question of whether a study's conclusions can be generalized to other situations. In a laboratory study, the typical problem is to be able to generalize from a population that has developed a unique exposure history—for example, a pretest that may sensitize a respondent and thus bias his subsequent behavior—to the general population, which has had no such history. The establishment of external validity is especially a problem when a study attempts to investigate a meaningful segment of social behavior (e.g., how an individual recognizes the faces of other individuals) within the confines of the laboratory setting (e.g., testing subjects by using photographs of a preselected group of faces). In the face recognition example, only a full-fledged field demonstration would satisfy the conditions for external validity. (For an example of face recognition as studied in the laboratory, see Yin, 1969.) Campbell (1969) has enumerated six threats to external validity: the effect of testing, the interaction between subject selection and treatment conditions, the reactive effects of experimental arrangements (e.g., the "Hawthorne" effect), inferences based on

Table 2-2
Level of Confidence for Five Key Decentralization Outcomes

| | Level of Confidence for All Answers | | | |
| | Sure | | Not Sure | |
Topic Covered by Question	No.	Percent	No.	Percent
1. Flow of information	154	71.6	61	28.4
2. Attitudes of agency officials	84	39.1	131	60.9
3. Attitudes of clients	85	39.5	130	60.5
4. Changes in services	140	65.1	75	34.9
5. Changes in client control over services	111	51.6	104	48.4

multiple treatments, irrelevant responsiveness of measures, and irrelevant replicability of treatments.

Of the two validity categories, the present study failed to develop any usable criteria for external validity. Several questions in the checklist were attempted (Qs. 15-21), but the reader-analysts simply found no adequate rationale for deciding when the conditions for a specific case study could be said to be generalizable to other situations. Any decentralization effort involves a specific community, with a specific set of leaders and history, at a certain period of time. Under these conditions, which are vastly different from the laboratory situation, the rules for establishing external validity are not clear. There is no satisfactory way of knowing how to generalize from community to community or from one time period to another (Weiss and Rein, 1970).

As for establishing internal validity, two questions were used. The two questions (Qs. 12 and 13) were concerned with the nature of the research instruments used in the case study and with the study's research design. Because of the highly nonexperimental nature of the decentralization literature, only a very weak criterion was set, in which studies having *either* "no explicitly cited measures or observations," *or* "no specific innovation focus" were rejected from the final analysis. Table 2-4 shows the responses to the two relevant questions. *A total of 54 of the 269 cases failed to achieve the criterion, and there were thus 215 case studies in the final caseload.*[h] Because of the weak criterion, the final caseload included many studies that would not otherwise have been acceptable under strict experimental procedures. These studies were basically one-shot case studies that made

[h] The final caseload of 215 studies covered 149 discrete innovations, since several innovations were reported in more than one case study.

Table 2-3
Distribution of Answers for Questions with Low Level of Confidence[a]

Question 1. *As a result of the innovation, the attitudes of service officials toward the service or clients appear to have:*

| | Level of Confidence[b] | |
	Percent Sure ($n = 84$)	*Percent Not Sure* ($n = 131$)
a. Improved	13.1	12.2
b. Deteriorated	6.0	6.1
c. Remained unchanged or no information	80.9	81.7
Total ($n = 215$)	100.0	100.0

Question 2. *As a result of the innovation, the attitudes of clients toward the services or officials appear to have:*

| | Level of Confidence[c] | |
	Percent Sure ($n = 85$)	*Percent Not Sure* ($n = 130$)
a. Improved	27.0	23.1
b. Deteriorated	10.6	5.4
c. Remained unchanged or no information	62.4	71.5
Total ($n = 215$)	100.0	100.0

Question 3. *The innovation resulted in increased client influence over services to the extent that:*

| | Level of Confidence[d] | |
	Percent Sure ($n = 111$)	*Percent Not Sure* ($n = 104$)
a. Clients implemented some of their own ideas in service delivery	26.1	18.3
b. All other	73.9	81.7
Total (n = 215)	100.0	100.0

[a]The χ^2 is used throughout the data analysis even though the collection of case studies is not a random sample. The reader is therefore cautioned to examine the raw observations closely and to use the χ^2 calculations only as a guideline for interpreting the data.

[b]$\chi^2 = 0.04$, $df = 2$, not significant.

[c]$\chi^2 = 2.86$, $df = 2$, not significant.

[d]$\chi^2 = 1.89$, $df = 1$, not significant.

no attempt to establish control groups or to provide pre- and post-measures. The studies follow a research design that Campbell (1957) describes as "pre-experimental"—that is, carrying none of the weight of a true or even a quasi-experimental design. As Table 2-4 also indicates, if only those cases with acceptable research designs were used (either experimental and comparison groups with pre- and post-observations, or experimental and comparison groups with only a single observation period), there would have been no more than 33 case studies under review. The main point about the case survey, however, is that the investigator selects his rejection criteria explicitly and can select rigorous or loose criteria, depending upon the nature of the investigation.

Comparison of Cases of Different Research Quality. A further benefit of making the rejection criteria explicit is that the effects of the rejection procedure can also be examined. In short, one can study the extent to which the rejection procedure, no matter how valid from a methodological view, has resulted in changes in the aggregate characteristics of the cases under review. The answer can be obtained if the original 269 cases are divided into three categories:

1. *Lower Quality Cases*, which covers the 54 cases originally excluded on the basis of *either* no explicitly cited measures *or* no specific innovation focus (see Table 2-4, Q. 1, response d; and Q. 2, response e);
2. *Medium Quality Cases*, which covers an additional 127 cases that contained no clearly operational measures (see Table 2-4, Q. 1, response c);
3. *Higher Quality Cases*, which covers the remaining 88 cases.

Appendix D contains the percentage response distributions for these three categories for a selected number of key checklist questions. It is important to note those questions for which the variation in research quality apparently makes little difference, as well as those for which the variation produces strong differences.

The major pattern that emerges is for studies of higher quality to produce only slight variations in the frequency with which each of the five service areas (police, education, health, economic development, and multiservice programs), size of city, or seven major decentralization strategies were studied. Some differences were found, however, with regard to other case study characteristics: studies of higher quality tended to be conducted *more* by authors with academic affiliations and *less* by authors employed by independent research organizations; to be supported *more* by federal agencies and *less* by private sources; and to be more frequently judged by their authors as reflecting a *successful* innovation.

Most important, the differences in research quality appear to produce consistent differences in the assessment of the five decentralization out-

Table 2-4
Checklist Questions Used for Excluding Case Studies

Question 1. *The type of measures used in the case study were:*

	Cases	
	No.	*Percent*
a. Operational outcome measures[a]	69	25.7
b. A mixture of operational measures and other measures	24	8.9
c. No operational measures, but other measures or observations that were used informally	127	47.2
d. No explicitly cited measures or observations[b]	49	18.2
Total	269	100.0

Question 2. *The type of research design used in the case study was:*

	Cases	
	No.	*Percent*
a. Experimental and comparison groups, with pre- and postobservations	9	3.3
b. Experimental and comparison groups, but with only a single observation period	24	8.9
c. An experimental group with pre- and postobservations	19	7.1
d. An experimental group, with only a single observation period	209	77.7
e. No specific experimental group or no clear observation period[b]	8	3.0
Total	269	100.0

[a]Described in sufficient detail that a new investigator could repeat the investigation. Five of these cases also fell into Q. 2 (alternative e) and were thus excluded.
[b]Three cases fell into both these alternatives; therefore the final number of cases excluded was 54.

comes: *Higher quality studies were associated with higher rates of success.* This is especially true in the assessment of changes in client attitudes. The higher quality studies appear more often to have found such attitudes changed in a positive direction as a result of the decentralization innovation (see Table 2-5).

In general, this pattern suggests that the effects of rejecting low quality cases does not change the scope of the study in terms of the services covered, the size of the city studied, or the strategies studied. It does, however, produce a slightly higher rate of success among the outcomes, and hence a slightly more positive interpretation of the decentralization

Table 2-5
Assessed Change in Client Attitudes as a Result of Decentralization

	Quality of Case Study					
	Higher		Medium		Lower	
Client Attitudes	No.	Percent	No.	Percent	No.	Percent
Improved	33	37.5	20	15.7	4	7.4
Remained unchanged	29	33.0	67	52.8	26	48.1
Deteriorated	4	4.5	12	9.4	9	16.7
No information	22	25.0	28	22.0	15	27.8
Total	88	100.0	127	100.0	54	100.0

$\chi^2 = 27.98$, $df = 4$, $p < .001$.
Note: $N = 269$; "no information" cases are excluded.

literature.[1] This pattern thus reveals the potential significance in any literature review of the effects of excluding studies. However, the pattern also
provides an especially important finding about the decentralization literature: Contrary to popular beliefs, higher quality studies are associated with
more successful cases of decentralization. Whether this is because better
researchers seek out successful innovations, because better researchers
fail to report about innovations that turn out to be unsuccessful, or because
one of the byproducts of a successful innovation is the ability to stand up to
more stringent evaluative efforts, the fact remains that decentralization
results are more positive when research quality is higher. (The critiques of
12 illustrative case studies presented in Appendix E focus mainly on
methodological concerns, apparent author biases, and nature of the author's conclusions.)

References

Abrahamson, Julia. 1959. *A Neighborhood Finds Itself*. Harper, New
York.
Alinsky, Saul D. 1946. *Reveille for Radicals*. University of Chicago Press,
Chicago.
_____. 1971. *Rules for Radicals*. Random House, New York.
Altshuler, Alan A. 1970. *Community Control: The Black Demand for
Participation in Large American Cities*. Pegasus, New York.
Averch, Harvey et al. 1972. *How Effective Is Schooling? A Critical Review*

---

[1] No systematic analysis was made of the relationship between the quality of the study and the
interactions among the checklist questions.

and Synthesis of Research Findings. The Rand Corporation, R-956-PCSF/RC, Santa Monica, Calif.

Barss, Reitzel and Associates, Inc. 1970. "Reports from the 100-City CAP Evaluation." Cambridge, Mass.

Booz, Allen Public Administration Services, Inc. 1971. "Citizen Participation in the Model Cities Program." Prepared for the U.S. Department of Housing and Urban Development. Washington, D.C.

Campbell, Donald T. 1957. "Factors Relevant to the Validity of Experiments in Social Settings." *Psychological Bulletin* 54, pp. 297-312.

_____. 1969. "Reforms as Experiments." *American Psychologist* 24 (April), pp. 409-29.

_____and Julian C. Stanley. 1966. *Experimental and Quasi-Experimental Designs for Research*. Rand-McNally, Chicago.

Caporaso, James A. and Leslie L. Roos, Jr., eds. 1973. *Quasi-Experimental Approaches*. Northwestern University Press, Evanston, Ill.

Cole, Richard L. 1974. *Citizen Participation and the Urban Policy Process*. Lexington Books, D.C. Heath, Lexington, Mass.

Daniel Yankelovich, Inc. 1967. "Detailed Findings of Study to Determine Effects of CAP Programs on Selected Communities and Their Low Income Residents." New York.

Davies, J. Clarence, III. 1966. *Neighborhood Groups and Urban Renewal*. Columbia University Press, New York

Davis, James W. and Kenneth M. Dolbeare. 1968. *Little Groups of Neighbors: The Selective Service System*. Markham, Chicago.

Etzioni, Amitai. 1969. "The Fallacy of Decentralization." *The Nation*, August 25, pp. 145-7.

Farkas, Suzanne. 1971. "The Federal Role in Urban Decentralization." *American Behavioral Scientist* 15 (September-October), pp. 15-35.

Ferman, Louis, ed. 1969. "Evaluating the War on Poverty." *The Annals* 385 (September), entire issue.

Godschalk, David R. 1967. "The Circle of Urban Participation," in H. Wentworth Eldredge, ed., *Taming Megalopolis*. Doubleday, Garden City, New York.

Greenstone, J. David and Paul E. Peterson. 1973. *Race and Authority in Urban Politics: Community Participation and the War on Poverty*. Russell Sage, New York.

Hallman, Howard W. 1973. *Government by Neighborhoods*. Center for Governmental Studies, Washington, D.C.

Hollister, Robert M. et al. 1974. *Neighborhood Health Centers*. Lexington Books, D.C. Heath, Lexington, Mass.

Holsti, Ole R. 1969. "Content Analysis," in G. Lindzey and E. Aronson, eds., *The Handbook of Social Psychology,* Vol. 2. Addison-Wesley, Reading, Mass.

Hyman, Herbert. 1972. *Secondary Analysis of Sample Surveys*. John Wiley, New York.

Kaufman, Herbert. 1969. "Administrative Decentralization and Political Power." *Public Administration Review* 29 (January-February), pp. 3-15.

Keyes, Langley C., Jr. 1969. *The Rehabilitation Planning Game: A Study in Diversity of Neighborhood*. M.I.T. Press, Cambridge, Mass.

Kramer, Ralph M. 1969. *Participation of the Poor: Comparative Community Case Studies in the War on Poverty*. Prentice-Hall, Englewood Cliffs, N.J.

Kristol, Irving. 1968. "Decentralization for What?" *The Public Interest* 11 (Spring), pp. 17-25.

Light, Richard and Paul Smith. 1971. "Accumulating Evidence." *Harvard Educational Review* 41 (November), pp. 429-71.

Marris, Peter and Martin Rein. 1967. *Dilemmas of Social Reform*. Atherton, New York.

President's Task Force. 1969. "Model Cities: A Step toward the New Federalism." Presented to the White House December 16.

Reiss, Albert, Jr. 1971a. *Police and the Public*. Yale University Press, New Haven.

Reiss, Albert, Jr. 1971b. "Systematic Observation of Natural Social Phenomena," in Herbert Costner, ed., *Sociological Methodology 1971*. Jossey-Bass, San Francisco.

Rossi, Peter H. and Robert A. Dentler. 1961. *The Politics of Urban Renewal: The Chicago Findings*. Glencoe, Ill.

Rossi, Peter H. and Walter Williams, eds. 1972. *Evaluating Social Programs*. Seminar Press, New York.

Selznick, Philip. 1949. *TVA and the Grass Roots*. University of California Press, Berkeley.

Shalala, Donna E. and Astrid E. Merget. 1973. "Decentralization: Implications for Urban Services," unpublished manuscript. Teachers College, Columbia University, New York.

Staff and Consultants' Reports. 1967. *Examination of the War on Poverty*. Prepared for the Subcommittee on Employment, Manpower and Poverty of the Committee on Labor and Public Welfare, U.S. Senate, 90th

Congress, 1st Session. U.S. Government Printing Office, Washington, D.C.

Strange, John H. 1972. "Citizen Participation in Community Action and Model Cities Programs." *Public Administration Review* 32 (October), pp. 655-69.

Suchman, Edward A. 1967. *Evaluative Research*. Russell Sage, New York.

Sundquist, James L. 1969. *Making Federalism Work: A Study of Program Coordination at the Community Level*. Brookings Institution, Washington, D.C.

U.S. Department of Housing and Urban Development. 1973a. *The Model Cities Program: A Comparative Analysis of City Response Patterms and Their Relation to Future Urban Policy*. U.S. Government Printing Office, Washington, D.C.

_____. 1973b. *The Model Cities Program: A Comparative Analysis of Participating Cities: Process, Product, Performance, and Prediction*. U.S. Government Printing Office, Washington, D.C.

_____. 1973c. *Ten Model Cities: A Comparative Analysis of Second Round Planning Years*. U.S. Government Printing Office, Washington, D.C.

_____. 1970. *The Model Cities Program: A Comparative Analysis of the Planning Process in Eleven Cities*. U.S. Government Printing Office, Washington, D.C.

Warren, Roland et al. 1974. *The Structure of Urban Reform*. Lexington Books, D.C. Heath, Lexington, Mass.

Washnis, George. 1974. *Community Development Strategies: Case Studies of Major Model Cities*. Praeger, New York.

Weiss, Robert A. and Martin Rein. 1970. "The Evaluation of Broad-Aim Programs: Experimental Design, Its Difficulties, and an Alternative." *Administrative Science Quarterly* 15 (March), pp. 97-109.

Whiting, John W. M. 1968. "Methods and Problems in Cross-Cultural Research," in Gardner Lindzey and Elliot Aronson, eds., *The Handbook of Social Psychology*, Vol. 2. Addison-Wesley, Reading, Mass.

Wilson, James Q. 1966. "Planning and Politics: Citizen Participation in Urban Renewal," in James Q. Wilson, ed., *Urban Renewal: The Record and the Controversy*. M.I.T. Press, Cambridge, Mass.

Yin, R. K. 1969. "Looking at Upside-Down Faces." *Journal of Experimental Psychology* 81, pp. 141-5.

Yin, R. K., W. A. Lucas, P. O. Szanton, and J. A. Spindler. 1973. *Citizen Organizations: Increasing Client Control over Services*. The Rand Corporation, R-1196-HEW. Santa Monica, Calif.

3

The Outcomes of Urban Decentralization

The overriding initial concern about urban decentralization has to be with its outcomes. Regardless of one's theory of governmental organization or interest in a particular municipal service, the logical first question remains: In the aggregate, what were the decentralization outcomes reported by the case studies? The present chapter deals primarily with this question by examining the outcomes alone as well as by comparing different decentralization strategies in relation to the outcomes. However, since the collective evidence and the conclusions to be drawn from it are no better than the basic evidence presented by each case study, we first describe the nature of this evidence and how it was used in the case survey.

Nature of the Evidence

Five checklist questions (Qs. 98, 102-104, and 89) served as the keys to each of the five decentralization outcomes: increased flow of information, improved agency attitudes, improved client attitudes, improved services, and increased client control. Whenever one of these questions was answered affirmatively, a positive outcome was tallied. (However, for Q. 98, whenever the question was answered affirmatively, this meant—because of the wording of the question—that a *negative* outcome was tallied.) Individual studies could obviously report more than one outcome or none at all. In addition, the remainder of our investigation attends only to the rate of positive outcomes, and does not attempt to distinguish (as in the previous chapter) among positive, negative, and no outcomes.

The case study evidence that was sufficient to register an affirmative answer varied from verbal report (of the case study's author) to evidence from service records to evidence from resident surveys. However, the decentralization innovation in many cases was deemed to have no outcome if there was an absence of evidence and if other facts of the case (for example, the innovation had been in operation for only a few months and no outcomes had been expected at that time) also suggested that no positive outcomes had occurred. The following sections present the rationale for and concrete examples of the types of evidence for each outcome.

49

The Five Outcomes

1. Increased Flow of Information. The appropriate question in the checklist that defined this outcome dealt with increased social contact or the passage of information between servers and served (Q. 98 in the checklist). Such increased information has been seen as a basic objective for decentralization and bringing government closer to people (*Report of the National Advisory Commission on Civil Disorders*, 1968; National Commission on Urban Problems, 1968; and Washnis, 1971). The following excerpts are examples of evidence from specific case studies:

The Public Information Office handles some 4,000 complaints and 8,000 walk-in requests for information annually . . .

. . . *the kids have been allowed to honk the horns, listen to the police radios, turn on the red lights and sirens, get in the car, sit on the cycle, and look at and play with the handcuffs.*

During the first three months, the paraprofessional receptionists served 20,000 clients.

Block captains were residents who agreed to maintain a regular liaison with police.

. . . mounting statistics point toward vastly increased contact between health aides and members of the community.

. . . *outreach workers helped clients to complete forms and prepare letters on the client's behalf.*

. . . the health education aides carried out a community survey to determine residents' perceived health problems.

The school . . . produced a widely acclaimed community information manual which was distributed to every parent or family.

Other ways in which studies recorded increases in the flow of information included notations concerning the occurrence of neighborhood meetings between residents and officials, the provision of referral and informational services, the frequency of parents' visits to schools, and the passing out of posters and other publicity about a new service.

In the vast majority of cases, the evidence about increased flow of information consisted of the author's verbal report. The major exception was in studies of grievance procedures where the number of grievances handled had often been recorded and was therefore presented in tabular form. Table 3-1 presents the total number of responses to the question of increased flow of information, broken down by the source of evidence: the author's report, presentation of service records that reflected service input or output activities, surveys of residents or officials, and none of the above or no information.[a] A total of 132 or *61.4 percent of all the studies indicated that an increase in information had occurred* as a result of the decentralization innovation.

2. Improved Service Officials' Attitudes. The appropriate checklist question (Q. 103) dealt with any evidence that service officials had a more positive attitude toward either the service being rendered or the clients as a result of the innovation. Excerpted examples of evidence for both positive and negative outcomes from specific case studies are as follows:

The mayor and councilmen see branch city halls as performing a valuable service and helping to dispel feelings of remoteness.

. . . spokesmen for the building and police departments state that officials in the neighborhood service centers have improved communications with residents.

[As assessed on a questionnaire], teachers and administrators perceived [the decentralized schools] to have a stronger, freer intellectual atmosphere and a more growth-inducing climate.

. . . police officers responded "yes" when asked whether they thought [the unit] had improved police-community relations.

The [new decentralized police] teams never became popular with non-team members, . . . and [there were] recruiting difficulties.

[Survey results show] agencies which work within little city hall facilities generally feel the program has helped them relate to the city and reach citizens more effectively by their proximity.

The evidence on the second outcome was most frequently based on the author's report or on some formal survey of agency officials. Most of the surveys were not designed with much sophistication. For instance, ratings of the innovation or of officials' performance often called for verbal responses like "more effective," "less effective," or "no change." When surveys were carried out, the author usually presented the results of the survey in tabular form. Table 3-2 presents the summary responses on service officials' attitudes, again broken down by the source of evidence. A total of 27 or *12.6 percent of the studies indicated that service officials' attitudes had improved* as a result of the decentralization innovation. This positive response rate was the lowest for all of the outcomes, which is not unexpected because so few studies even attended to the reactions of service officials in the first place.

3. Improved Client Attitudes. A third checklist question (Q. 102) dealt with changes in client attitudes, either toward service officials or the services

---

[a] Table 3-1 and the following four tables represent cross-tabulations of the checklist questions for each outcome and the parallel question concerning the source of the evidence from Qs. 109-114 of the checklist.

Table 3-1
Outcome 1: Increased Flow of Information

| | Increased Flow of Information | | |
| | Yes | No | No Information |
Source of Evidence			
Author's Report	107	0	0
Service Records	21	1	0
Surveys	4	0	0
None of Above or No Information	0	76	6
Total	132	77	6

rendered, in a manner similar to the previous question on agency attitudes. Since client attitudes are typically of greater concern as a decentralization issue,[b] more of the case studies attempted to assess client attitudes. The following excerpts are examples of this outcome:

[A majority of the] residents surveyed expressed agreement with the statement, "I believe the program makes my neighborhood safe."

Interviews and questionnaires from residents reveal that [they] feel they are "gaining on the system" in the sense of learning what services are available and how to get them.

Citizens view branch city halls as a convenience to them in those areas where service is good. The branches reinforce community identity.

. . . Students [in the decentralization program] responded positively to forty statements about the police, requiring responses from favorable to unfavorable on an 11-point scale.

Community board members surveyed gave a high rating for the community officer program.

[The extent of school vandalism] has been construed as providing a good clue as to whether the community has a sense of partnership and participation in the local school. [Vandalism, however, had not declined.]

Patients were asked to rate their satisfaction with services and to note whether they knew the staff person who had served them.

As with the assessment of service officials' attitudes, the major sources of evidence were the author's report or the results of a survey of residents or clients. The quality of the surveys again varied, with many of the surveys covering only a brief set of questions from a small and not necessarily well defined sample of clients. Table 3-3 shows the summary responses for

[b] The literature abounds with works on government and alienation (see Yin and Lucas, 1973); for an especially sensitive and carefully thought out statement of the problem and the expectations, see Richardson (1967).

Table 3-2
Outcome 2: Improved Service Officials' Attitudes

| | Improved Attitudes | | |
Source of Evidence	Yes	No	No Information
Author's Report	17	30	0
Service Records	0	2	0
Surveys	10	10	1
None of Above or No Information	0	87	58
Total	27	129	59

improvements in client attitudes and also shows that a total of 53 or *24.7 percent of the studies indicated that client attitudes had improved* as a result of the decentralization innovation.

4. Improved Services. The fourth outcome concerned improvements in neighborhood services that could be attributable to the decentralization innovation.[c] Service improvements were assessed by answers to Q. 104 of the checklist, and the case study evidence that constituted a service improvement could consist of either service inputs—for example, increased patient or client utilization of a service, increased availability of funds or resources for a service, or increased manpower —or service outputs—for example, improved reading scores for education, improved health status, lower crime rates, or more jobs as a result of economic development. Both inputs and outputs were scored in the same manner, with both being counted as evidence for service improvement. (One type of service input *not* scored as a service improvement was an increase in grievances investigated. This outcome was considered only an increase in information flow and not a service improvement.) Examples of evidence for this outcome from specific case studies are the following:

[40 percent of the student's physical problems were treated, and] . . . most children received immunizations for the first time. Free eyeglasses were provided.

. . . *achievement in the community controlled schools apparently improved over the three-year period of their existence.*

[There were] 945 interventions, involving 665 families.

---

[c] The concern for improved services as a major outcome of decentralization is found throughout the literature. For a start, see the several articles in the special issue of *Public Administration Review* (1972), "Curriculum Essays on Citizens, Politics, and Administration in Urban Neighborhoods."

Table 3-3
Outcome 3: Improved Client Attitudes

	Improved Attitudes		
Source of Evidence	Yes	No	No Information
Author's Report	27	26	2
Service Records	1	1	0
Surveys	25	14	3
None of Above or No Information	0	71	45
Total	53	112	50

Over a three-year period roughly $2 million [in loans] have been provided to forty-eight local firms.

. . . more than 1,450 houses have been renovated in a program that has employed over 900 formerly unemployed and unskilled youths.

[Before the clinic was expanded, there were] 350 patients per month. Afterwards, the average was 550 patients per month.

1,000 patient visits were analyzed for the average number of diagnostic and treatment actions, and compared with those of three non-poverty clinics.

For calendar 1970, 1887 individuals were registered at the center and participation [in its service activities] totaled 47,438.

The results of the 1971 test were lower even than those of the tests given to the same schools in 1967.

[The decentralization program has resulted in] . . . 135 ditches being cleaned, 55 streets being repaired, 45 lots being cut and cleaned.

As these examples readily indicate, the significance of the service improvement varied substantially, both in the number and kind. Ideally, it would have been desirable to distinguish the more important improvements from the less important ones, just as the decentralization efforts themselves should have been divided into those with many versus few resources. The case studies, however, rarely permitted such distinctions about either the level of effort or the significance of the outcome. As a result, any improvement, no matter how large or small, was tallied as a positive response. Table 3-4 shows that a total of 142 or *66.1 percent of the case studies indicated an improvement in services* attributable to the decentralization innovation. The table also shows that unlike the other four outcomes, the vast majority of the studies provided evidence other than verbal report.

5. Increased Client Control. The fifth and last outcome was reflected in the checklist question on the clients' experience in implementing their own

Table 3-4
Outcome 4: Improved Services

| Source of Evidence | Improved Services | | |
	Yes	No	No Information
Author's Report	49	7	6
Service Records	87	13	0
Surveys	6	0	0
None of the Above or No Information	0	35	12
Total	142	55	18

ideas in organizing services (Q. 89). An affirmative answer to this question meant that the case study had pointed to some decision that had been made or heavily influenced by the clients. Client control over governmental services has obviously been one of the most important objectives of decentralization (Kotler, 1969; Altshuler, 1970; Hallman, 1970; and Frederickson, 1973). Examples excerpted from this evidence for both positive and negative outcomes are as follows:

When the School Board proposed that a community school coordinator should have a salary of $14,000 and academic requirements that would have eliminated [neighborhood] residents from consideration, the [local board] came in with a counterproposal. Finally, a compromise was reached that there should be a $10,000 coordinator and a $6,000 assistant coordinator as a resident-in-training for the job.

Residents helped to develop the neighborhood youth center and the drug abuse and new careers programs.

The [citizen board] chose the site . . . and reviewed staff appointments for the new health center.

. . . the community boards won the right to appoint their own local superintendent to either 2- or 4-year contracts. Previously the local superintendents were named, virtually for life, by the central board.

. . . a regional board acceded to the demands of a group of black parents to remove a principal in clear violation of the school system's contract with the principals' union.

To date, minimal success has been experienced in establishing lay advisory groups or councils.

[The Patient Advisory] Committee does not have much influence over service policies . . . professionals treat [the committee] paternalistically and/or use [it] for their own ends.

. . . forty [neighborhood] residents elected in neighborhood elections and seventeen appointed agency representatives serve on the . . . board, which plans and governs the. . . program.

In the economic development case studies, an important distinction was made between profit-making organizations with shareholders at large (no increased control), nonprofit organizations run by a very small group of self-selected members (no increased control), and nonprofit organizations run by a large group of board members with at least one-third client representation (increased control). This distinction had to be made independent of the boards' actual functions, which all tended to include governing powers. In general, as with the outcome of improved services, the outcome of increased control included significant as well as minor types of control, with either type leading to an affirmative response. Table 3-5 shows that a total of 48 or *22.3 percent of the case studies indicated an increase in client control* as a result of the decentralization innovation. As one might expect, the source of evidence was most frequently the report of the author.

Summary

In summary, the two dominant outcomes for all 215 case studies were improved services and increased flow of information. In other words, about 66 percent of all the studies reported an association between decentralization and an improvement in services, whether of a major or minor sort, and about 61 percent of the studies reported an association between decentralization and an improved flow of information. The other three outcomes each occurred in less than 25 percent of the studies (see Figure 3-1). These rates of outcomes, especially of improved services, suggest that *the case studies have on balance reported a fairly positive picture for the decentralization experience*. Certainly the results do not warrant any of the strongly negative interpretations of the overall decentralization experience, a point that we shall discuss further in Chapter 10.

The Pattern of Outcomes

Lack of Tradeoffs among Outcomes

The aggregation of outcomes also makes it possible to compare those studies (and their characteristics) that have positive outcomes and those studies that have no positive outcomes. This procedure first means that the five outcomes can be examined for any potential tradeoffs—that is, a prevailing question about decentralization is whether certain outcomes tend to occur only at the expense of other outcomes. (Some of the more critical views of decentralization, including possible tradeoffs among out-

Table 3-5
Outcome 5: Increased Client Control

Source of Evidence	Increased Control		
	Yes	No	No Information
Author's Report	42	46	2
Service Records	4	1	0
Surveys	2	11	1
None of the Above or No Information	0	87	19
Total	48	145	22

comes, are discussed in Schmandt, 1972.) In particular, increased citizen control may occur to the exclusion of improved services, or vice versa. To test this and similar hypotheses regarding the relationship among the five outcomes, cross-tabulations were carried out for the 215 case studies, with each paired combination of the five outcomes being examined.

The results of such cross-tabulations showed the following *significant* relationships:

1. The occurrence of increased client control, as an outcome, is *positively* related to the occurrence of improved services (see Table 3-6).
2. The occurrence of improved service officials' attitudes is *positively* related to the occurrence of improved client attitudes (see Table 3-7).

None of the other cross-tabulations among the five outcomes showed a significant relationship in a positive or negative direction. These results thus show that when the five outcomes are considered in each possible pair of combinations with each other, there are no negative tradeoffs among any of the outcomes, as the only significant relationships are positive.

Relationship of Outcomes to Decentralization Strategies

The systematic aggregation of outcomes also means that the rate of positive outcomes can be associated with the frequency of occurrence of other case study characteristics. In particular, the seven decentralization strategies can be compared in terms of these outcomes. Table 3-8 presents a summary overview of the success rates associated with each of the seven strategies in regard to the five outcomes. Each number in the table represents the percentage frequency a given strategy was associated with a given outcome. The effectiveness of each strategy may thus be judged both in

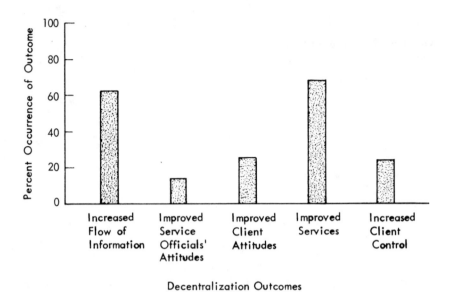

Figure 3-1 Results for Five Decentralization Outcomes

comparison to the other strategies as well as in comparison to the overall success rate for all of the studies, shown in the last row of the table. For instance, the first percentage in Table 3-8 indicates that, of the 87 studies with a community relations strategy, 96.6 percent had an increase in information flow, which was the highest success rate for that outcome.

This overall comparison of strategies reveals that no single strategy is consistently related to high rates of success on all outcomes. There is a tendency, however, for the first four (or weaker) strategies to be associated with higher frequencies of increased information, and for the last three (or stronger) strategies to be associated with higher frequencies of both improved services and increased control.

Relationship to Weak, Moderate, and Strong Strategies

Unfortunately, for analytic purposes this strategies-by-outcomes matrix oversimplifies the real strategy-outcome relationship, because many decentralization innovations involve more than one strategy. An economic development innovation, for instance, might simultaneously include the establishment of a nonprofit neighborhood organization (new neighborhood institution), the election of a resident-dominated governing board

Table 3-6
Relationship Between Increased Client Control and Improved Services, for All Case Studies

	Improved Services		
Increased Client Control	Yes	No	No Information
Yes	37	7	4
No	91	45	9
No Information	14	3	5

$\chi^2 = 4.77$, $df = 1$, $p < .05$.
Note: N = 215; excludes "no information" cases.

Table 3-7
Relationship Between Improved Client Attitudes and Improved Service Officials' Attitudes, for All Case Studies

	Improved Service Attitudes		
Improved Client Attitudes	Yes	No	No Information
Yes	19	23	11
No	4	105	3
No Information	4	1	45

$\chi^2 = 40.56$, $df = 1$, $p < .001$.
Note: N = 215; excludes "no information" cases.

(political decentralization), and the development of an employment program to use residents to fill the organization's positions (employment). As another example, a school decentralization innovation could include the granting of greater discretionary authority to the district superintendent (administrative decentralization), the election of a resident-dominated district board (political decentralization), and the initiation of a formal campaign to inform parents of school activities and encourage their visiting of the schools (community relations). In these innovations with multiple strategies, the case survey made no attempt to converge on a single overriding strategy, but merely noted the occurrence of each strategy that was involved. For this reason, the total number of strategies in the aggregate is larger than the total number of case studies, and any simple comparison between single strategies may be misleading.

Table 3-8
Outcomes for Seven Decentralization Strategies

Decentralization Strategy[a]	More Information	Percentage Occurrence of Outcome			
		Improved Agency Attitudes	Improved Client Attitudes	Improved Services	More Client Control
Community relations (n = 87)	96.6	17.2	33.3	63.2	19.5
Physical Redeployment (n = 67)	88.1	12.0	23.8	65.6	10.4
Grievance Mechanisms (n = 58)	93.1	18.9	25.8	58.6	34.5
Administrative decentralization (n = 43)	72.1	18.6	28.0	69.8	32.6
Employment of Neighborhood Residents (n = 99)	50.5	14.2	24.2	79.9	31.3
New Neighborhood Institutions (n = 116)	50.0	5.2	18.1	75.8	19.8
Political Decentralization (n = 93)	51.6	9.7	23.7	74.2	45.2
All Case Studies	1.4	12.6	24.7	66.1	22.3

Note: N = 215.
[a]Total number of strategies is greater than the number of studies because of multiple occurrences of strategies within single studies.

An alternative procedure is to divide the strategies into *mutually exclusive categories* so that each case study falls into only one such category. Since the major concern of our study is on the comparison of weak, moderate, and strong decentralization strategies as defined in Chapter 2, the three categories were defined in the following manner:

1. *Weak Decentralization*, which includes any case study dominated by the community relations, physical redeployment, grievance mechanisms, or administrative decentralization strategies. For instance, if a case study had three of these strategies in addition to the employment and new neighborhood institution strategies, the innovation was categorized as representing weak decentralization.
2. *Moderate Decentralization*, which includes any case study dominated by the employment or new neighborhood institution strategies. If a case study had either of these and only one or two of the above weak forms, it was categorized as representing moderate decentralization.
3. *Strong Decentralization*, which includes any case study in which the political decentralization strategy occurred, regardless of the other strategies that might also have been involved in the innovation.

These three categories therefore served as a way of grouping all of the case studies. In total, 66 case studies fell into the weak category, 56 into the moderate category, and 93 into the strong category.

When these weak, moderate, and strong groups are compared in terms of the frequency of the five outcomes produced, the results show that:

1. *Strong forms of decentralization are associated with higher frequencies of improved services and increased client control.*

2. *Weak forms are associated with increased information.*

3. *No significant differences are observed for improved agency attitudes and improved client attitudes.* (See Table 3-9.)

For both the service and control outcomes, strong decentralization is associated with the highest success rate, moderate decentralization is associated with an intermediate success rate, and weak decentralization is associated with the lowest rate.[d] In other words, strong decentralization can be more successful than weak decentralization in achieving *both* the service improvement and client control outcomes, which have usually been of greater concern than the other three outcomes in assessing the effect of decentralization.

The lack of any relationship between the strength of the decentralization strategy and either service officials' or clients' attitudes is consistent with a theme found in the past—that decentralization innovations probably have little effect on attitudes about government (Yin and Lucas, 1973). Such attitudes appear to be based on many factors, not those concerned merely with a specific local service, and cannot be expected to be changed on the basis of innovations in a specific service. Media coverage, national and even foreign affairs, and simple awareness of local events and service changes are all as likely as the innovation itself to be important in shaping attitudes toward a specific local service such as police protection, education, or health services. The results presented throughout the following chapters all reinforce this theme, as none of the factors examined appears to bear any relationship to changes in attitudes.

Relationship to Service Areas

If strong decentralization strategies have been so clearly related to positive

---

[d] We made a separate investigation of the possibility that differences in strategy complexity, and hence possibly in level of effort, could account for these results (i.e., "weak" decentralization strategies might more frequently be strategies tried singly and reflect less of an effort at decentralizing; hence fewer outcomes would be expected). When the outcomes are compared for studies involving different numbers of strategies simultaneously (i.e., studies with one strategy versus studies with two strategies versus studies with three strategies, and so forth without regard to the type of strategy), slight differences were found that could account for some but not all of the pattern of outcomes for strong versus weak strategies.

Table 3-9
Weak, Moderate, and Strong Decentralization Strategies, by Five Outcomes

Type of Decentralization Strategy	Total Number of Studies	Percentage Occurrence of Outcome[a]				
		More Infor- mation	Improved Agency Attitudes	Improved Client Attitudes	Improved Services	More Client Control
Weak	66	84.8	16.7	27.3	54.5	1.5
Moderate	56	60.7	12.5	23.2	66.1	8.9
Strong	93	45.2	9.7	33.7	74.2	45.2
All Studies	215	61.4	12.6	24.7	66.1	22.3

[a]χ^2 differences for the outcomes are significant at the $p < .01$ level for more information, improved services, and more client control.

outcomes for improved services and increased client control, then it is important to understand why this is so and the conditions under which strong decentralization can take place. One of the most important factors here appears to be the nature of the service bureaucracy and the specific service being decentralized. Different services are characterized by different decentralization outcomes. For the five service areas covered in the present study, Figures 3-2 through 3-6 show that the service areas varied significantly not only in terms of their overall levels of positive outcomes but also in their patterns of success for weak, moderate, and strong strategies. On the increased flow of information, for instance, the economic development studies had the lowest overall rate of success, but none of the successful cases involved weak strategies, whereas the opposite tended to be true for the safety and multiservice areas (see Figure 3-2). Conversely, the safety studies had the lowest overall rate of success for improved services, but few of the successful cases involved strong strategies, whereas the opposite tended to be true for economic development and education (see Figure 3-5). In all of these figures, the rates of success for each service area are attributable to a combination of *two factors*: (1) the effectiveness of a given type of strategy in producing a given outcome, and (2) the frequency of occurrence of a given type of strategy in each service. For instance, we have noted that the safety studies show a low rate of success for improved services; the particularly low rate for strong strategies is attributable *both* to the fact that the strong strategies did not do as well in safety *and* to the fact that few strong strategies were attempted in safety in the first place.

Thus it appears that *variations in these five service areas account for major differences in decentralization strategies attempted and outcomes achieved*. One possible reason for these service differences is that the

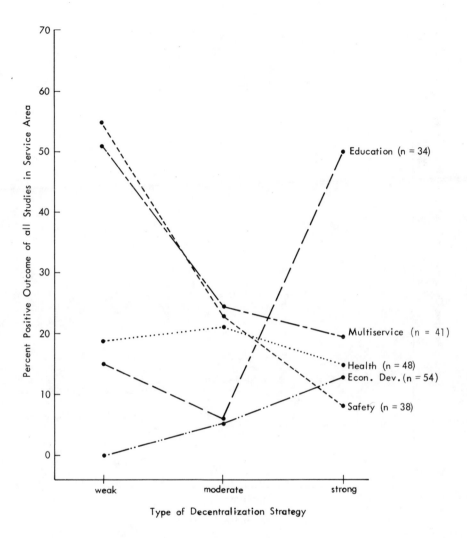

Figure 3-2. Relationship between Type of Decentralization Strategy and Increased Flow of Information

server-served relationship in each service is somewhat different. Police protection and health are dominated by a highly professional server group that sets the rules for service delivery. Clients have traditionally had little policy influence over these services, even though considerable discretion may be exercised in individual police-citizen or doctor-patient relationships. In multiservice programs there is no dominant professional server group, but there has also been no traditional mechanism for clients to

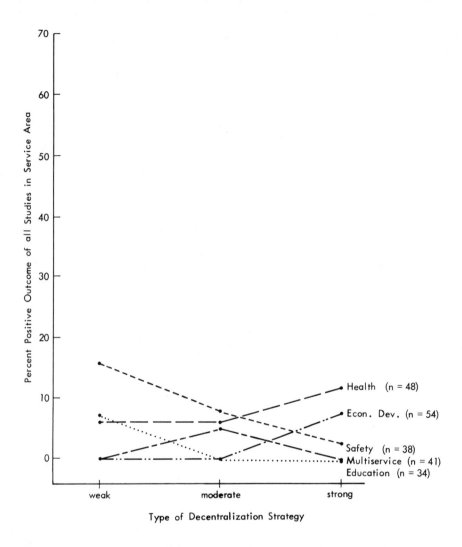

Figure 3-3. Relationship between Type of Decentralization Strategy and Improved Service Officials' Attitudes

participate in policymaking. A nonprofessional server group has taken advantage of bureaucratic devices and has minimized participatory mechanisms. The development of such mechanisms, however, would presumably be easier than in police protection or health, where strong resistance from the server group would also be based on both professional and bureaucratic grounds. In education and economic development, clients have had greater opportunities for influencing policymaking. In education,

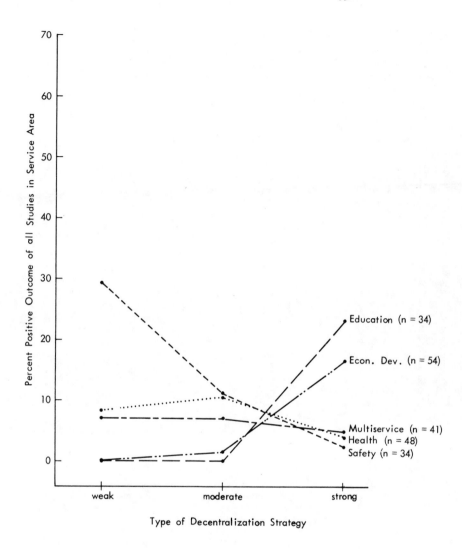

Figure 3-4. Relationship between Type of Decentralization Strategy and Improved Client Attitudes

the traditional openness of the service (the school facility) to parents and the establishment of joint parent-teacher organizations and activities have provided a basis for the exchange of ideas between servers and served as well as for the potential influence of parents in school policy. In economic development, the public service is fairly new on the urban scene, but the basic tenet of organization has been an even stronger sharing of responsibility between servers and served.

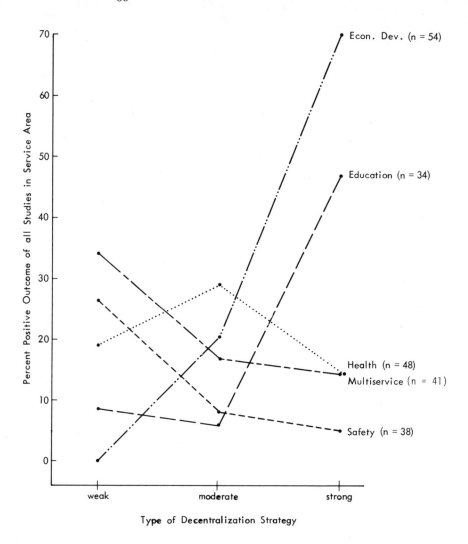

Figure 3-5. Relationship between Type of Decentralization Strategy and Improved Services

There thus appear to be two important elements at work here: the degree of professionalism and the scope of bureaucratic control. The more a service area possesses these two characteristics, the more *closed* it will be to client influence; the less a service possesses these characteristics, the more *open* it will be. Given these two elements, the five services in our study could be ranked as shown in Tables 3-10. This basic nature of the service bureaucracy will not only affect the outcomes of any decentraliza-

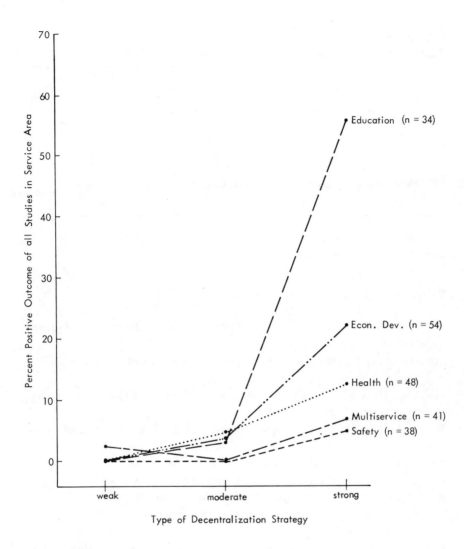

Figure 3-6. Relationship between Type of Decentralization Strategy and Increased Client Control

tion but will also affect the types of decentralization innovations tried in the first place. The following chapters therefore describe the events surrounding decentralization in each of the five service areas and particularly how the service characteristics may have conditioned the decentralization experience. These services are discussed in the order of their ranking, and each chapter deals with the specific results of the case survey in the given service area. Chapter 9, which follows the five service chapters, then

Table 3-10
Ranking of Five Service Areas by Server-Served Relationship

	Degree of Server Control over Policies	
Service	Professional	Bureaucratic
Safety	High	High
Health	High	Moderate
Multiservice Programs	Low	High
Education	Moderate	Moderate
Economic Development	Low	Low

summarizes the findings and attempts to place them within a general explanation of the outcomes of decentralization.

References

Altshuler, Alan. 1970. *Community Control: The Black Demand for Participation in Large American Cities. Pegasus, New York.*

Frederickson, George, ed. 1973. *Neighborhood Control in the 1970s.* Chandler, New York.

Hallman, Howard W. 1970. *Neighborhood Control of Public Programs.* Praeger, New York.

Kotler, Milton. 1969. *Neighborhood Government: The Local Foundations of Political Life.* Bobbs-Merrill, Indianapolis.

National Commission on Urban Problems. 1968. *Building the American City.* U.S. Government Printing Office, Washington, D.C.

Public Administration Review. 1972. "Curriculum Essays on Citizens, Politics, and Administration in Urban Neighborhoods." Special issue, vol. 32, (October).

Report of the National Advisory Commission on Civil Disorders. 1968. Bantam, New York.,

Richardson, Elliot. 1967. "Significant Individual Participation: The New Challenge in Government." *The University of Chicago Law School Record* 15 (Autumn), pp. 37-44.

Schmandt, Henry J. 1972. "Municipal Decentralization: An Overview." *Public Administration Review* 32 (October), pp. 571-88.

Washnis, George J. 1971. *Little City Halls.* Center for Governmental Studies, Washington, D.C.

Yin, R. K. and W. A. Lucas. 1973. "Decentralization and Alienation." *Policy Sciences* 4 (September), pp. 327-36.

4   Public Safety

Prelude to Decentralization

As the guardians of neighborhood safety in a democratic society, police and fire officers have unusual responsibilities but also enjoy very special privileges. These public safety officers must be prepared to give their lives and risk serious injuries in carrying out their duties. As part of these duties, society legitimately grants these officers the discretionary use of force over citizens and property, whether to apprehend suspected criminals, destroy private property, or prevent the spread of a nearby fire. Both the responsibilities and the privileges are subject to abuse and excesses. Fire officers, for instance, may be called upon to risk their lives unnecessarily by fighting fires in vacant buildings that frequently involve several fires in the same building on the same night. However, there have also been clear incidents where police or fire officers have abused their privileged use of force.

During the 1960s, both the role of the public safety officer and his relationship to neighborhood residents were put to a severe test. Crime rates and fire alarm rates rose precipitously in large cities, and there was a general increase in demand for public safety service in cities across the country. At the same time, there was also a sharp increase in the number of assaults by residents on the very public safety officers who were serving their neighborhoods. For firemen, these assaults mostly took the form of harassment—bricks and rocks thrown at the firemen while they were responding to calls or fighting fires. (Such harassment incidents were responsible for the addition, in a few cities, of rear canopies attached to the fire trucks, which can still be seen on the trucks today even though the harassment incidents appear to have subsided.) For policemen in the 1960s, physical assaults with intent to kill were no longer unique incidents.

The civil disorders that occurred in many cities in the mid-1960s highlighted the strained relationship between residents and their public safety officers. Although the disorders were undoubtedly reactions to many social problems—including poverty, unemployment, deteriorated housing, and racial discrimination—police and fire officials bore the brunt of the hostilities. As a result, national attention focused on *the improvement of the relationship between citizens and their police and fire officers.* Nowhere more than in public safety was the loss of social symmetry between servers and served more apparent. The challenge became, as one author put it, one of restoring the *civil* relationship between citizens and safety officers, in

69

which people behave with a sense of concern and responsibility for the interests of others, citizens grant legitimacy to the intervention of police in citizen affairs, and the police are accountable to civil authority and the people protected from police tyranny (Reiss, 1971). The police, because of their wider range of functions, potential use of lethal force, and greater numbers, received the greater attention; however, it should be remembered that fire departments suffered similar problems.[a]

Blacks and the Police

Surveys during the 1960s consistently showed that the poor relationship between the public safety officer and the resident primarily involved a communication gap between the white policeman and the black resident. The subsequent attempts to improve the relationship between citizens and public safety officers have really been attempts to deal with this particular communication gap.

The surveys showed that the police usually reflected the more conservative political leanings of the broader community. They tended to stereotype blacks as troublemakers, as an ungrateful minority dissatisfied with its already privileged position, and as a minority willing to use violence to attain its objectives (Bayley and Mendelsohn, 1968; Mendelsohn, 1970; Groves and Rossi, 1970; and Norris, 1973). In other studies, black residents, on their part, were found to be more dissatisfied with their police services than any other group of citizens (Campbell and Schuman, 1971, p.8). The dissatisfaction held by black residents generally covered four aspects of police work: (1) police discrimination in enforcing the law and in choosing which laws to enforce; (2) police provision of poorer service to blacks than to other neighborhoods; (3) police harassment, verbal abuse, and brutality against black residents; and (4) lack of effective resources for residents to make complaints about police behavior or service (Gourley 1954; Angell et al., 1967; President's Commission on Law Enforcement and Administration of Justice, 1967; *Report of the National Advisory Commission on Civil Disorders,* 1968, pp. 299-322; Bayley and Mendelsohn, 1968; Bouma, 1969; Wallach et al., 1971; and Hahn, 1971a). The four aspects of blacks' dissatisfaction cover both of the major functions of police work, as stated in James Wilson's (1968) terms, order maintenance and law enforcement. It is important to remember, however, that much of the discontent with the police also reflected discontent with the legal system in

---

[a] It should also be pointed out that private police also play an important role in preserving neighborhood safety, but they are not included in the following discussion. A recent study found that private security personnel constitute about one-half of all security personnel (Kakalik and Wildhorn, 1971).

general, and that attention often focused on police service only because it was the most frequent occasion for citizen interaction with the law (Hahn, 1971a).

To a certain extent, the poor relationship between black residents and the police also existed among other population subgroups. These included the Spanish-speaking, youths in general, and people with low incomes in general (see, for instance, *Task Force Report: The Police*, 1967). While each population subgroup may have had slightly different dissatisfactions, and while the specific service factors undoubtedly varied from city to city and neighborhood to neighborhood, there nevertheless emerged several basic approaches for improving the relationship between citizens and their public safety officers. These approaches became the basis for a variety of innovations and intervention programs. Before we assess the outcome of these interventions, we shall describe the rationale for each approach.

Strategies for Change

There have been five basic approaches to improving the relationship between citizens and the police:

1. Improving the *informal communications* between citizens and the police;
2. Changing *police personnel* through recruitment, training, and promotion policies;
3. Changing the *procedures in police operations*;
4. Making the entire police apparatus responsible to *external review or control*;
5. Developing entirely *separate, community-based patrol* capabilities.

Each of these approaches, as we shall see, uses at least one of the seven decentralization strategies that are the main concern of our study.

Informal Communications. The first approach calls for the development of some sort of community relations program within a police department. The rationale for such a program is that better communications between the servers and the served will increase mutual trust—that is, if police and residents have better information about each other, then they may better appreciate their roles and reduce their mutual antagonisms. More information, in other words, will lead to actual changes in the attitudes of both the police and the residents, and these attitude changes will restore satisfactory services, since the police and residents would no longer have hostile stereotypes of each other (Kreps and Weller, 1973.)

The development of a community relations program occasionally involves activities on a department-wide basis. More often, however, it involves the formation of a special organizational entity, a police-community relations unit, to report separately to the city's top police commander. The first city to develop a formal community relations program was St. Louis in 1955. Other cities eventually adopted their own programs, with strong urging by such national commissions as the President's Commission on Law Enforcement and Administration of Justice (the Katzenbach Commission).[b] The community relations programs that have been created have emphasized any number of educational and interactive activities including:

Police relations on the part of the police;

Police training about contemporary social issues;

Residents' education about police practices;

Meetings between police and residents that may vary from formal sensitivity training sessions to occasions for questions and answers;

Police-sponsored recreation programs for youths; and

Provision of actual information and referral services by the police in helping residents to cope with the problems in their daily lives.[c]

Community relations programs were the most common response made by police departments to the problem of improving citizen-police relations (Earle, 1967; Momboisse, 1967; and Brandstatter and Radelet, 1968.) By 1970, the vast majority of cities with over 500,000 people had developed some sort of community relations program (see Table 4-1). To their credit, the community relations programs in many cases focused directly on the most inflammatory incidents in an attempt to prevent civil disorders and to reduce citizen-police tensions.

Police Personnel. A second approach is based on the rationale that the most effective means of improving citizen-police relations is merely to hire and promote better police. This approach assumes that poor police services and abuse of ghetto citizens are attributable to poorly trained officers exercising bad judgment. Better trained police, acting in a more professional manner—and also more sympathetic with or knowledgeable about ghetto conditions—would thus alleviate the problem.

Many changes in police personnel policies have therefore been advocated in order to foster both professionalization and greater understanding of ghetto problems among police officers. These changes include:

---

[b] See the Commission's report, *The Challenge of Crime in a Free Society* (1967), but note, however, that police-community relations units were *not* recommended by the National Advisory Commission on Civil Disorders (Kerner Commission) in its report a year later.

[c] A brief description and typology of community relations programs can be found in Brown (1971). Again, although little has been written about them, it should be remembered that fire departments also established community relations programs along similar lines.

Table 4-1
Cities with Police-Community Relations Programs, 1970

Population Group	Number of Cities Surveyed	Cities Responding	
		Number	Percent
Total, All Cities	2,072	667	32
City Population			
Over 500,000	27	24	89
250,000-500,000	27	23	85
100,000-250,000	96	80	83
50,000-100,000	232	144	62
25,000-50,000	477	138	29
10,000-25,000	1,213	258	21

Source: International City Management Association, "Recent Trends in Police-Community Relations," *Urban Data Service* 2, no. 3, (March 1970).

Increasing police pay to attract better qualified candidates;

Recruiting heavily from minority and black residents;

Designing intensive training programs to raise the general level of education among officers;

Establishing new apprentice-level positions to recruit neighborhood youths into the police department;

Increasing lateral entry for officers at all levels.

Among these personnel policies, the one that most directly involves a decentralization strategy is an employment program, the establishment of apprentice-level positions for neighborhood youths. These positions, usually known as Community Service Officers, were recommended by both the Katzenbach and Kerner Commissions (President's Commission, 1967; and *Report of the National Advisory Commission on Civil Disorders,* 1968). The new recruits were hired to learn about police operations and to carry out all duties not requiring the use of weapons. In theory, these apprenticeship positions could also lead to advancement into full-time officer positions.

Police Operations. The third approach arises from the observation that citizen-police encounters in law enforcement situations are often the immediate source of citizen dissatisfaction and of police and citizen stereotyping (e.g., Bayley and Mendelsohn, 1968, pp. 68-76). The use of motorized patrol, for instance, has been frequently cited as resulting in fewer informal contacts between individual patrolmen on the beat and neighborhood residents. This practice, combined with aggressive patrol and field interrogation, has meant that most police-citizen contacts occur under hostile conditions and produce antagonistic feelings (Bordua and Tifft, 1971). If encounters with potential criminals are the only contacts police have in a neighborhood, it may be easy for them to stereotype that neighborhood as being filled with criminal types (Condlin, 1969-70). One actual survey of police found that 31 percent of the police did not know a single important teenage or youth leader in their precincts well enough to speak with whenever they saw him (Groves and Rossi, 1970). The approach thus assumes that changes in these patrol operations will improve citizen-police relations. This approach also implies that the traditional police-community relations programs, training programs, and personnel policies as previously described are all likely to fail. As one author states:

[T]he relations between police and citizens are a result of the effort of the police to attain their major objectives—crime prevention, criminal apprehension, and order maintenance. . . .

The chief policy implication of this argument is that police-community relations cannot be substantially improved by programs designed to deal with the citizen in settings other than encounters with patrolmen. . . . Nor can the behavior of patrolmen be modified other than providing him with incentives and instructions relevant to his central task [Wilson, 1972].

The most common innovation stemming from this approach has been a combination of physical redeployment and administrative decentralization. Whole patrol units, or teams, are given greater responsibility for policing small geographic areas. The team commander may have considerable discretion in deploying the team members, and team responsibilities may include both patrol and investigative (detective) functions. The hope is that the team members will communicate closely and be able to provide relevant services to a particular area and that the consistency of personnel will mean that, over a period of time, team members and residents will get to know each other on a more personal basis (Bloch and Specht, 1973; and Sherman et al., 1973). In some cases, teams may even hold informal meetings with residents. The important difference between these and community relations meetings is that the residents are dealing directly with the team members or officers who patrol their neighborhood.

External Control. The fourth approach looks outside rather than inside the police department for reform. Its major rationale again appears intuitively plausible: If police are held accountable to citizens through some external control mechanism, then police operations and citizen-police relations should change in a desirable direction. Two types of external control mechanisms—grievance investigation and community control—have dominated discussion in the literature, though in fact few innovations have actually taken place.

Grievances against police misconduct have been responsible for the call to develop citizen-dominated grievance investigation procedures. The felt

need for external control reflects dissatisfaction with the traditional grievance procedures, which involve a police department's own internal review
of police behavior and investigation of citizen complaints. These internal
review procedures often leave much to be desired, as procedural for-
malities discourage citizens from filing complaints, hearings may be held in
secrecy, recommendations are seldom disclosed to the public or the comp-
lainant, and there have been few meaningful disciplinary actions (*Virginia
Law Review*, 1969). Although the police can rightfully claim that they have
the best expertise to investigate any complaints against their services
(Locke, 1967), an internal review procedure unfortunately fails, as with
most self-investigations by public agencies (Reiss, 1970), to guarantee an
impartial investigation.

Recommendations to develop external complaint procedures have been
made from many quarters, including the Kerner Commission. The proposed external procedures have involved a civilian review board that
would hold hearings and make recommendations on a complaint, or a
citywide (or multiagency) ombudsman who would do the same but investigate complaints against any number of agencies, not just the police. Civilian review boards tend to raise considerable controversy. For one thing,
they unfairly focus attention only on the police; most proposals to develop
review boards have met with strong resistance from the police, and
Philadelphia appears to be the only city in which a review board operated
for any length of time. Ombudsmen, however, while not focusing just on
the police, may not have the option of using conciliation to settle citizen-
police differences. (*Virginia Law Review*, 1969; and Berleman, 1972).
(Since ombudsmen are usually multiservice agents, further discussion of
this innovation will be found in Chapter 6.)

The second type of external control has been direct community control
or political decentralization. The idea here is that precinct commanders
could be made responsible to a neighborhood-elected board, but they
would also coordinate activities with the rest of the department. The major
difficulty, of course, is in applying uniform standards of enforcement while
serving diverse neighborhood needs (Hahn, 1971b). Not surprisingly,
community control of the police has not been accomplished in any city,
although a pilot project was started in Washington, D.C., and police forces
controlled by communities of different sizes have been studied in Indianapolis (for Washington, see Kelley et al., 1972; for Indianapolis, see
Ostrom and Whitaker, 1973).

Community Police. The fifth and last approach is also external to the police
department and simply calls for a separate police force—responsible to the
community—that serves as a new neighborhood institution. This approach
assumes that the question of citizen-police relations may be bypassed
entirely, with the community receiving police services from a separate

force (Waskow, 1970). Although this approach at first glance seems to raise the specter of severe political clashes between the existing and new police forces, in actuality the experiments that have been conducted have only called for a narrow definition of the community patrol's responsibilities. In some cases, community patrols have evolved in order to deal with riots and reduce community tensions (Knopf, 1969). In other cases, community patrols have served to protect specific residential blocks or housing projects and have even gained cooperation from the existing police departments (Marx and Archer, 1971).

Summary of Change Strategies

The variety of strategies tried in public safety has actually mirrored, in one fashion or another, each of the seven decentralization strategies that is the broader concern of our study—that is to say, the community relations strategy is reflected in the community relations program; the physical redeployment and administrative decentralization strategies are reflected in team policing; grievance mechanisms in civilian review boards; employment in the community service officer programs; and new neighborhood institutions or political decentralization in the various innovations with community patrols or community-controlled police. However, as the case survey will show, not all of these strategies have been attempted with equal frequency. The essentially closed nature of the police service, which reflects both a high degree of professional police organization as well as a tight control over the service bureaucracy by the police, has created a service environment in which clients have traditionally had very little influence over service policymaking. Clients, for instance, have typically had little to say over the circumstances under which they interact with the police, whether in the street or in the precinct house. Only recent decisions by the Supreme Court have affected the ground rules for these interactions. As a result of the high degree of server control, the police decentralization innovations have been marked by weak strategies.

Results of the Case Survey

The case survey reviewed 38 studies of public safety innovations. The studies covered 33 discrete innovations and included reports on every well known police-community relations program across the country, many reports of team policing experiments, and several independent studies of the two familiar civilian review board innovations in Philadelphia and New York. In addition, there were also studies of community patrols and of police aide employment programs. Table 4-2 lists the major innovations, their characteristics, and the prominent outcomes.

Strategies Attempted

Each of the seven decentralization strategies was found in the 38 studies, with many of the innovations involving a combination of strategies.[d] Whenever such multiple strategies occurred, the same case study was characterized once for *each* of the component strategies. Table 4-3 shows the frequency with which each strategy was represented and also shows that the number of studies declines consistently with increasingly stronger forms of decentralization, which suggests that the safety innovations in general have not usually involved strong forms of decentralization. In terms of the three previously defined mutually exclusive sets of strategies, there were 24 cases of weak decentralization, 10 cases of moderate decentralization, and only 4 of strong decentralization. This pattern of strategies attempted is not surprising, given the strong control of the police over their own service. Nearly every aspect of police operations precludes any civilian control, and the most severe conflicts have occurred in cities where civilian review or control of any sort has been proposed, much less implemented.

Outcomes[e]

Among the outcomes, the case studies most frequently indicated an increased flow of information and least frequently an increased client control over services. In a comparison of these outcomes with those in the service areas reported in the next four chapters, three features stand out: The public safety studies had a substantially higher rate of improved client attitudes, a substantially lower rate of improved services, and a lower rate

---

[d]The frequent combinations of strategies were attributable to such innovations as team policing, which involved the redeployment of personnel (physical redeployment), downward shifts in command authority from the precinct house to a team leader (administration decentralization), and special attention to community affairs (community relations), all at the same time. Another frequent combination was attributable to the civilian review boards and other grievance mechanisms, which often simultaneously involved a complaint procedure (grievance mechanism) and the appointment of a citizen board (new neighborhood institution). In this and the following chapters, wherever such multiple strategies occurred, the same case study was categorized once for *each* of the component strategies. No attempt has been made to reduce every study to a single, dominant strategy.

[e]The outcomes of the public safety innovations were assessed in different ways. First, most studies indicated an increase in contact between policemen and the public. Any evidence of increased social contact or transmission of written materials was coded as an increase in

Table 4-2
Major Neighborhood Safety Innovations

Date	Location	Area of Coverage	Main Innovation	Major Reported Outcomes
1955	St. Louis	3 police districts subsequently expanded to a total of 12 districts.	Organization of a citizen-police community relations program in 3 high-crime districts, including a citizens' steering committee; development of district projects on burglary prevention; new citizens' panels on juvenile delinquency.	Improvement in communications between the police department and social service administrators; improvements in coordination of social service agencies to deal with school truancy; increased positive contact between police and citizens.
1958	Philadelphia	Citywide.	Police Advisory Board of five citizens appointed by the mayor to investigate citizen complaints against police officials.	Disposed of 67 of 107 complaints received; recommendations generally have little effect on police services.
1962	San Francisco	Citywide.	A police-community relations program to promote greater public cooperation with the police department; staffed by 13 police officers.	Increase in conflict within the police department; development of rapport with minority groups; investigation of citizen service complaints.
1966	Boston	13 police districts.	Development of a police-community relations program and the formation of citizen committee in each of 13 police districts.	Learning of Spanish language by officers; organization of youth panels on community crime; employment of youths in a police cadet program; increased communication about neighborhood problems.

1967	New York City	1 precinct (85,000 population).	Implementation of police-family intervention teams involving 18 patrolmen (blacks and whites) trained in conflict management techniques through a local university program.	945 interventions involving 665 families; families increased utilization of the service; patrolmen showed increased "compassion" and developed greater understanding of the "complexities" of family problems; developed more positive attitudes of their police roles.
1968	Washington, D.C.	Single police precinct.	A pilot police project to improve police services by improving in-service training and increasing citizen control over some non-law enforcement functions, with an elected citizens' board to direct the project.	In-service training program failed; increase to social services to citizens; 12% of the local community aware of the program after a 3-year existence; conflict between police and community leaders.
1968	Richmond, California	Citywide.	Development of a team patrol program comprising 5 primary and 3 relief teams. Each team was directed by a sergeant and ranged in size from 8-15 men, with assignments determined by sergeants.	Increased contact with citizens through attending local meetings; failure to provide adequate training for teams; inadequate supervision by sergeants because of conflicting responsibilities.
1971	New York City	Selected small areas.	Development of 30 Neighborhood Police Teams with approximately 30 men to each team; team commanders have greater authority in deploying members.	Antagonism with police department between team and officers; lack of geographic stability of assignments; poor communications within teams; increase in contacts with community groups.

Table 4-3
Decentralization Strategies Found among Public Safety Studies

Strategy	Number of Studies[a]
Community Relations	24
Physical Redeployment	17
Grievance Mechanisms	8
Administrative Decentralization	8
Employment of Neighborhood Residents	8
New Neighborhood Institutions	8
Political Decentralization	4

Note: N = 38.

[a]Total is greater than the total number of studies because of multiple occurrences of strategies within single studies.

of increased client control. Table 4-4 displays the frequencies for each of the five main outcome questions. As with the seven strategies, many studies had multiple outcomes, and where this occurred, the same case study was similarly categorized once for *each* of the component outcomes.

Given the strong control of the police over their own bureaucracy and the low frequency of strong decentralization strategies attempted, this pattern of outcomes is not surprising. In fact, the closed nature of the bureaucracy may explain not only the obvious failure to produce increased client control but also the low rate (in comparison with the other services) of all outcomes not counting a mere increase in the flow of information. This can be shown by comparing the outcomes associated with those strategies that involve the line functions in police operations (Physical redeployment, administrative decentralization, and political decentralization) with those that do not (primarily community relations) in terms of their association with outcomes other than mere increases in the flow of information. Table 4-5 shows the results of this comparison by grouping each study into four *mutually exclusive* sets of strategies and by dividing the outcomes into two mutually exclusive sets. Although the cell sizes are small, the conclusions from this table are that strategies that involve the

---

information flow. Second, many case studies interviewed target populations of youths or the public, or interviewed policemen engaged in the innovation. Wherever this was done, the outcome was coded in terms of changes in the attitudes of clients or service officials. Other studies reported on street crime rates, juvenile delinquency rates, changes in patrol patterns, or changes in other manpower resources. Such outcomes were coded in terms of changes in service. Finally, a very few studies indicated some change in control by clients over the program innovation and were coded accordingly. The generally weak nature of the evidence in the case studies, however, should be underscored. Most studies did not use adequate research designs, so that baseline or control group comparisons were usually absent. Moreover, positive or negative results were often recorded even though the overall effect of the innovation may have been minor—for example, involving only a small group of people or operating for only a year-long period but not on a permanent basis.

Table 4-4
Decentralization Outcomes Found among Public Safety Studies

Outcome	Number of Studies			
	Yes	No	No Information	Percent Yes
More Information	33	5	0	86.3
Improved Agency Attitudes	10	19	9	26.3
Improved Client Attitudes	16	12	10	42.1
Improved Services	15	23	0	39.5
Increased Client Control	2	35	1	5.3

Note: N = 38.

line functions in police operations tend to be associated with substantive outcomes other than an increased flow of information, while community relations and other strategies such as grievance mechanisms not involving line functions tend to produce an "information only" outcome. In other words, substantive outcomes of any sort result only from innovations involving day-to-day police operations. Because police decentralization has so frequently taken the form of community relations programs, which is both the weakest type of decentralization and the type not involving routine police operations, the decentralization experience has resulted in negligible client control and a low rate of other substantive outcomes.

In summary, decentralization generally led to the following results in public safety:

1. Only the weaker decentralization strategies and, in particular, community relations programs tended to occur in public safety studies, and only a very low rate of increased client control was found.

2. More of the studies reported a positive outcome in terms of improved attitudes than in terms of improved services.

3. Studies with strategies involving line functions in police operations tended to indicate more success in outcomes other than "information only." but these strategies also occurred less frequently than community relations and hence explain the low overall rate of other-than-information outcomes in all the safety studies.

4. Studies involving a combination of grievance mechanisms and new neighborhood institutions reported the least successful outcomes, which suggests that attempts to bypass the police bureaucracy entirely, as in civilian review board cases, will probably have few positive consequences.

Table 4-5
Comparison of Strategies Involving Line Functions in Police Operations

	Total Number of Studies	None or Information Only		All Other Outcomes	
Strategy		Number	Percent	Number	Percent
Tend to involve line functions in police operations:					
Physical redeployment, administrative or political decentralization	7	1	14.3	6	85.7
Above plus community relations	13	2	15.4	11	84.6
Tend not to involve line functions:					
Community relations without above	11	3	27.3	8	72.7
All remaining strategies[a]	7	6	85.7	1	14.3
Total	38	12	31.6	26	68.4

$\chi^2 = 12.20$, $df = 3$, $p < .01$.

[a]Primarily new neighborhood institutions and grievance mechanisms.

Citizen Participation

The public safety studies also reported a lower frequency of formal citizen participation than any of the other four service areas. If formal citizen participation is defined as involving either a specific paraprofessional program or some type of board structure, then only 16, or 42.1 percent, of the safety studies reported citizen participation as part of the innovation, whereas there was an 81.9 percent rate of citizen participation for the four other service areas. The low rate again reflects the extremely tight control of the police. Although citizen boards might be expected to have been an intolerable innovation, the low overall rate also means that the police could not even develop paraprofessional programs, which tend not to involve the more volatile aspects of strong client control.

Other observers have also pointed out the low rate of citizen participation in public safety programs (see, for example, Myren, 1972). The low rate is probably attributable to the closed nature of municipal fire and police bureaucracies. Of all the municipal service areas, both police and fire departments have had the fewest innovations that attempt to provide clients or users of services with a meaningful role other than as recipients of the services. Any substantial form of citizen participation is believed to be incompatible with effective police or fire services. In the 38 studies surveyed here, innovations with citizen participation appeared to produce a slightly higher rate of client control, but lower rates of improved agency or client attitudes; none of these differences, however, was statistically significant. Table 4-6 shows the success rates for the citizen participation versus non-citizen participation studies, judged by the five major outcomes (each percentage represents the frequency that citizen participation was associated with a given outcome).

Decentralization and Public Safety

Comparing Case Survey Results with Other Findings

The main results of the case survey indicate that the police have primarily engaged in community relations, a weak decentralization strategy not involving the *line operations* of the police department and thus producing a low rate of increased client control and of all other outcomes except for increased flow of information. Second, the public safety innovations have involved an exceptionally low rate of citizen participation.

These results are difficult to compare with those of the existing literature. In the first place, most previous studies have not emphasized evaluative findings. For instance, a recent comprehensive review of decentralization in the criminal justice system, although fully elaborating the major strategies tried, made no attempt to assess the decentralization experience or give any operational definitions for success (Myren, 1972). Similarly, reviews of police-community relations programs either discuss individual programs without attempting to draw general lessons or limit themselves to the development of a generic (but not evaluative) typology of the many programs (Brown, 1969; and Johnson and Gregory, 1971). Other reviews focus on the process of developing community relations programs but do not attempt to assess the existing array of programs (Harlow, 1969; and Gabor and Low, 1973).

Our findings are in general agreement with those few studies that have arrived at evaluative conclusions. Such previous studies have covered the effectiveness of team policing (Sherman et al., 1973) and the difficulties encountered by the civilian review board experiences (Gellhorn, 1966, pp. 170-195). The studies have also covered the ineffectiveness of community relations programs by citing such cases as the abortive San Francisco

Table 4-6
Outcomes for Citizen Participation, Public Safety Studies

Type of Citizen Participation	Total Number of Studies	Percentage Occurrence of Outcome[a]				
		More Infor- mation	Improved Agency Attitudes	Improved Client Attitudes	Improved Services	More Client Control
Paraprofessionals, Boards, or Both	16	87.5	18.8	31.3	43.3	12.5
No Citizen Participation	22	86.4	31.8	50.0	36.4	0
All Public Safety Studies	38	86.8	26.3	42.1	39.5	5.3

Note: N = 38.

[a]None of the differences is statistically significant.

program (Perry and Sornoff, 1972; and Condlin, 1969-70). Community relations programs are seen negatively because (1) they involve only a few policemen, (2) the few policemen become estranged from the rest of the department, and (3) the community relations efforts tend to be oriented toward improving public relations rather than creating operational changes (Wasserman et al., 1973).

At the same time, other studies have not emphasized the enormous expectations for decentralization. In the public safety area, decentralization and citizen participation innovations were clearly undertaken with the expectation that the *quality of life*—reflected in the level of neighborhood safety—would be changed. Decentralization was supposed to reduce rapidly rising crime rates and the estrangement between citizens and police, and to prevent riots. Moreover, decentralization programs were expected to produce these results with a minimum of new resources and within a fairly short period of time. It is against these expectations that decentralization probably can be said to have failed. Although in fact the rapid rise in fire and crime rates appears to have tapered off in the early 1970s, and although the frequency of civil disturbances has gone down considerably, such changes in the nature and extent of the safety *problem* are probably not attributable to decentralization or to any other internal changes in particular police *services*.

The Prospects for Decentralization

The major consequence of the decentralization innovations in the last decade, rather than having a positive or negative effect on the public safety problem, has probably been to increase the awareness of both police and residents about the complexity, fragility, and sensitivity of their mutual relationship. However, whereas the immediate reaction in the past has been to devise special police-community relations and other programs in an attempt to deal directly with the relationship, the experiences of the past few years suggest that improving this relationship cannot be divorced from making client-oriented changes in police operations. To this extent, the termination of the National Institute on Police-Community Relations (1955-1970), and the National Center on Police and Community Relations (1965-1973), and the broadened mandate of the Center for Criminal Justice Systems, all based at Michigan State University, are probably changes in the right direction, since community relations programs will no longer be considered a special part of police work, but should be integrated with other police innovations (Radelet, 1974).

Many of the new innovations, such as team policing, do in fact tend to combine a concern for improved police operations through decentralized command with a concern for improving police encounters with citizens. A further step in this direction of operational decentralization is reflected in new research suggesting that smaller police departments can provide higher levels of service than larger departments, even though larger departments support a greater variety of specialized skills (Ostrom and Whitaker, 1973; and Ostrom et al., 1973). The possible return to a preference for generalists rather than specialists might be the new theme for the coming decade and might even lead to new experiments with traditional forms of policing, such as the use of foot patrol.[f] Any trend in such a direction is bound to increase nonhostile contacts between police and citizens; it may also give individual patrolmen greater responsibilities and discretionary power and hence represent the decentralization spirit carried one step further (Danzig, 1973).

References

Angell, John E. et al. 1967. *A National Survey of Police and Community Relations.* Prepared for the President's Commission on Law Enforcement and Administration of Justice. U.S. Government Printing Office, Washington, D.C.

---

[f]The use of foot patrol has consistently been considered the best way of improving contacts between the police and neighborhood residents (see *Task Force Report,* 1967); Wilson (1972). An interesting note about foot patrol is that it is always conceived as being more expensive than motor patrol, but only because coverage of a physical area is deemed important. The authors are unaware of any research comparing this criterion with an alternative: *acquaintance with neighborhood residents.* It might be that crime prevention is more effective the more a policeman knows the people on his beat; if this were true, motor patrol would become the more expensive and ineffective type of patrol.

Bayley, David H. and Harold Mendelsohn. 1968. *Minorities and Police: Confrontation in America.* Free Press, New York.

Berleman, William C. 1972. "Police and Minority Groups." *Crime and Delinquency* 18 (April), pp. 160-7.

Bloch, Peter B. and David Specht. 1973. *Neighborhood Team Policing.* The Urban Institute, Washington, D.C.

Bordua, David J. and Larry L. Tifft. 1971. "Citizen Interviews, Organizational Feedback, and Police-Community Relations Decisions." *Law and Society Review* 6 (November), pp. 155-82.

Bouma, Donald. 1969. *Kids and Cops: A Study in Mutual Hostility.* Eerdmans, Grand Rapids, Mich.

Brandstatter, A.F. and Louis A. Radelet, eds. 1968. *Police and Community Relations: A Sourcebook.* Glencoe Press, Beverly Hills, Calif.

Brown, Lee P. 1969. "Police Community Relations Evaluation Report." Law Enforcement Assistance Administration, U.S. Department of Justice, Washington, D.C.

_____. 1971. "Typology Orientation of Police-Community Relations Programs." *Police Chief* 38 (March), pp. 17-21.

Campbell, Angus and Howard Schuman. 1971. *Racial Attitudes in Fifteen American Cities.* Survey Research Center, University of Michigan, Ann Arbor, Mich.

Condlin, Robert J. 1969-70. "Citizens, Police and Polarization: Are Perceptions More Important Than Facts?" *Journal of Urban Law* 47, no. 3, pp. 653-72.

Danzig, Richard. 1973. "Toward the Creation of A Complementary, Decentralized System of Criminal Justice." *Stanford Law Review* 26, (November), pp. 1-54.

Earle, Howard H. 1967. *Police-Community Relations: Crisis in Our Time.* Charles C. Thomas, Springfield, Ill.

Gabor, Ivan R. and Christopher Low. 1973. "The Police Role in the Community," *Criminology* 10, (February), pp. 383-414.

Gellhorn, Walter. 1966. *When Americans Complain.* Harvard University Press, Cambridge, Mass.

Gourley, G. Douglas, 1954. "Police Public Relations." *The Annals* 291, (January), pp. 135-42.

Groves, W. Eugene and Peter H. Rossi. 1970. "Police Perceptions of a Hostile Ghetto," in Harlan Hahn, ed., *Police in Urban Society,* Sage, Beverly Hills, Calif.

Hahn. Harlan, 1971a. "Ghetto Assessments of Police Protection and Authority." *Law and Society Review* 6 (November), pp. 183-94.

Hahn, Harlan. 1971b. "Local Variations in Urban Law Enforcement," in P. Orleans and W. R. Ellis, eds., *Race, Change, and Urban Society*. Sage, Beverly Hills, Calif.

Harlow, Eleanor. 1969. "Problems in Police-Community Relations: A Review of the Literature." *Information Review on Crime and Delinquency* 1, no. 5 (February), pp. 1-40.

Johnson, Deborah and Robert J. Gregory. 1971. "Police-Community Relations in the United States: A Review of Recent Literature and Projects," *Journal of Criminal Law, Criminology and Police Service* 62 (March), pp. 94-103.

Kakalik, James S. and Sorrell Wildhorn. 1971. *Private Police in the United States*. The Rand Corporation, R-869-DOJ. Santa Monica, Calif.

Kelly, Rita M. et al. 1972. "The Pilot Police Projects: A Description and Assessment of a Police-Community Relations Experiment in Washington, D.C." American Institute for Research, Kensington, Md.

Knopf, Terry Ann. 1969. *Youth Patrols: An Experiment in Community Participation*. Lemberg Center for the Study of Violence, Brandeis University, Waltham, Mass.

Kreps, Gary A. and Jack M. Weller. 1973. "The Police-Community Relations Movement." *American Behavioral Scientist* 16 (January-February), pp. 402-12.

Locke, Hubert G. 1967. "Police Brutality and Civilian Review Boards." *Journal of Urban Law* 44 (Summer), pp. 625-33.

Marx, Gary and Dane Archer. 1971. "Citizen Involvement in the Law Enforcement Process." *American Behavioral Scientist* 15 (September-October), pp. 52-72.

Mast, Robert. 1970. "Police-Ghetto Relations: Some Findings and a Proposal for Structural Change." *Race* 3 (April), pp. 447-62.

Mendelsohn, Robert A. 1970. "Police-Community Relations: A Need in Search of Police Support," in Harlan Hahn, ed., *Police in Urban Society*, Sage, Beverly Hills, Calif.

Momboisse, Raymond M. 1967. *Community Relations and Riot Prevention*. Charles C. Thomas, Springfield, Ill.

Myren, Richard A. 1972. "Decentralization and Citizen Participation in Criminal Justice Systems." *Public Administration Review* 32 (October), pp. 718-38.

Norris, Donald F. 1973. *Police-Community Relations: A Program that Failed*. Lexington Books, D.C. Heath, Lexington, Mass.

Ostrom, Elinor and Gordon Whitaker. 1973. "Does Local Community Control of Police Make a Difference?" *American Journal of Political Science* 17 (February), pp. 58-77.

Ostrom, Elinor et al. 1973. "Do We Really Want To Consolidate Urban Police Forces?" *Public Administration Review* 33 (September-October), pp. 423-32.

Perry, David C. and Paula Sornoff. 1972. "Street Level Administration and the Law: The Problem of Police-Community Relations." *Criminal Law Bulletin* 8 (January-February), pp. 43-61.

President's Commission on Law Enforcement and Administration of Justice. 1967. *The Challenge of Crime in a Free Society*. U.S. Government Printing Office, Washington, D.C.

Radelet, Louis A. 1974. "Police-Community Relations." *Police Chief* 41 (March), pp. 24-32.

Reiss, Albert J., Jr. 1971. *The Police and the Public*. Yale University Press, New Haven, Conn.

———. 1970. "Servers and Served in Services," in John P. Crecine, ed., *Financing the Metropolis*. Sage, Beverly Hills, Calif.

Report of the National Advisory Commission on Civil Disorders. 1968. Bantam, New York.

Sherman, Lawrence W. et al. 1973. *Team Policing: Seven Case Studies*. Police Foundation, Washington, D.C.

Task Force Report: The Police. 1967. A volume of President's Commission on Law Enforcement and Administration of Justice, *The Challenge of Crime in a Free Society*. U.S. Government Printing Office, Washington, D.C.

Virginia Law Review. 1969. "Grievance Response Mechanisms for Police Misconduct." Vol. 55 (June), pp. 909-51.

Wallach, Irving A. et al. 1971. "Perceptions of the Police in a Black Community." Research Analysis Corporation, McLean, Va.

Waskow, Arthur I. 1969. "Community Control of Police." *Transaction* 7 (December), pp. 4-7.

Wasserman, Robert et al. 1973. *Improving Police-Community Relations*, U.S. Department of Justice, Washington, D.C.

Wilson, James Q. 1972. "The Police in the Ghetto," in Robert F. Steadman, ed., *The Police and the Community*. Johns Hopkins Press, Baltimore, Md.

———. 1968. *Varieties of Police Behavior*. Harvard University Press, Cambridge, Mass.

5 Health

Prelude to Decentralization

The Traditional Organization of Health Services

Since the end of World War II, there has been increased acceptance of public responsibility for the planning and delivery of health services, especially for low-income groups and the elderly. Health care, traditionally a commodity whose consumption depended on a person's ability to pay, has gradually been redefined as a right of every citizen. However, in spite of the increasing involvement of federal and local governments in providing health services, two features still characterize the health care scene: the importance of the physician[a] and the dominance of the private sector.[b] Both of these characteristics make health services considerably different from the other neighborhood services in the present study and have influenced the ultimate decentralization strategies.

Among health care personnel, only 323,000 (or about 8 percent) of those employed are physicians. This small minority possesses ultimate control over the provision of health services. Only the physician has the technical knowledge and skills, ethical right, and legal power to heal the body and the mind. His wisdom and primacy are respected both by other health professionals and by consumers. Physicians, for the most part, have determined whether and how care is delivered; and more than in any other service, this professional credo has produced status gaps between the providers and consumers of service. While physicians have always accepted their social responsibility to care for poor patients for a nominal charge, such charity cases tend to be viewed as less desirable and even as less deserving. At the same time, the traditional public sector of the health delivery system has typically offered only preventive and educational health services; among

[a] Until the recent advent of physician's assistants and nurse practitioners, only physicians had the authority to diagnose and to prescribe medication. Even the new medical professionals have had difficulty in establishing their legal independence from a physician supervisor. For a discussion of the legal issues raised by physician assistants, see Cooper and Willig (1971).

[b] As for the dominance of the private sector, 67 percent of all active physicians are in private practice, and 64 percent of all hospitals are private (see American Medical Association, 1972, p. 9; and National Center for Health Statistics, 1973, p. 483).

the few curative functions have been those for tuberculosis and venereal disease, allowed specifically by public statutes (Stoeckle and Candib, 1969). The outpatient clinics, emergency clinics, and inpatient wards of municipal hospitals have operated to care for the poor, but such care has usually been regarded as inferior to that of the private medical sector (Roth, 1969, pp. 222-4).

Mental health services are also a part of the health care system but have been more frequently supported by public institutions. According to Hollingshead and Redlich's well-known study, over two-thirds of all psychiatric patients in New Haven were treated in state mental hospitals (Hollingshead and Redlich, 1958, pp. 137-68). However, socioeconomic class status has also been associated with the use of the public or private sector in mental health services, with state mental hospitals generally used only when a lack of money prohibits the use of psychiatrists in private practice. People who can afford to pay for mental health care, if hospitalized at all, are placed in private institutions and for shorter periods of time (Ozarin, 1966; and Roth, 1969).

The Crisis of the 1960s

By the 1960s, public officials were becoming increasingly concerned with the personal health care needs of low-income Americans and of the inadequacy of existing resources. First, there was a strong association between income and health status indices, which illustrated the relatively poor health status of low-income groups.[c] Similarly, in mental health, despite controversy over class-biased labeling procedures, most studies had found that low-income groups had a higher incidence of mental illness (Fried, 1969; Hollingshead and Redlich, 1958, pp. 194-219; and Srole et al., 1962). As for mortality, although overall death rates had fallen since 1900, there was a large differential between racial groups, and hence between income groups, especially for maternal and infant deaths (Office of the Assistant Secretary for Planning and Evaluation, 1967, pp. 15-17). Finally, numerous studies of variations in health status among neighborhoods within cities showed sharp differences between middle- and low-income neighborhoods.[d]

Second, low-income groups consistently received less health care than middle-income groups. Rates of utilization of physicians and dentists, for

[c] For instance, the National Health Survey indicated higher morbidity rates among persons at the low-income levels (see National Center for Health Statistics, 1964).

[d] For instance, the New York City Health Department found significant differences between a middle- and lower-class neighborhood in mortality rates for a variety of conditions responsive to medical care-for example, pneumonia-influenza, tuberculosis, cervical cancer (see James, 1964). Similarly, the Chicago Board of Health (1966) found a 75 percent higher mortality rate in poverty census tracts of the city than in nonpoverty tracts.

instance, showed a positive relationship to family income level. During 1963-64, only 59 percent of the people of all ages with a family income under $2,000 had been treated by a physician within a year, whereas 73 percent of the people with incomes over $10,000 had been treated (National Center for Health Statistics, 1965). For the population under 17 years, the pattern was more dramatic; at family incomes under $2,000 only 7.5 percent had seen a pediatrician within a year, while at incomes of $10,000 or more 33 percent of the young population made such a visit (National Center for Health Statistics, 1966).

Third, low-income people were less likely than higher-income people to be covered by hospital insurance; not only did they less frequently have insurance that paid any part of the bill, but their coverage was usually less adequate (National Center for Health Statistics, 1964). Although family size appeared to be one cause of lower health insurance coverage among low-income families, the poor were also less likely to have the kinds of jobs that offered group rates or employer contributions to defer some of the cost of a policy (Office of the Assistant Secretary for Planning and Evaluation, 1967, p. 29).

Financial Innovations

As a result of these health and health care conditions, the federal government launched a series of major health programs, thereby creating change in both health financing and service.[e] The Community Mental Health Centers Act of 1963 assisted states in the provision of mental health service through comprehensive community care facilities. The Economic Opportunity Act of 1964 established a number of programs to meet the special needs of the poor, among them health care. Under Titles XVIII and XIX of the Social Security Amendments of 1965, financing mechanisms for the health care of the aged (Medicare) and the poor (Medicaid) were created. The Comprehensive Health Planning and Health Services Amendments of 1966 offered grants to encourage the efficient use of existing health resources and to develop new ones. Simultaneously with these federal initiatives, the number of health personnel expanded considerably. However, patient care facilities did not keep pace with the increased manpower and increased medical need. The number of hospitals and hospital beds per 1,000 population has actually been decreasing slightly, in spite of the construction activities supported by the Hill-Burton Act of 1946.

---

[e] Only some of the important pieces of legislation are mentioned below; for a more exhaustive description of federal programs affecting health care services for the poor, see Office of the Assistant Secretary for Planning and Evaluation (1967, pp. 42-44). Also, a recent discussion of the history and problems of some of these federal health care initiatives of the 1960s is offered in Klarman (1974).

Despite the large federal expenditures under Titles XVIII and XIX—
$11 billion in fiscal year 1971 (Social Security Administration, 1973, p.
57)—financial barriers to health care have not been entirely overcome. For
Medicaid, income eligibility limits in many states have excluded many of
the medically needy. Care under Medicare has presented other problems,
for many of the low-income aged cannot afford to pay the monthly premium
that buys supplementary insurance for outpatient care. Even if Medicaid
and Medicare *could* eliminate the financial barriers to care, urban low-
income populations remain residentially segregated and therefore have
inadequate access to doctors and health care facilities. The scarcity of
private physicians in low-income and black areas, for instance, has been
noted in many research studies (Davis, 1971; Elesh and Schollaert, 1971;
Haynes and McGarvey, 1969; and Marsden, 1966). As evidence of the
inaccessibility of a family doctor, many of the medically indigent have
turned to hospital emergency rooms for nonurgent care. For instance,
users of a New Haven emergency room were more frequently nonwhite,
inner-city residents, and were of a lower-income status than the general
New Haven population; only 37 percent of the patients interviewed named
a private physician as their usual source of care; about one-half indicated
the lack of *any* regular source of care (Weinerman et al., 1966).

Cultural barriers have also acted to segregate low-income groups from
the mainstream of medical care (Irelan, 1971). For one thing, low-income
residents are less likely to have factual information about the causes,
treatment, and outcomes of various diseases. Therefore, they are more
likely than middle-income groups to be uninformed about preventive measures; to be fatalistic about tooth decay, disease symptoms, and mental
disturbance; to seek treatment at a later stage; and to practice self-
medication. Similarly, social distance between classes can also explain the
less frequent use of health services. Most physicians come from families
with incomes over $10,000 (Smith and Crocker, 1970); further, only 2
percent of physicians are black (Health Resources Administration, 1974, p.
1). The social distance between low-income patients and white health
professionals causes distrust and makes the patient less accessible to the
health information efforts of these professionals.

Strategies for Change

To combat the inequity evident in health care, great expectations have been
invested in new health service programs. The programs are intended to
make health services more accessible, comprehensive, personal, and of
higher quality. Between 1965 and 1971, about 80 neighborhood health
centers and other comprehensive health services projects were funded

under the Economic Opportunity Act of 1964 (Zwick, 1972; and Hollister et al., 1974). An additional thirty such projects and hundreds of community mental health centers were initiated by the Department of Health, Education, and Welfare. The projects are based on an old concept in rendering medical care to the indigent—*neighborhood centers*—which are assumed to be one of the few ways of overcoming the cultural and geographic access problems (Robinson, 1967; and Stoeckle and Candib, 1969). Like their predecessors in the early 1900s, neighborhood health centers (NHCs) and community mental health centers (CMHCs) attempt to bring services closer to urban low-income groups, and they represent in principle a decentralization effort in the broadest sense—from the federal government directly to the neighborhood resident. Although the development of neighborhood health centers first and foremost involves the decentralization strategy of *new neighborhood institutions*, in fact all but one of the seven decentralization strategies have been involved in health innovations.

If a municipal health department is a grantee for neighborhood health center or community health center funds, this does not constitute a new neighborhood institution but is an extended form of *administrative decentralization*. Here, the health department usually opens a new local center as a new organizational unit within the municipal system, and thus this type of administrative decentralization involves more than command decentralization. Two other decentralization strategies have also been used frequently in conjunction with the establishment of either a new neighborhood institution or a new organizational unit: *employment of indigenous paraprofessionals* and *community relations*. These two strategies share common objectives. Paraprofessionals can perform a variety of functions, including patient care, health education, and social advocacy (Domke and Coffey, 1966; Kent and Smith, 1967; Luckham and Swift, 1969; Wise et al., 1968; and Wood, 1968). Since the paraprofessionals are also residents of the community they serve, they can act as advocates for the client, expediting services and organizing the neighborhood by overcoming the cultural barriers evident in traditional medical care delivery. Thus, in their many roles, the indigenous paraprofessionals also serve a critical community relations function (Zwick, 1972).

A fifth decentralization strategy, *territorial decentralization*, occurs as part of the general location of neighborhood institutions to make health services more accessible to low-income residents. Typical of such attempts is the opening of storefront clinics by municipal or university hospitals to break geographic barriers and gain the confidence of the client population.

A sixth decentralization strategy, *political decentralization*, is reflected in the citizen board structures required by OEO regulations for NHCs. The regulations require one of two alternative representations of low-income residents: a one-third representation of neighborhood residents on a gov-

Table 5-1
Major Neighborhood Health Innovations

Start Data	Location	Area of Coverage	Main Innovation	Major Reported Outcomes
1965	Dorchester, Mass.	Low-income public housing community (5,500 population).	Development of a neighborhood health center to provide comprehensive health services as part of a community health action program, and jointly sponsored by a local medical school.	Increase in utilization of health services; improvement in attitudes on ambulatory care; increase in positive attitudes toward doctors.
1966	Denver	Black, low-income neighborhood (20,000 population).	Comprehensive neighborhood health facility with 15 full-time doctors and "action councils" elected by residents; employment of indigenous paraprofessionals.	Increase in patient load; screening of neighborhood aide trainees by action council, and acceptance of trainees by the local civil service; family-based treatment and registration; patients indicate appreciation of the facility.

1968	Rochester	Low-income neighborhood (21,000 population).	A program designed to provide comprehensive medical and dental care to local citizens, jointly administered by a local medical school and a community organization, under a neighborhood advisory board.	Patient interviews indicate improved access to health care and high level of satisfaction with physicians; patients generally unaware of the organizations involved in administering the program.
1968	New Haven	Black, low-income neighborhood.	Neighborhood health center providing free health care to neighborhood children, with a neighborhood-controlled board of directors.	Increased utilization by residents from 2,000 in 1968 to 2,000 per week in 1972; selection of staff by board personnel committee; high turnover rate of professional staff.
1969	St. Louis	Low-income service district (65,000 population).	A community health center operated by a 60-member elected community corporation to provide health services, health education, and paraprofessional training.	Satisfactory employment of paraprofessionals; but low citizen participation in board elections; continuing focus on improving the delivery of health services.

erning (i.e., policymaking) board, or a 50 percent membership on advisory boards (Herzog, 1970).

Throughout all these changes, however, the pre-eminent role of the physician in determining service policies has continued. Whether the issue is a new piece of national legislation or the fine-tuning of a specific health clinic's procedures, the traditional training, education, and status gaps between the physicians and their patients have made any client influence over service policies extremely difficult to carry out. The federal government has attempted to broaden the participation base, as in the development of jobs for health paraprofessionals, but physicians have always asserted their authority. Whether such strong control by the server group is justifiable is not the issue here. The main point is that the dominance of the physician has an obvious effect on decentralization and its outcomes.

Results of the Case Survey

A total of 48 studies of health and mental health innovations were reviewed in the case survey. These studies covered 39 discrete innovations, with about twice as many health cases as mental health cases. Although there were some examples of county health department efforts, most of the innovations were the direct result of the federal service programs, which funded Neighborhood Health Centers, Comprehensive Health Services Projects, and Community Mental Health Centers. Unlike any other service area in this study, the health case studies that were included in the case survey represented only a portion of those available. Because of the many studies that were uncovered, a 50 percent sample was randomly selected for inclusion in the case survey, so that the number of studies reviewed would be more comparable to the number in the other service areas. Table 5-1 lists the major innovations of health decentralization.

Strategies Attempted

In the 48 health studies, the seven strategies for decentralizing services were represented in varying degrees (see Table 5-2). All but 11 studies exhibited a combination of two or more strategies. The most common strategy was the establishment of a new neighborhood institution, which typically involved the opening of a community-based health or mental health center operated in conjunction with a medical school, hospital, or other existing health facility. This new institution was outside the municipal bureaucracy, and not only offered health care services but also gave residents the opportunity to be trained to work on health teams and to have a voice in center operations. An illustrative example of such a comprehen-

Table 5-2
Decentralization Strategies Found Among Health Studies

Strategy	Number of Studies[a]
Community Relations	15
Physical Redeployment	11
Grievance Mechanisms	3
Administrative Decentralization	13
Employment of Neighborhood Residents	22
New Neighborhood Institutions	26
Political Decentralization	13

[a]Total is greater than the total number of studies because of multiple occurrences of strategies within single studies.
Note: N = 48.

sive innovation in health is the Tufts-Columbia Point Neighborhood Health Center in Boston. Established to serve a low-income population geographically isolated from other health services, the neighborhood health center was sponsored by Tufts University School of Medicine and supported by the U.S. Office of Economic Opportunity. The center provides comprehensive ambulatory services with a health team that includes indigenous community aides. Through a Community Health Association, residents share in the policy decisions about services.

Administrative decentralization, involving 13 studies, was the main alternative strategy. Among health and mental health studies, this strategy took on a meaning beyond mere delegation of administrative responsibility to local service officials. In most instances, it represented the establishment of new health centers as organizational units within the municipal bureaucracy. The one feature usually distinguishing these centers from the new neighborhood institutions was that the service officials or providers were employees of the city or county government. Denver's health program is an example of this type of administrative decentralization. With federal funds and the cooperation of the University of Colorado Medical School, the Denver Department of Health and Hospitals opened two decentralized health facilities to serve low-income residents of the city. Neighborhood aide trainees and action councils elected by the residents also characterize the two centers. Similarly, San Francisco's Mission Community Mental Health Center is located within the city's General Hospital, staffed with civil service employees and administered by the city. The center offers comprehensive community mental health services (diagnostic, emergency, rehabilitative, hospitalization, outpatient). Although few indigenous paraprofessionals are used, there is a community policy board. Thus, new neighborhood institutions and administrative decentralization as currently defined exhibit similar characteristics whether they are within or outside the municipal bureaucracy.

Table 5-2 shows that the employment of neighborhood residents also occurred frequently. However, like the remaining strategies of political decentralization, physical redeployment, grievance mechanisms, or community relations, the employment strategy seldom occurred in isolation. Understandably, the frequent strategy combinations were largely attributable either to the establishment of new neighborhood institutions or to administrative decentralization.

Outcomes[f]

Table 5-3 summarizes the occurrence of the five outcomes among the 48 health service studies. Five of the studies showed no positive outcomes of any sort. The most frequent outcome was an improvement in services, and this seems to suggest that consistent with their prime objective, new neighborhood institutions and other health innovations had an effect on health care. Improved flow of information was the other major outcome. In 14 studies, this outcome occurred in combination with service improvements. Few studies indicated a positive outcome for agency attitudes, client attitudes, and client control. Given the strong federal initiatives for establishing resident boards, the low percentage of increased client control must be viewed as somewhat disappointing. However, the low percentage is less disappointing when it is realized that there was only a small minority of strong decentralization strategies in health studies.

Table 5-4 divides the case studies into mutually exclusive categories of strong, moderate, and weak decentralization strategies and presents the relationship among these strategies and the three outcomes of increased control, improved services, and increased flow of information. Only 13 of the 48 studies involved strong decentralization, but when strong decentralization occurred, a significantly greater rate of increased client control also occurred. However, the type of decentralization strategy did not have

---

[f]The health case studies were assessed according to the five major outcomes in the following manner: Since the main objective of new neighborhood health institutions was to provide more accessible services of higher quality to the medically needy, any increase in utilization rates by indigent residents, decreases in hospitalization rates due to more timely ambulatory care, or such other indicators as suicides prevented were noted as service improvements. Second, such measures as increased client-service communication through outreach workers; increased client knowledge about the service center; and use of paraprofessionals to interpret the medical, mental, and social needs of residents to professionals were all considered evidence of an increased flow of information. Third, a few studies indicated improvements in patient satisfaction, either with the physician or with the quality of care delivered, and these were assessed in terms of changes in client attitudes. Similarly, interviews focusing on provider satisfaction formed the basis for assessing changes in service officials' attitudes. Finally, a few studies had client boards effectively implementing their ideas over health center priorities, budget, hiring, and personnel review, and these were noted as increases in client control.

Table 5-3
Decentralization Outcomes Found among Health Studies

Outcome	Number of Studies			Percent Yes
	Yes	No	No Information	
More Information	26	20	2	54.2
Improved Agency Attitudes	3	10	35	6.2
Improved Client Attitudes	11	12	25	22.9
Improved Services	30	10	8	62.5
Increased Client Control	8	26	14	16.7

Note: N = 48.

any relationship to the frequency of either the service or information outcomes.

The health studies were also examined according to another set of mutually exclusive categories involving new neighborhood institutions or administrative decentralization, since these two strategies dominated the health innovation. A comparison of these two strategies in isolation from each other, however, shows that neither is significantly more effective than the other in producing the five outcomes (see Table 5-5).

In summary, decentralization led to the following results in health services:

1. The predominant strategy for decentralization was the formation of new neighborhood institutions.
2. The most frequent outcome was an improvement in services, but only a low proportion of studies indicated increases in client control.
3. The low rate may have been attributable to the fact that weak and moderate, but not strong, decentralization strategies dominated the health studies.
4. Administrative decentralization and new neighborhood institutions, the main alternatives for developing new health centers, appear equally effective in being associated with all outcomes.

Citizen Participation

A total of 36 of the health studies indicated the presence of some formal citizen participation, with either an indigenous paraprofessional program or a formal citizen board structure. However, this high incidence of citizen participation included 12 studies with paraprofessional programs only, so that only half of the health studies indicated a citizen board form of participation (see Table 5-6). This moderate occurrence of boards is cer-

Table 5-4
Type of Decentralization Strategy and Control, Service, and Information Outcomes

Type of Strategy	Total Number of Studies	Increased Control[a]			Increased Services[b]			Increased Information[b]		
		Yes	No	No Info	Yes	No	No Info	Yes	No	No Info
Weak	14	0	13	1	9	3	2	9	4	11
Moderate	21	2	7	12	14	5	2	10	10	11
Strong	13	6	6	1	7	2	4	7	6	0
Total	48	8	26	14	30	10	8	26	20	2

[a]$\chi^2 = 8.84$, $df = 2$, $p < .05$ for the differences among strategies on this outcome.
[b]The differences are not statistically significant.

Table 5-5
New Neighborhood Institutions and Administrative Decentralization Strategies Compared

Strategy	Total Number of Studies	Percentage Occurrence of Outcome[a]				
		More Information	Improved Agency Attitudes	Improved Client Attitudes	Improved Services	More Client Control
New Neighborhood Institutions	25	52.0	0.0	20.0	64.0	20.0
Administrative Decentralization	12	50.0	16.7	16.7	58.3	16.7
Both	1	0.0	0.0	0.0	100.0	0.0
Neither	10	70.0	10.0	40.0	60.0	10.0
Total	48	54.2	6.2	22.9	62.5	16.7

[a]None of the differences is statistically significant.

tainly greater than that found in the safety area, but it is not as great as in other services, as we shall see, where the server group is not so dominant.

Table 5-7 compares the relationship between studies with and without boards and the five major outcomes. The results show that increased client control occurs more frequently when boards are involved, but that service improvements occur more frequently when boards are not involved. Although these relationships are significant only at the $p < .10$ level, they nevertheless reflect again the possible reluctance with which health professionals accept the intrusion of clients in the delivery of services.

Table 5-6
Types of Citizen Participation for Health Studies

Type of Participation	Number of Studies
None	12
Paraprofessionals Only	12
Boards Only	11
Boards and Paraprofessionals	13

Note: N = 48.

Table 5-7
Relationship of Citizen Participation to the Five Outcomes

	Percentage of Occurrence of Outcomes				
Type of Participation	More Information	Improved Agency Attitudes	Improved Client Attitudes	Improved Services[a]	More Client Control[a]
None or no boards (n = 24)	62.5	8.3	20.8	79.2	4.2
Boards (n = 24)	45.8	4.2	25.0	45.8	29.2
Total (n = 48)	54.2	6.2	22.9	62.5	16.7

[a]Both differences are significant at the $p < .10$ level.

Decentralization and Health Services

Comparing Case Survey Results with Other Findings

The results of the case survey indicate that nearly two-thirds of the health decentralization cases showed an improvement in services, but only a few cases showed an increase in client control. Moreover, the occurrence of citizen participation was found to be associated both with higher rates of increased client control and with lower rates of improved services. These findings correspond generally with the emphasis and findings of other health studies that themselves have been based on surveys of several centers. Their evidence has usually included site visits, interviews, and a large quantity of data concerning health center operations. Such multi-case studies in health have also usually taken the form of formal evaluations of federal programs (Langston, 1974), and for the most part, their assessments have been favorable in terms of improved services and equivocal in terms of increased client control. For instance, the OEO-sponsored studies of neighborhood health centers have assessed center performance along such dimensions as utilization, patient satisfaction, comprehensiveness and continuity of care, and cost efficiency. The quality of care has been found equal to or better than that given by established providers of care, such as hospital outpatient departments (Langston et al., 1972; Morehead et al., 1971; Sparer and Johnson, 1971; and Strauss and Sparer, 1971). Further, although certain critics of neighborhood health centers suggest that service is being provided at unreasonable costs (the average center in 1971 had a budget of about $2.9 million), one study showed the costs of mature centers with over 10,000 registrants to be competitive with those of other institutional providers, including prepaid group practices (Sparer and Anderson, 1972). There is always some question, however, whether different accounting procedures might make the centers appear less competitive from a cost standpoint (Klarman, 1974).

Evaluation of participation efforts in health centers has been less frequent and less favorable (for a descriptive but not very analytic review, see Howard, 1972). Among federally supported health programs, citizen participation on boards has been found to be highest for neighborhood health centers, with community aides being used in over half of the centers (Community Change, Inc., and Public Sector, Inc., 1972). However, although there is general agreement that some control has been redistributed as a result of this participation, there is much ambiguity both as to the nature of the control and as to whether it satisfies similarly ambiguous federal guidelines, all of which has left some confusion, conflict, and frustration (Torrens, 1971). The extent of participation and its effectiveness in community mental health centers has generally been so minimal that such potential conflicts have not even become an issue. The development of community mental health centers occurred as a result of trends in psychiatric care and not in relation to the antipoverty program (Joint Commission on Mental Illness and Health 1961), as was the case with the neighborhood health centers. Thus, it is not surprising that citizen participation, much less any increase in citizen control, has been very infrequent in any of the centers (Health Policy Advisory Center, 1971). The mental health centers have simply made little use of either indigenous paraprofessionals or citizen boards.

Lasting Changes in Health Services

The institutional form of health services in the future will depend partly on continued federal support for neighborhood health centers and mental health centers. Such support has not yet stabilized because of the federal government's gradual shift away from a services strategy and toward various health insurance and other income-supplementing strategies. The institutional forms will thus also depend on future legislation that is still an emerging area of public policy. At the same time, it is not clear whether the large investment of money and effort between 1964 and 1974 has produced any significant changes in health status. What is needed is a five- to ten-year longitudinal comparison of health status changes among two groups of selected low-income residents—one group that has had access to neighborhood health centers and a control group that was eligible for but did not have access to such centers. Until these types of evaluation have been made, it will be difficult to interpret the importance of the apparent service gains that decentralization has produced.

References

American Medical Association. 1972. *Reference Data on the Profile of Medical Practice*. Chicago.

Chicago Board of Health 1966. *Preliminary Report of Medical and Health Care in Poverty Areas of Chicago and Proposed Health Programs for the Medically Indigent*. Chicago.

Community Change, Inc., and Public Sector, Inc. 1972. *A Study of Consumer Participation in the Administrative Processes in Various Levels of HSMHA's Service Projects*. Final Report to HSMHA. Sausalito, Calif.

Cooper, James K. and Sidney H. Willig. 1971. "Non-Physicians for Coronary Care Delivery: Are They Legal?" *American Journal of Cardiology* 28, pp. 363-5.

Davis, James W. 1971. "Decentralization, Citizen Participation, and Ghetto Health Care." *American Behavioral Scientist* 15, no. 1 (September-October), pp. 94-107.

Domke, Herbert R. and Gladys Coffey. 1966. "The Neighborhood-Based Public Health Worker: Additional Manpower for Community Health Services." *American Journal of Public Health* 56 (April), pp. 603-8.

Elesh, D. and P. T. Schollaert. 1971. "Race and Urban Medicine Factors Affecting the Distribution of Physicians in Chicago," discussion paper. Institute for Research on Poverty, University of Wisconsin, Madison.

Fried, Marc. 1969. "Social Differences in Mental Health," in J. Kosa et al., eds., *Poverty and Health: A Sociological Analysis*. Harvard University Press, Cambridge, Mass.

Haynes, M. Alfred and Michael R. McGarvey. 1969. "Physicians, Hospitals, and Patients in the Inner City," in J. C. Norman, ed., *Medicine in the Ghetto*. Appleton-Century-Crofts, New York.

Health Policy Advisory Center, Inc. 1971. *Evaluation of Community Involvement in Community Mental Health Centers*. New York.

Health Resources Administration, U.S. Department of Health Education, and Welfare. 1974. *How to Pay for Your Health Career Education*, DHEW Publication No. (HRA)74-8. U.S. Government Printing Office, Washington, D.C.

Herzog, Barry A. 1970. "Participation by the Poor in Federal Health Programs." *Wisconsin Law Review*, vol. 1970, no. 3, pp. 682-725.

Hollingshead, August B. and Fritz C. Redlich. 1958. *Social Class and Mental Illness*. Wiley, New York.

Hollister, Robert M. et al., eds. 1974. *Neighborhood Health Centers*. D.C. Heath, Lexington, Mass.

Howard, Lawrence C. 1972. "Decentralization and Citizen Participation in Health Services." *Public Administration Review*. 32 (October), pp. 701-17.

Irelan, Lola M. 1971. "Health Practices of the Poor," in L. M. Irelan, ed., *Low-Income Life Styles*. Social and Rehabilitation Services, Office of Research and Demonstration, U.S. Department of Health, Education, and Welfare, SRS-ORD-175-1971, Washington, D.C.

James, George. 1964. *Poverty as an Obstacle to Health Progress in Our Cities*. APHA Annual Meeting.

Joint Commission on Mental Illness and Health. 1961. *Action for Mental Health*. Wiley, New York.

Kent, James A. and C. Harvey Smith. 1967. "Involving the Poor in Health Services through Accommodation—The Employment of Neighborhood Representatives." *American Journal of Public Health* (June), pp. 997-1003.

Klarman, Herbert E. 1974. "Major Public Initiatives in Health Care." *The Public Interest*, no. 34 (Winter), pp. 106-123.

Langston, Joann H. 1974. "OEO Neighborhood Health Centers: Evaluation Case Study," in J.G. Abert and M. Kamrass, eds., *Social Experiments and Social Program Evaluation*. Ballinger, Cambridge, Mass.

Langston, Joann H. et al. 1972. *Study to Evaluate the OEO Neighborhood Health Center Program at Selected Centers*. Final Report to OEO, GEOMET Report No. HF-71. Washington, D.C.

Luckham, Jane and David W. Swift. 1969. "Community Health Aides in the Ghetto: The Contra Costa Project." *Medical Care* 7 (July-August), pp. 332-9.

Marsden, A.S. 1966. "Physician and Attorney Office Activities, Seattle: A Functional, Spatial, and Linkage Analysis," master's thesis. University of Washington, Seattle.

Morehead, Mildred A. et al. 1971. "Comparisons between OEO Neighborhood Health Centers and Other Health Care Providers of Ratings of the Quality of Health Care." *American Journal of Public Health* 61, no. 7 (July), pp. 1294-306.

National Center for Health Statistics, U.S. Department of Health, Education, and Welfare. 1966. *Characteristics of Patients of Selected Types of Medical Specialists and Practitioners, United States, July 1963-June 1964*, Series 10, No. 28. U.S. Government Printing Office, Washington, D.C.

————. 1973. *Health Resources Statistics: Health Manpower and Health Facilities, 1972-73*, DHEW Publication No. (HSM)73-1509. U.S. Government Printing Office, Washington, D.C.

————. 1964. *Medical Care, Health Status, and Family Income*, Series 10, No. 9. U.S. Government Printing Office, Washington, D.C.

————. 1965. *Physician Visits, Interval of Visits, and Children's Routine Check-up, United States, June 1963-June 1964*, Series 10, no. 19. U.S. Government Printing Office, Washington, D.C.

Office of the Assistant Secretary for Planning and Evaluation, U.S. Department of Health, Education, and Welfare. 1967. *Delivery of Health Services for the Poor*. U.S. Government Printing Office, Washington, D.C.

Ozarin, Lucy D. 1966. "The Community Mental Health Center—A Public Health Facility." *American Journal of Public Health* 56 (January), pp. 26-31.

Robinson, Mariana. 1967. "Health Centers and Community Needs," in F.C. Mosher ed., *Governmental Reorganization: Cases and Commentary*. Bobbs-Merrill, New York.

Roth, Julius. 1969. "The Treatment of the Sick," in J. Kosa et al., eds., *Poverty and Health: A Sociological Analysis*, Harvard University Press, Cambridge, Mass.

Smith, Louis C.R., and Anna R. Crocker. 1970. *How Medical Students Finance Their Education*. National Institutes of Health, U.S. Department of Health, Education, and Welfare, U.S. Government Printing Office, Washington, D.C.

Social Security Administration, U.S. Department of Health, Education, and Welfare. 1973. *Compendium of National Health Expenditure Data*, DHEW Publication No. (SSA)73-11903. U.S. Government Printing Office, Washington, D.C.

Sparer, Gerald and Anne Anderson. 1972. "Cost of Services at Neighborhood Health Centers." *New England Journal of Medicine* 286, no. 23 (June 8), pp. 1241-5.

Sparer, Gerald and Joyce Johnson. 1971. "Evaluation of OEO Neighborhood Health Centers." *American Journal of Public Health* 61, no. 7 (July), pp. 1294-306.

Srole, Leo et al. 1962. *Mental Health in the Metropolis*. McGraw-Hill, New York.

Stoeckle, John D. and Luey M. Candib. 1969. "The Neighborhood Health Center—Reform Ideas of Yesterday and Today." *New England Journal of Medicine* 280 (June 19), pp. 1385-91.

Strauss, Mark A. and Gerald Sparer. 1971. "Basic Utilization Experience of OEO Comprehensive Health Services Projects." *Inquiry* 8, no. 4 (December), pp. 36-49.

Torrens, Paul R. 1971. "Administrative Problems of Neighborhood Health Centers." *Medical Care* 9, no. 6 (November-December), pp. 487-97.

Weinerman, E. Richard et al. 1966. "Yale Studies in Ambulatory Medical Care: V. Determinants of the Use of Hospital Emergency Services." *American Journal of Public Health* 56 (July), pp. 1037-56.

Wise, Harold B. et al. 1968. "The Family Health Worker." *American Journal of Public Health* 58 (October), pp. 1828-38.

Wood, Eugene C. 1968. "Indigenous Workers as Expeditors." *Hospital Progress* 49 (September), pp. 64-68.

Zwick, Daniel I. 1972. "Some Accomplishments and Findings of Neighborhood Health Centers." *Milbank Memorial Fund Quarterly* 50 (October), pp. 387-420.

6

Multiservice Programs

Prelude to Decentralization

Needs for Multiservice Programs

Of all the service groups covered in this study, the multiservice programs are the most heterogeneous and difficult to define. On the one hand, the programs include citywide innovations, such as an ombudsman or citizen complaint office. On the other hand, they include operations at the neighborhood level, such as a new neighborhood facility designed to accommodate several services. Three criteria, however, dominated the search for case studies that were ultimately defined as multiservice programs. First, most of these programs were of a "helping" or informational nature. They provided referral or access for using other services. In this sense, a grievance investigation program does not itself provide a substantive service; it merely facilitates, through successful referral and investigation, the citizen's use of some other public service, such as housing, health, or employment. Second, most of the multiservice programs dealt with social services. The whole field of social services, covering employment, training, and other welfare programs, is itself poorly defined (Kahn 1973). However, except for actual payments programs—for example, welfare assistance—social services are predominantly "helping" in nature, since they involve information and referral, counseling, and followup. Third, the multiservice programs included any efforts that were made to coordinate services at the neighborhood level. For example, a genuine attempt at neighborhood government, where a locally elected body allocates resources and directs neighborhood services, was included as a multiservice program.

Multiservice programs have not traditionally been identified with either a dominant server profession or with active client influence over service policy. Many services provided in multiservice programs, such as welfare or housing assistance, do involve municipal bureaucracies that have not been well known for their accessibility and responsiveness to clients. However, these services are not dominated by a server group, as in public safety or in health, that has an extremely large status gap in relation to the served. Client influence has come only through recent and fairly sporadic

107

efforts such as welfare rights and tenants' organizations. No traditional form of client participation or influence has been institutionalized.

Local and federal governments made a considerable effort during the 1960s to develop multiservice programs. The perceived need for these programs was caused by overly specialized and fragmented public services, to the point that citizens often did not know where to address their problems. This need for a single, well-publicized point of entry for the citizen appeared not only to increase with the increasing specialization of services or with the size of a given neighborhood, but also with the decline of private neighborhood institutions and neighborhood-based political organizations that traditionally dealt with such problems. The private settlement house, for instance, had emerged at the very end of the nineteenth century to deal with the problems of the immigrant city. However, by the 1960s, the churches, private welfare agencies, and community centers that in the past had served some of the "helping" functions were fast disappearing from urban neighborhoods; disappearing as well were such neighborhood artisans as the ward leader, the druggist, the doorman, and the superintendent, who similarly might have provided the necessary service or information. The urban neighborhood of the 1960s not only often consisted of a new set of residents, then, but also of a new array of neighborhood institutions (Hallman, 1973b; and Post, 1973). In this light, the need for developing new multiservice programs may have been part of a broader need to refurbish the institutional structure of central-city neighborhoods (National Commission on Urban Problems, 1968, especially pp. 346-54).

Major Multiservice Programs

As a result of these needs, local and federal governments launched a series of multiservice programs. While some such programs, such as mayor's complaint offices, had already existed for several years[a] the first wave of genuine concern for new neighborhood programs came with the initiation of major federal programs. The extent of these federal and local government efforts has been comprehensively surveyed (Stenberg, 1973) and will be discussed under four categories: federal multiservice programs, neighborhood action task forces and rumor control centers, grievance investigation programs, and neighborhood governance programs.

Federal Multiservice Programs. Federal activities at the neighborhood level had begun, of course, with the Community Action Program. But in addition to the CAPs and later the Model Cities Program, the federal

---

[a] In Chicago, for instance, Mayor Daley had established an Office of Inquiry and Information in 1955. For a description of this innovation, see Wyner (1973).

government also sponsored a variety of other neighborhood-oriented programs. Perhaps the best publicized of these was the Neighborhood Centers Pilot Program, designed in response to President Johnson's call in 1966 for one-stop neighborhood centers in every ghetto (Hallman, 1970, pp. 138-62; Abt Associates, 1969; and Lawson, 1972). However, the pilot program was actually initiated only in a few cities, as the costs of having centers in every neighborhood were found to be prohibitive; moreover, even in the few test cities the program had only minimal resources and had difficulty working with existing neighborhood-based programs.

A second program was the neighborhood facilities program, authorized by Section 703 of the Housing and Urban Development Act of 1965 and designed to provide physical facilities to house neighborhood programs. This program came under criticism by the General Accounting Office in 1971 for not fulfilling its primary goal of housing multiservice operations. However, a subsequent survey of these facilities showed that most of them were indeed used to provide more than seven types of services, with recreation programs being the most common (U.S. Department of Housing and Urban Development, 1971). This program thus provided a new neighborhood institution in 190 neighborhoods across the country.

Other federal programs did not call for the development of separate facilities but were integrated into existing local services. Typically, grants were made to support the hiring of indigenous paraprofessionals for new services such as visiting home care, parent education, and general outreach functions. These grants were supposed to be used in conjunction with other federal social service programs, though later surveys showed only minimal cooperation between the social science programs and the neighborhood multiservice centers (O'Donnell, 1971). The multiservice centers found themselves dealing mostly with unemployment and housing problems and generally acting on individual complaints (O'Donnell and Reid, 1971 and 1972).

Neighborhood Action Task Forces and Rumor Control Centers. In addition to the dominantly federal initiatives, local governments also attempted to develop a wide array of multiservice programs. Some were a direct response to the urban riots of the 1960s. The Kerner Commission report, for instance, cited the lack of effective grievance mechanisms and poor communication between black residents and local authorities as two of the underlying conditions of the urban riots. The Commission recommended that cities develop local neighborhood action task forces (*Report of the National Advisory Commission on Civil Disorders*, 1968, pp. 289-94). These task forces were to be small-scale storefront operations in predominantly low-income neighborhoods, with a prominent city official or mayoral representative supervising the investigation of individual grievances. In addition to grievance functions, the task forces were to maintain street-level contact with neighborhood activities and thus provide early warning of new hostilities among residents or between residents and local authorities. Finally, the task forces were designed to focus on the activities of youths and to provide whatever counseling and recreational programs possible with very limited budgets.

Related to the task forces was another new type of institution, the rumor control center. The first centers were opened in Chicago and in the Watts section of Los Angeles in 1967 (Ponting, 1973; and Williams and Erchak, 1969). Nearly all centers were operated by city government but did not necessarily have strong informational ties with other relevant city agencies, such as the police. The main function of the centers was to investigate rumors and to disseminate accurate information. Following the decline in the incidence of major urban riots, however, the rumor control center has slowly faded from the urban scene.

Grievance Investigation Programs. At the same time, the task force philosophy provided the roots for more broadly based grievance investigation programs. These programs not only cut across many services but are also not usually confined to low-income neighborhoods. The programs have taken many forms: little city halls, which involve neighborhood walk-in facilities; citywide ombudsmen or complaint officers; and complaint bureaus or special telephone numbers for receiving calls about public service problems. All the complaint mechanisms attempt to provide citizens with a single, highly visible point for interacting with government; in most cases, the ensuing complaints cover local, county, state, and federal services, so that the complaint unit must be able deal with several different governments as well as different services within each government.

Only a few cities have developed any sort of little city halls program (National League of Cities and U.S. Conference of Mayors, 1973; for the location and characteristics of existing little city hall programs, see Grollman, 1971). The most extensive program has been in Boston, where 14 little city halls have been in operation since 1968. They investigate citizen complaints but also provide a few "helping" services: citizens may pay local taxes; pick up permits and registration forms; register to vote; request birth, death, and marriage certificates; and obtain informal counseling on social security programs and federal income tax returns at the little city halls (Nordlinger, 1973). Other cities have started similar programs, mainly in the context of existing neighborhood facilities, such as the branch public library, with one prototype being the British Citizens' Advice Bureau, which began during World War II and now exists in over 450 locations (Kahn et al., 1966). The library-based programs have emphasized information dissemination and referral functions, however, rather than grievance investigation (Bolch et al., 1972; Turick, 1973; and Yin et al., 1974).

Ombudsmen programs are also quite new to the urban scene (Wyner, 1973). The main distinction between the urban ombudsman and the traditional European ombudsman is that the urban ombudsman is normally appointed by the municipal executive rather than by the legislative branch. The urban ombudsman thus has direct ties with the mayor's office and derives his informal power by relying on the mayor's ability to influence change within the local bureaucracy.

Finally, many cities have established special complaint bureaus or telephone numbers for referring complaints (Gellhorn, 1966; Wyner, 1973; Kaiser, 1971; Krendel, 1970; and Gusdorf et al., 1971). Most of these offices operate on an informal basis—that is, they have small staffs and make only weak attempts to attract a large number of complaints. Somewhat like the rumor control centers, these complaint investigating efforts become more important in times of crisis—for example, power shortages or public union strikes.

Neighborhood Governance Programs. In contrast to both the federal and the grievance investigation programs, neighborhood governance programs usually involve less ephemeral and more irreversible innovations. This is because the innovations call for changes in the existing service delivery system, either by administrative regulations or by changes in the city charter. The neighborhood governance programs generally fall into either administrative or political decentralization.[b] Administrative decentralization gives district service officials more decisionmaking authority so that they can be more responsive to the needs of local residents. If many services decentralize decisionmaking authority in a similar manner at the same time, the decentralization can also potentially improve the district coordination of these services. Administrative decentralization thus provides multiservice contact between citizens and their government at the neighborhood level and has been tried to varying degrees in several cities (Washnis, 1972).

Political decentralization adds one important change to administrative decentralization. The neighborhood polity gains some direct electoral authority over the local district services. Political decentralization thus involves the creation of new general purpose units of government at the neighborhood levels (Advisory Commission on Intergovernmental Relations, 1968). Such fundamental changes do not occur in isolation; they may

[b] The best distinction between these two strategies is found in Hallman (1971). Hallman uses the term "citizen control" rather than "political decentralization," but the conceptual meaning is the same. Others have also discussed this distinction. For instance, see Frederickson (1973). Two authors who find the distinction not very useful are Shalala and Merget (1973).

be accompanied by other governmental restructuring, such as shifting citywide functions to a metropolitan level of government. (The whole question of the proper balance among tiers of government is given excellent treatment in an essay by Ylvisaker, 1959.) In theory, such neighborhood governments should have revenue-raising as well as service delivery powers. In practice, only a few cities in the United States[c] have attempted any such changes, and these usually involve neighborhood governments or councils with very limited resources and functions (Dayton's Priority Boards are an example; see Sterzer, 1971). The major American cities that have considered some form of neighborhood councils are Washington, D.C., Detroit, Honolulu, New York, Indianapolis, Chicago, and Pittsburgh (Richardson, 1970; Zimmerman, 1972; and Center for Governmental Studies, March 1974). Other cities—Los Angeles, for example—have considered such changes but have not produced sufficient interest to get a proposal on the ballot (Wilson, 1971).

Strategies for Change

Our brief review of multiservice programs indicates that cities have in fact tried all of the seven strategies for decentralization that have been described in previous chapters. The federal neighborhood facilities programs, for instance, involve new neighborhood institutions (the facility itself) and physical redeployment (local agencies relocating staff from downtown to the neighborhood facility), and may also include community relations, employment, and grievance strategies. Little city halls programs, as another example, may be based mainly on the grievance strategy and physical redeployment (establishment of offices at neighborhood locations) but may also include administrative decentralization and community relations. We shall now examine the case study findings and review the results of these innovations.

Results of the Case Survey

There were 41 multiservice case studies, covering 37 different innovations. Table 6-1 lists the major multiservice innovations in the case survey and their characteristics.

---

[c]The best example of contemporary neighborhood government is the borough system in London (see Foley, 1972; and Rhodes, 1972). See Shalala and Merget (1973) for comparisons of the most prominent cases of political decentralization, including London.

Strategies Attempted

Table 6-2 shows the frequency of strategies tried in the multiservice case studies. Although every decentralization strategy was attempted at least once, there were many studies with multiple strategies, and four strategies occurred with much greater frequency than the rest: community relations, physical redeployment, grievance mechanisms, and new institutions. This indicates that in a large number of studies, a new neighborhood facility, operating either entirely outside the municipal bureaucracy or within the bureaucracy but without substantial command decentralization, was initiated. The multiservice studies, in effect, were dominated by outreach facilities and services, and generally did not involve substantial redistribution of political or administrative authority. In terms of the different types of strategies, there were 23 studies with weak decentralization, 10 with moderate decentralization, and eight with strong decentralization. The large number of weak decentralization strategies is somewhat surprising, given the lack of a dominant professional server group. Clients working on strong governing boards, for instance, could easily have administered many of these innovations. The weak strategies found, however, may very well be attributable to the urban reaction to the Community Action and Model Cities programs, with few officials anxious to stir up the same participatory controversies and few residents available to participate in the multiservice programs because of continuing engagements with the still active CAPs and Model Cities, where the stakes were higher.

Outcomes

Since most of the multiservice programs served a "helping" function and involved outreach facilities but only few changes in authority relationships, the frequencies of the five outcomes of our study are not surprising—that is, in 95 percent of the studies, there was some improvement in the flow of information, which reflects the dissemination of information about services (for example, about eligibility rules and accessibility), the investigation of complaints, or counseling. In 66 percent of the studies, there was some service improvement, which reflects such results as the satisfactory clearance of complaints (not merely the notation of the number of complaints), the provision of day care services, increased participation in recreation activities, or successful referrals for new employment opportunities. The three other outcomes—dealing with changes in officials' or clients' attitudes, or with increases in client control—all occurred much less frequently. Table 6-3 shows the overall occurrence of the five outcomes in the multiservice studies.

Table 6-1
Major Multiservice Innovations

Start Date	Location	Area of Coverage	Main Innovation	Major Reported Outcomes
1955	Detroit	Low-income residents covering entire city.	Development of new programs with several service agencies, health evaluation clinic for senior citizens, prototype preschool programs, comprehensive mental health service, community leadership training program, youth services corp.	Increased utilization rate; increase in information available about services.
1968	Boston	14 neighborhoods covering whole city.	Creation of little city halls to deal with grievances; accept payments for water, sewer, and real estate taxes; register voters; and give information and referrals.	Increased grievance and utilization rates; increased awareness of facilities and satisfaction with their services; improved communications between neighborhood officials and service agencies.
1969	Norfolk, Va.	Berkeley neighborhood (10,800 target population).	New neighborhood facility to provide health care and social service information; employment of local residents.	Continued development of central intake and referral service for residents.

1970	Seattle	Low-income neighborhood.	Development of single center to coordinate manpower and training services; governing board consisting of service officials and citizen representatives.	Minimal improvements in information about services; failure to develop center management; failure to develop citizen participation.
1970	Erie, Penn.	Low-income neighborhood.	New neighborhood facility to provide day care services, lunch program for 40 children attending a neighborhood school, and cultural and recreational programs; residential board of directors.	Increased utilization rates for facility; increase in participation by senior citizens.
1971	Dayton	All residents of city	Establishment of local ombudsman to deal with citizen complaints regarding government services and functions.	Increases in number of complaints and complaints successfully investigated; satisfaction with service by residents and service officials; wide publicity about service activities.
1971	New York City	Initially 5 neighborhoods, eventually extended to 16 neighborhoods (about 150,000 residents each).	Increased authority for district commanders in major municipal services; appointment of district manager for coordination.	More responsive services in relation to neighborhood requests for special cleanups, repair of street facilities; current monitoring of citizen attitudes.

Table 6-2
Decentralization Strategies Found among Multiservice Studies

Strategy	Number of Studies[a]
Community Relations	25
Physical Redeployment	35
Grievance Mechanisms	20
Administrative Decentralization	4
Employment of Neighborhood Residents	6
New Neighborhood Institutions	27
Political Decentralization	8

Note: N = 41.
[a]Total is greater than the total number of studies because of multiple occurrences of strategies within single studies.

Table 6-3
Decentralization Outcomes Found among Multiservice Studies

	Number of Studies			
Outcome	Yes	No	No Information	Percent Yes
More Information	39	1	1	95.1
Improved Agency Attitudes	2	35	4	4.8
Improved Client Attitudes	8	30	3	19.5
Improved Services	27	12	2	65.9
Increased Client Control	4	36	1	9.8

The uneven division among weak, moderate, and strong strategies, as well as the poor distribution of outcomes except for improved services, made any further analysis of the multiservice cases difficult. Too many combinations of strategies and outcomes had either a very low or very high frequency and were not susceptible to statistical analysis. As for the improved services outcome, it should be pointed out that the three types of decentralization strategies were all associated with about the same frequency of positive outcomes.

In sum, the multiservice studies showed the following results:

1. The dominant strategies were of weak decentralization.
2. The frequent outcomes were an increased flow of information (95 percent of the studies) and improved services (66 percent of the studies).

3. Strong decentralization and increased client control both occurred only infrequently.

Citizen Participation

Sixteen of the multiservice studies had no citizen participation, and another eight had only paraprofessional programs. Thus, fewer than half of the multiservice studies had citizen boards, which is not surprising since the studies were mostly of weak decentralization strategies. Table 6-4 shows the outcomes associated with the various types of citizen participation, though the differences are again not statistically significant because of the poor distribution of outcomes. (The percentages in Table 6-4 represent the frequency with which a given type of participation was associated with a given outcome.)

Decentralization and Multiservice Programs

Comparing Case Survey Results with Other Findings

The most salient characteristic of other studies on multiservice programs is a lack of evaluative discussions. In only a few isolated cases, as in a study of Boston's little city halls (Nordlinger, 1973), have authors attempted to draw conclusions about the decentralization innovation. However, most major studies of multiservice programs, each covering several innovations, have failed to provide any conclusions with which the case survey results can be compared. Two studies of neighborhood governments, for instance, after describing an array of innovations, merely summarize their general characteristics, without any further analysis (Washnis, 1972; and Zimmerman, 1972).

The case survey results do appear consistent with the common beliefs expressed by reformers that decentralization with elected or selected neighborhood residents can achieve service improvements (Hallman, 1973b, pp. 205-26; Frederickson, 1973; and Hallman, 1973a). Further, the results are not inconsistent with the major criticisms made by these reformers that the decentralization innovations have not really been of major proportions, have not led to substantial increases in client control, and have certainly not met the levels of expectations created at the start of federal programs (see, for instance, Davis, 1973). The issues that the case survey results do not address well are those dealing with specific problems of designing or installing specific innovations. For instance, very little was

Table 6-4

Outcomes for Citizen Participation, Multiservice Studies

Type of Citizen Participation	Total Number of Studies	More Infor- mation	Improved Agency Attitudes	Improved Client Attitudes	Improved Services	More Client Control
			Percentage Occurrence of Outcome[a]			
None	16	87.5	0.0	12.5	62.5	0.0
Paraprofessionals only	8	100.0	12.5	37.5	50.0	12.5
Boards Only	14	100.0	7.1	14.2	71.4	7.1
Boards and Paraprofessionals	3	100.0	0.0	33.3	100.0	66.7
All	41	95.1	4.8	19.5	65.9	9.8

[a]None of the differences is statistically significant.

found in the case surveys on the topic of organizational transition from centralized to decentralized services. Yet for multiservice programs, this transitional stage can be very important, since much of the municipal bureaucracy and polity can be involved (Shalala and Merget, 1973). Similarly, the case survey was not examined for the specific characteristics of board membership or function, mostly because of the low number of cases.

The Prospects for Decentralization

In multiservice programs more than in any of the other service areas, continued decentralization is possible in the future because local governments have become so large and complex that many, under the appropriate political conditions, may attempt some kind of decentralization. Physical redeployment, administrative decentralization, and the development of neighborhood councils are all possible changes, though strong forms of decentralization are unlikely. In New York City, as an example, multiservice decentralization programs that emphasize administrative decentralization are continuing in several neighborhoods and are being evaluated, in terms of both service changes and changes in residents' attitudes.[d] Whereas in the past federal programs have provided the incentive and resources for inducing multiservice decentralization, future efforts are likely to rely on local governments and possibly federal revenue-sharing

[d] For an early description of these activities, see Yin, Hearn, and Shapiro (1974). The full evaluation is being carried out by Stanley J. Heginbotham, Bureau of Applied Social Research, Columbia University.

funds, but not federal programs. King County in Washington state, for instance, has recently opened new decentralization facilities with partial support by revenue-sharing funds, and other county governments have begun to consider ways of bringing services closer to clients (Center for Governmental Studies, May 1974).

One exception here may be the continued federal interest in *services integration*, as embodied in demonstration projects supported by the U.S. Department of Health, Education, and Welfare. In these projects, local agencies are encouraged to integrate the administration of categorical grant programs in order to increase managerial efficiencies and to make service operations more responsive to client needs. The levels of integration vary, but several of the projects do operate in a neighborhood context. The demonstration projects are the beginning of a potentially expanded effort that would take place under the aegis of the Allied Services Bill (S. 3643 and H.R. 15838), first introduced during the 92nd Congress in 1972. The services integration framework could then be one basis for encouraging further multiservice decentralization, although decentralization is by no means an essential part of services integration (Spencer, 1974).

In general the main characteristic of multiservice decentralization in the future is likely to be the nonfederal nature of the innovations. More pointedly, the innovations are also not likely to build on the CAP or Model Cities projects[e] that are currently being phased out. This is perhaps an ironic development, since the new innovations may benefit a great deal in learning from the CAPs' and Model Cities' experiences.[f] The major lesson may be that local governments, having expanded considerably over the last 15 years, may at last feel that the political conditions for decentralization are appropriate partly *because* of the declining federal role. Federal initiatives in the past that served as a threat to local power structures may in effect have created a trend toward centralization that is only now being dissipated. Whether this resurgent localism will include any provision for increasing client influence over multiservice programs remains to be seen.

References

Abt Associates. 1969. *The Neighborhood Pilot Center Program.* Cambridge, Mass.

---

[e] Community development corporations are also unlikely to serve as the foundation for the new efforts. See Chapter 8 for further discussion.

[f] For example, the New York State Charter Revision Commission, in studying new decentralization changes for New York City, has completed a study of the CAP experience in New York just to identify the major lessons for the future. See the State Charter Revision Commission (1973).

Advisory Commission on Intergovernmental Relations. 1968. *New Proposals for 1969*. Washington, D.C.

Bolch, Eleanor et al. 1972. *Information and Referral Services: An Annotated Bibliography*. Institute for Interdisciplinary Studies, Minneapolis.

Center for Governmental Studies. 1974. "Neighborhood Decentralization." January; March; May. Washington, D.C.

Davis, James. 1973. "Citizen Participation in a Bureaucratic Society" in George Frederickson, ed., *Neighborhood Control in the 1970s*. Chandler Publishing Co., New York.

Foley, Donald L. 1972. *Governing the London Region*. University of California Press, Berkeley.

Frederickson, George. 1973. "Epilogue," in George Frederickson, ed., *Neighborhood Control in the 1970s*. Chandler Publishing Co., New York.

Gellhorn, Walter. 1966. *When Americans Complain: Governmental Grievance Procedures*. Harvard University Press, Cambridge, Mass.

Grollman, Judith. 1971. "Decentralization of Municipal Services." *Urban Data Service Reports* 3, no. 2 (February), pp. 1-9.

Gusdorf, Nigel et al. 1971. "Puerto Rico's Citizen Feedback System." M.I.T. Operations Research Center, Cambridge, Mass.

Hallman, Howard W. 1971. "Administrative Decentralization and Citizen Control." Center for Governmental Studies, Washington, D.C.

_____. 1973a. *Government by Neighborhoods*. Center for Governmental Studies, Washington, D.C.

_____. 1973b. "The Neighborhood as an Organization Unit: A Historical Perspective'" in George Frederickson, ed., *Neighborhood Control in the 1970s* Chandler Publishing Co., New York.

_____. 1970. *Neighborhood Control of Public Programs: Case Studies of Community Corporations and Neighborhood Boards* Praeger, New York.

Kahn, Alfred J. 1973. *Social Policy and Social Services*. Random House, New York.

Kahn, Alfred J. et al. 1966. *Neighborhood Information Centers*. Columbia University School of Social Work, New York.

Kaiser, John A. 1971. *Citizen Feedback: An Analysis of Complaint Handling in New York City*. Office of the Mayor, New York.

Krendel, Ezra S. 1970. "A Case Study of Citizen Complaints as Social Indicators." *IEEE Transactions on Systems Science and Cybernetics* SSC-6 (October), pp. 265-72.

Lawson, Simpson. 1972. "The Pitiful History of the Pilot Neighborhood Center Program." *City* 6 (March-April), pp. 53-57.

National Commission on Urban Problems. 1968. *Building the American City*. U.S. Government Printing Office, Washington, D.C.

National League of Cities and U.S. Conference of Mayors. 1973. *Little City Halls: Selected Readings and References*. NLC and USCM, Washington, D.C.

New York State Charter Revision Commission. 1973. "The Community Action Experience." New York City.

Nordlinger, Eric A. 1973. *Decentralizing the City: A Study of Boston's Little City Halls*. M.I.T. Press, Cambridge, Mass.

O'Donnell, Edward J. 1971. "Service Integration." *Welfare in Review* 9 (July-August), pp. 7-15.

O'Donnell, Edward J. and Otto M. Reid. 1971. "Citizen Participation on Public Welfare Boards and Committees." *Welfare in Review* 9 (September-October), pp. 1-9.

_____. 1972. "The Multiservice Neighborhood Center." *Welfare in Review* 10 (May-June), pp. 1-18.

Ponting, J. Rick. 1973. "Rumor Control Centers." *American Behavioral Scientist* 16 (January-February), pp. 391-401.

Post, Joyce. 1973. "Background Reading on Total Community Service." in Guy Garrison, ed., *Total Community Library Service*. American Library Association, Chicago.

Report of the National Advisory Commission on Civil Disorders. 1968. Bantam, New York.

Rhodes, Gerald, ed. 1972. *The New Government of London: The First Five Years*. International Arts and Sciences Press, White Plains, N.Y.

Richardson, Charles T. 1970. "Decentralization of Metropolitan Government." *Journal of Law Reform* 4 (Winter), pp. 311-35.

Shalala, Donna E. and Astrid E. Merget. 1973. "Decentralization: Implications for Urban Services," unpublished manuscript. Teachers College, Columbia University, New York.

Spencer, Lyle, Jr. 1974. "The Federal Approach to Services Integration." *Urban Social Change Review* 7 (Winter), pp. 7-12.

Stenberg, Carl W. 1972. "Decentralization and the City." *Municipal Yearbook, 1972*. International City Management Association. Washington, D.C.

Sterzer, Earl. 1971. "Neighborhood Grant Program Lets Citizens Decide." *Public Management* 53 (January), pp. 10-11.

Turick, Dorothy. 1973. "The Neighborhood Information Center." *RQ* 12 (Summer), pp. 341-63.

U.S. Department of Housing and Urban Development. 1971. *Neighborhood Facilities: A Study of Operating Facilities*. Community Development Evaluation Series No. 1. U.S. Government Printing Office, Washington, D.C.

Washnis, George J. 1972. *Municipal Decentralization and Neighborhood Resources*. Praeger, New York.

Williams, Larry and Gerald Erchak. 1969. "Rumor Control Centers in Civil Disorders." *Police Chief* 36 (May), pp. 26-32.

Wilson, Kenneth D. 1971. "Neighborhood Proposal Aimed at Citizen Participation." *Public Management* 53 (January), pp. 12-13.

Wyner, Alan S. 1973. "Complaining to City Hall: The Chicago Approach," in Alan S. Wyner, ed., *Executive Ombudsmen in the United States*. Institute of Governmental Studies, Berkeley, Calif.

Yin, Robert K., R.W. Hearn, and P.M. Shapiro. 1974. "Administrative Decentralization of Municipal Services." *Policy Sciences* 5 (March), pp. 57-70.

Yin, Robert K., Brigitte Kenney, and Karen Possner. 1974. *Neighborhood Communications Centers: Planning Information and Referral Services in the Urban Library*. The Rand Corporation, R-1564-MF, Santa Monica, Calif.

Ylvisaker, Paul. 1959. "Some Criteria for a Proper Areal Division of Governmental Powers," in Arthur Maass, ed., *Area and Power: A Theory of Local Government*. The Free Press, New York.

Zimmerman, Joseph F. 1972. *The Federated Ctiy: Community Control in Large Cities*. St. Martin's Press, New York.

7

Education

Prelude to Decentralization

Early Municipal Reform and the Schools

The history of public education in American cities has been dominated by the development and increasing control of large, centralized bureaucracies. A major concern has therefore been the types of structural and administrative arrangements most conducive to the delivery of educational services, and a common theme has been the proper mix between professional and citizen control over institutional arrangements and procedures. Thus, unlike the three previous service areas, education has had a rich tradition of server-served interaction over policy issues, whether this has taken the form of elections of school officials, the formation of school organizations, or informal communications. In fact, early efforts to provide educational services were largely the prerogatives of neighborhood residents and organizations (Cronic, 1973).[a] Local control, however, was regarded with suspicion since jobs, contracts, and even curriculum development were often linked to the operations of local, ward-based politicians. As a result, the reform movement that began in the late nineteenth century included efforts to remove public education from the direct influence of ward politics. Administrative *centralization,* involving the development and expansion of central education boards, became the established procedure for divorcing public education from local politics. The centralization of authority led to the implementation of uniform fiscal policies and procedures, standardization of the curriculum, and nonpartisan employment standards. The success of the reform movement meant that by 1900, most of the older cities had eliminated ward or community school boards and had transferred power to centralized authorities. Such reforms remained fairly stable for the 30-year period following 1925 (Cronin, 1973, p. 12).

---

[a] For an excellent history of the New York City School System, see Ravitch (1974); for a history of the early development of schools in Massachusetts, see Lazerson (1971); and for an early history of the New York system, see Kaestle, (1973).

The Crisis of the 1960s

The Supreme Court's landmark decision of 1954 (*Brown* v. *Board of Education of Topeka*) created pressures for the racial integration of schools and gradually forced changes in school systems everywhere. In large cities, the primary response to the demand for integrated education was to increase the authority of the citywide superintendent and his staff, which was intended to force principals and local school administrators to comply with centrally issued mandates for integrated education (Rogers, 1968; and Meranto, 1970). The central school authorities also developed new compensatory education programs, especially in reading and math, in an attempt to reduce dropout rates and improve educational performance in ghetto schools (Fantini et al., 1970, Ch. 2).

By the mid-1960s, big city schools had still failed either to achieve more integration or to improve the quality of education (Stein, 1971). The controversial Coleman Report documented the inequities attributable to continued de facto segregation and also questioned the value of compensatory programs to improve the education of black children Coleman, 1966; the results were also supported by a reanalysis of the data found in U.S. Commission on Civil Rights, 1967). In another study, the Kerner Commission found that ghetto schools were producing a syndrome of educational failure and that parents were distrustful of officials responsible for formulating and implementing education policy (Report of the National Advisory Commission on Civil Disorders, 1968, p. 451). Armed with such evidence, local groups and civil rights advocates continued to opt for integrated schools, but the prospect for school integration declined as the proportion of blacks in central cities continued to increase. Moreover, it is often forgotten that in any given city, the percentage of blacks enrolled in the public school system is inevitably much higher than the percentage of blacks in the population as a whole. Table 7-1 illustrates this difference by comparing the school enrollment reported in 1967 with the citywide proportions of blacks reported three years later in the 1970 census for 16 selected cities.

The difficulties in producing racial integration produced a new focus on direct community participation in public education. The most well-known example of this transition took place in 1966 in New York City, as a result of the failure to integrate I.S. 201, a junior high school in Harlem (Fantini et al., 1970). When the citywide board of education failed to locate I.S. 201 so that it would have an integrated enrollment, parents and neighborhood groups pressed for community control and power-sharing in matters affecting the school.

Decentralization was a concept born in I.S. 201, in New York City, among a group

Table 7-1

Racial Composition of School Enrollment and of Total Population in 16 Selected Cities

City	Percentage of Nonwhite Students Enrolled, 1966-1967[a]	Percentage Blacks in Total Population, 1970 Census
Washington, D.C.	91	71.1
Baltimore	63	46.4
St. Louis	62	40.9
Philadelphia	58	33.6
Detroit	57	43.7
San Francisco	56	13.4
Chicago	54	32.7
Cleveland	53	38.3
Memphis	51	38.9
New York	50	21.2
Pittsburgh	38	20.2
Buffalo	36	20.4
Boston	26	16.3
Los Angeles	25	17.9
Milwaukee	24	14.7
San Diego	10	7.5

[a]Source: Research Council of the Great Cities Program for School Improvements, Status Report, 1967.

of parent activists who had struggled long and hard for an integrated school. In the summer of 1966, having failed to achieve their goal, they asked the New York City Board of Education to give them a direct voice in the operation of the school. They used the term "community control" for the first time [Fantini and Gittell, 1973, p. 45].

The new focus on community control developed somewhat separately from continued efforts to increase school integration directly through busing policies (on busing, see Glazer, 1972; Rubin, 1972; and Kelley, 1974). But the new focus was naturally reinforced by federal antipoverty efforts in the mid-1960s in developing participatory roles for various community groups and grassroots organizations.

Subsequent developments occurred mainly in New York, as the New York State Legislature requested the mayor to make a decentralization proposal for the whole city, which resulted in the Bundy Report of 1967 (*Reconnection for Learning: A Community School System for New York City,* 1967). Not surprisingly, the report provoked strong resistance from organized teacher groups—the United Federation of Teachers (U.F.T.) and the Council of Supervisory Associations. Also in 1967, the New York City Board of Education announced plans to experiment with local control in three demonstration districts: Ocean Hill-Brownsville, Two Bridges, and the school district for I.S. 201. In New York and elsewhere, the rationale for decentralization has been that it would improve the quality of educational services by creating accountability between the school and the local community. In other words, if ghetto schools were made more accountable to local citizens, such schools would be able to do a better job of educating students.[b] Moreover, citizen participation would also lead to a reduction in the feelings of powerlessness and institutional alienation.[c] For these reasons, schools in many cities contemplated or implemented some decentralization innovations.

Strategies for Change

For the most part, school decentralization involves some combination of locally elected school boards (or *political decentralization*) and the devolution of new discretionary authority to locally based school administrators (or *administrative decentralization*) (Lopate et al., 1970). Either change requires the full cooperation of the central school board. In addition, political decentralization usually requires legislative changes in state or local charters to install such new procedures as dividing the city into districts with local governing boards, establishing elections of local school boards, providing eligibility rules for voters and nominees, and giving local boards their powers and responsibilities. The local school board then acts as the governing unit for the school district and has specified powers over personnel, budgetary, and curricular activities. Administrative decentralization, in contrast, involves delegated authority from superiors to subordinates within the school bureaucracy, and these delegations can be made without legislative changes. In administrative decentralization, however, the local administrators may still be accountable to the citywide educational bureaucracy, or they may be made accountable to the locally elected school board. The lack of a standard organizational arrangement for school decentralization has produced some confusion in the use of terms as "community participation," "community control," and "decentralization," all of which have been used to characterize both political and administrative decentralization.

In addition to the two main strategies, school decentralization has also involved *community relations* and the *employment of neighborhood residents* as paraprofessionals. The employment of neighborhood residents

---

[b] For a discussion of the pros and cons of decentralization, see Ornstein (1971); Fantini (1969); and Buskin (1969).

[c] However, the opposing view is that increased levels of participation may result in a greater sense of powerlessness and frustration; see Bell and Held (1969).

has been undertaken in an attempt to narrow the communications gap between professional educators and the local community. The paraprofessionals may function as community relations officers or as aides to classroom teachers, and are sometimes a communications link between the local board and various neighborhood organizations.

The actual incidence of school decentralization innovations may be considered low. A 1969 survey found that 29 major urban school systems had begun some form of decentralization (*Decentralization and Community Involvement,* 1969, p. 2). Among the innovations, 13 of the school systems in the survey were administratively decentralized but had no formal provision for citizen participation. Sixteen school systems were planning or had implemented some type of political decentralization through locally elected school boards or advisory committee structures. However, although the incidence of decentralization has been low, the size and extent of each attempt has usually been of major proportions and has involved at a minimum a whole school, but often a school district and occasionally the whole school system. The large scale of each school decentralization innovation distinguishes the school innovations from those in the other four service areas. To this extent, the school innovations represent the most serious attempts at urban decentralization, and it is worth briefly reviewing the innovations in three cities—New York, Detroit, and Washington, D.C.

New York City. New York City has had two distinct decentralization phases. The first involved three demonstration districts, with each having a locally elected board (Berube and Gittell, 1969; and Gittell et al., 1972). The most well-known of these districts was Ocean Hill-Brownsville, where conflict over the local authority to shift teachers out of the district precipitated a confrontation with the U.F.T. This resulted in a district- and, ultimately, citywide teachers' strike in 1968. The second and current decentralization phase began in 1969 when the three districts were incorporated into the districtwide system mandated by the New York State School Decentralization Act of the same year (Zimet, 1973). The Act was the outcome of proposals by the mayor and the citywide school board, based partly on the Bundy Report but heavily diluted by the strong lobbying activities of the U.F.T. The new law divided the school system into 31 local districts. Although the election of the local boards was in theory designed to expand citizen control, all district residents—not merely parents with children in the schools—were eligible to vote, and this resulted in the disproportionate election of representatives from traditionally well-organized Catholic and Jewish interest groups. In addition, the local boards were given less authority over school affairs than the authority given the boards of the original three demonstration districts.

Detroit. In Detroit, a decentralization plan adopted in 1970 called for the creation of eight districts that covered the entire city. Each district had its own regional board, but the authority delegated to the boards was minimal as the functions of the boards, particularly in personnel actions, use of contract funds, and budget allocations, were still subject to the influence of the central school board. The Detroit decentralization plan did provide for significant influence of local boards in the area of curriculum development, rather than in the development of new educational programs. The members of the regional boards are elected by the residents of each district, and the experience has again been that although the schools are predominantly black, the board members are predominantly white.

Washington, D.C. Two illustrations of noncitywide innovations involving the election of local boards are the Morgan School and the Anacostia school district, both located in Washington, D.C. Changes in the Morgan School were initiated by the D.C. Board of Education in 1967 in conjunction with Antioch College, which provided technical assistance in designing and implementing curriculum changes (Lauter, 1968). The Morgan School experiment subsequently became known as the Adams-Morgan project, and the local board was granted authority over the selection of school personnel, curriculum development, and some control over the allocation of funds. This innovation, incidentally, was one of the few efforts in school decentralization to receive the support of a teachers' association, the predominantly black Washington Teachers Union. A completely separate decentralization effort was made in Anacostia, as part of a federal initiative to establish a model school district in the District of Columbia through a special $1 million appropriation. The project covered 11 local school boards and one districtwide board. The districtwide board included representatives from each of the 11 local boards, and all of the boards have formal powers similar to those exercised by the Adams-Morgan board.

We turn now to an analysis of the results from the case studies on these and other school decentralization innovations.

Results of the Case Survey

The case survey covered 34 studies of neighborhood education. Because many studies were of the same innovation, these studies as a whole covered only 14 separate innovations. Table 7-2 gives a list of the major innovations in school decentralization that were covered by the studies, with brief descriptions of the important characteristics and outcomes.

Strategies Attempted

The most outstanding feature of the strategies attempted is the high frequency of strong decentralization strategies. In total, there were 26 cases of strong decentralization, three cases of moderate decentralization, and five cases of weak decentralization. However, since most of the case studies covered a multiple combination of strategies, the array of simple strategies shows a variety of weak and strong forms (see Table 7-3).

The great number of multiple strategies is evidenced by the fact that the total number of simple strategies far outnumbers the total number of studies. The multiple combinations occurred, for example, in the New York City innovations, where decentralization to the school district level simultaneously called for administrative decentralization (a downward shift in educational authority from the central administration to district staff), political decentralization (the election of locally represented school boards on a district basis), and either some new grievance procedure or community relations (special attention to local community affairs). In general, the high frequency of multiple combinations was attributable to the fact that the major decentralization strategy involved locally elected school boards, and these boards often initiated complaint procedures and paraprofessional programs as part of their operations. Administrative decentralization was necessary in such cases as well, so that the school administrators would have some powers (though not necessarily significant ones) to respond to the local board's decisions.

Outcomes[d]

Table 7-4 gives the results for each of the five basic outcomes. Since strong decentralization strategies occurred frequently, it is not surprising that

---

[d] The outcomes involving neighborhood education innovations were evaluated in several ways. Most studies indicated increases in the number of contacts between school officials and local citizens, and such studies were coded as having resulted in an increase in the flow of information. Many of the studies also provided information based upon interviews with target populations of youth, local board representatives, teachers, and administrators involved in the innovation, or the educational bureaucracy in general. This information was coded for changes in the attitudes of service officials or of clients, whichever was appropriate. Several other studies reported information on teacher turnover, changes in educational service resources, school vandalism, and, less frequently, student achievement (e.g., reading scores). These outcomes were coded as service changes. Finally, most of the studies focused upon the decisionmaking powers of local boards, including local control over the innovation. Wherever there was evidence that the elected board members had an opportunity to implement some of their own ideas, this information was coded as an increase in citizen control. In general, it is important to remember the difficulty of assessing the magnitude of significance of an outcome, and that many positively coded outcomes may have involved minor changes.

Table 7-2
Major Neighborhood Education Innovations

Start Date	Location	Area of Coverage	Main Innovation	Major Reported Outcomes
1967	New York City	Ocean Hill-Brownsville school district (8 schools and 8,000 students).	Election by parents of a local school board; board authority over major personnel, budget, and curriculum functions.	Selection of district principal and staff; expansion of paraprofessional and minority employment; development of new educational programs; increased parent participation; major teacher strike.
1967	New York City	I.S. 201 school district (5 schools and 7,000 students).	Election by parents of a local school board; board authority over major personnel, budget, and curriculum functions.	Selection of district principal and staff by local board; development of new paraprofessional and educational programs; some improvement in student performance; increased parent participation.
1967	Chicago	Woodlawn school district (3 schools and 3,300 students).	Development of district board comprised of university officials, of representatives of local organizations, and of board of education. Board has full authority over federal monies, and some authority over personnel.	Screening of teaching appointments and use of administrative transfers; development of teacher aide program; development of new educational programs; increased parent participation.

1967	Washington, D.C.	Morgan School (1 elementary school).	Election of local board composed of parents, teachers, and at-large community representatives. Board has authority over new educational programs.	Employment by board of new project director and of teacher aides; determination of priorities for school budget; development of new curriculum; high turnover among teaching staff; increased parent participation.
1968	Washington, D.C.	Anacostia school district (11 schools and 13,500 students).	Election of 11 neighborhood boards and 1 communitywide board; board administers large federal grant.	Employment of paraprofessionals; increased parent participation.
1969	New York City	Citywide school decentralization.	Establishment of 31 local districts and election of district boards; boards have minimal personnel and budget responsibilities, but can select district superintendent.	Selection of district superintendents; development of some new educational programs; some influence over selection of school principals; increased control over Title I monies.
1969	Boston	King-Timilty school district.	Election of parent-dominated community advisory council; council has authority over some personnel functions.	Selection of school principal; some new educational programs; increased parent participation.
1970	Detroit	Citywide school decentralization	Establishment of 8 regions, each with a 5-member elected board; central board comprised of region representatives; regional boards have authority over some personnel functions.	Screening of administrative appointments; improved parent-school communication; some new educational programs.

Table 7-3
Decentralization Strategies Found among Education Studies

Strategy	Number of Studies[a]
Community Relations	20
Physical Redeployment	4
Grievance Mechanisms	23
Administrative Decentralization	18
Employment of Neighborhood Residents	15
New Neighborhood Institutions	1
Political Decentralization	26

Note: N = 34.
[a]Total is greater than the total number of studies because of multiple occurrences of strategies within single studies.

Table 7-4
Decentralization Outcomes Found among Education Studies

	Number of Studies			
Outcome	Yes	No	No Information	Percent Yes
More Information	24	7	3	70.6
Improved Agency Attitudes	8	16	10	23.5
Improved Client Attitudes	8	16	10	23.5
Improved Service	21	8	5	61.8
Increased Client Control	20	12	2	58.8

Note: N = 34.

increased client control occurred in 20, or 58.8 percent, of the studies. This was a substantially higher rate than was found in any of the other four service areas, where an average of 16 percent of the studies showed increased client control. Among the other outcomes, the education studies were not much different from the other service areas. What is important is that the higher rate of increased client control occurred without any substantial decrease in the other outcomes.

A potential distinction among the client control and improved services outcomes, however, is observed when the education studies are examined according to weak, moderate, and strong decentralization. Because of the high frequency of strong forms, the definitions of weak and strong decentralization were altered somewhat, so that weak decentralization involved only community relations and grievance strategies and strong decentralization involved only political decentralization, and the remaining mixed

Table 7-5
Weak and Strong Strategies for Decentralization Compared

		Outcome			
Strategy	Total Number of Studies	Increased Client Control	Improved Services	Both	Neither
Weak Decentralization (community relations or grievance mechanisms)	7	0	4	1	2
Strong Decentralization (political decentralization)	8	5	1	1	1
Both (studies where both weak and strong occur simultaneously)	18	1	2	12	3
Neither	1	0	0	0	1
Total	34	6	7	14	7

$\chi^2 = 21.95$, $df = 4$, $p < .001$. Both "neither" categories are excluded.

cases were grouped together, regardless of whether weak or strong dominated. Table 7-5 distinguishes among four *mutually exclusive sets of strategies*: (1) those studies in which community relations or grievance mechanisms were used but political decentralization was absent; (2) those in which political decentralization was used but the other two were absent; (3) those in which both were present; and (4) those in which both were absent. Table 7-5 also presents the outcomes in mutually exclusive categories: those cases in which increased client control and any other outcome except for improved services occurred; those cases in which improved services and any other outcome but not increased control occurred; those with both control and service outcomes; and those with neither. The results show that strong forms of decentralization are associated with client control but not with improved services, while weak forms of decentralization have the opposite effect. In education, multiple strategies of strong and weak forms appear necessary in order to maximize both service and control outcomes. This was the only occasion in our study when any tradeoff between control and service improvements was evident.

In summary, the case survey revealed that for the basic strategies and outcomes of the education studies:

1. A high frequency of strong decentralization strategies was attempted;

2. Among outcomes, the education studies indicated a substantially higher rate of increased client control (58.8 percent of the studies) than any of the other four service areas (which averaged only 16 percent);

3. An analysis of mutually exclusive strategies showed that weak and strong forms of decentralization are associated with complementary outcomes, with weak forms relating to improved services and strong forms relating to increased client control; and both weak and strong forms appear needed if improvements in services as well as increased client control are desired.

Citizen Participation

Unlike the preceding three service areas, every education study reported some type of citizen participation. Compared with the other service areas, the education studies have much more frequently included attempts to widen and increase citizen participation. However, although citizen participation may have occurred frequently, such participation may have been confined to a small number of community activists and not encompassed the mass of local residents. In particular, the voter turnover rates for districtwide school board elections have been very low and especially disappointing. (LaNoue and Smith, 1973, pp. 229-30; and Gittell et al., 1973, pp. 162-3).

Table 7-6 compares three categories of citizen participation according to the five main outcomes. The percentages in Table 7-6 again represent the frequency with which a given type of participation was associated with a given outcome. The results suggest a contrast between those studies with boards only and those with boards and paraprofessional programs. The boards-only category is associated with lower frequencies for all five outcomes. Although none of the differences is statistically significant, the results do reflect a broader pattern that appears consistently among the service areas and that will be discussed further in Chapter 9: Citizen participation appears to be more effective when boards are involved; however, the effectiveness of boards can be increased even further if they are used in combination with paraprofessional programs.

Decentralization and Education

Comparing Case Survey Results with Other Findings

The dominant concern in other studies of school decentralization has been the issue of community control. More than in any other service area, decentralization within school systems has explicitly raised the issue of the balance of power among servers and served. As a result, several observers

Table 7-6
Outcomes for Citizen Participation, Education Studies

Citizen Participation	Total Number of Studies	More Infor- mation	Percentage Occurrence of Outcome[a]			
			Improved Agency Attitudes	Improved Client Attitudes	Improved Services	More Client Control
Paraprofessionals Only	2	50.0	100.0	0.0	50.0	0.0
Boards Only	16	56.3	6.3	12.6	43.8	56.3
Paraprofessionals and Boards	16	87.5	31.3	37.5	81.4	68.8
All Neighborhood Education Studies	34	70.6	23.5	23.6	61.8	58.8

Note: N = 34.
[a]None of the differences is statistically significant.

have made the redistribution of power their main criterion for judging decentralization, with service improvements playing a secondary role. Most of the previous studies have thus concluded that decentralization has failed because local boards have only infrequently gained sufficient authority to affect personnel, budgetary, or curriculum policies (Fantini and Gittell, 1973; and Gittell et al., 1973). For instance, the citywide school decentralization changes that took place in New York City in 1969 are strongly criticized for having failed to alter the balance of power.

The case survey findings showed that increased client control did occur in a majority of the case studies. This more positive outcome is attributable to the fact that increased client control was credited in the case survey whenever a study indicated that residents had been able to implement some of their own ideas. Many of the case studies did indicate, for instance, that decentralization had given residents, through the local boards, the ability to hire and fire paraprofessional staff and to institute some curriculum changes. Although these functions increase client control, they indeed do not consitute genuine management of the schools by the local school board. The case survey finding of frequent increases in client control nevertheless highlights a very important conclusion in comparison with the other four service areas. *In no other service area has client control, even over minor administrative matters, been achieved as frequently as it has in education.*

The heavy emphasis on community control in the existing literature has relegated the concern for service improvements to a secondary position, although dissatisfaction with the quality of education was the original impetus for decentralization. Here, the case survey did indicate a high frequency of positive service outcomes, but in only one case did service improvement cover improvements in scores on achievement tests, which have become the standard shorthand for assessing the quality of education. Other studies have also admitted to the lack of any link between decentralization and achievement scores,[e] but decentralization advocates have ignored this shortcoming on the basis that improvements in achievement scores depend on many other factors operating over a long period of time (Fantini and Gittell, 1973; and Gittell et al., 1973).

Furthermore, the case survey results also suggested a possible relationship between client control and service improvements. The case survey suggested a tendency for weak forms of decentralization to produce service improvements but not increased client control (even of a weak nature) and for strong forms of decentralization to produce increased control but few service improvements (even of a minor nature). Only studies that had both weak and strong forms of decentralization simultaneously produced both improved services and increased client control. In contrast, other investigators have apparently assumed that desirable service improvements will eventually follow the establishment of community control (Fantini and Gittell, 1973; Gittell et al., 1973; LaNoue and Smith, 1973; and Zimet, 1973). Our results may be more in line with experts like Kenneth Clark who have admitted some disillusionment with decentralization. After witnessing the decentralization activities in New York, Clark indicated that he had less enthusiasm for decentralization, mainly because the quality of education appeared to be indifferent to changes in the organizational structure of the school system (*The New York Times*, 1972a). Clark accepts decentralization as an important political shift, but the question he raises is whether such a shift will ever have any effect on the quality of education. A serious, analytic inquiry is needed into this major decentralization assumption that organizational changes can produce—even in the long run—substantial changes in the quality of education.

The need for a more analytic inquiry into the school decentralization experience, beginning with this distinction between organizational changes and changes in educational quality, is reinforced by other recent decentralization events. In New York, the first full year of citywide decentralization was accompanied by a high rate of turnover among district superintendents, allegedly because of difficulties in working with the local boards (*The New York Times*, 1972b). High rates of turnover among the principals were also reported in an intensive study of one local School district (Zimet, 1973, pp. 158-9). The turnover, it might be argued on the one hand, is desirable because it produces institutional change. On the other hand,

---

[e] LaNoue and Smith (1973, p. 231), make this observation about other studies. See, for example, Ravitch (1972).

the turnover might be viewed as undesirable because it produces institutional instability. Our point is that studies of school decentralization merely assume one position or the other, rather than comparing the validity of these competing interpretations.

The Future of Decentralization

School decentralization, unlike organizational changes in other service areas, is difficult to implement. Creating new organizational changes for the smallest unit for decentralization, an elementary school, already requires much more time and resources than that required for innovations in other services. In addition, school decentralization usually involves bargaining and possibly conflict among at least three parties: the central school board, teachers and their organizations, and parents and their organizations. Given these conditions, it is actually a considerable achievement that several major cities have been able, within a brief period, to attempt any decentralization innovations at all.

This considerable level of effort means that considerable expectations are raised regarding outcomes. Major organizational changes are justified, it seems, only by major outcomes. The fact that more parents may be interested in school activities, for instance, is just not a sufficient justification for undertaking decentralization. In the case of school decentralization, the major outcomes have not occurred. A significant shift in the power structure would not only give the local boards major personnel and budgetary functions but would simultaneously take the same functions away from the central board. As Gittell et al. properly point out, "Indeed, under a truly decentralized school system, there is question whether a central Board of Education would any longer be needed. The state could assume the minimal duties of a central Board" (Gittell et al., 1973, p. 159). Since all the major components of the traditional school system have still survived in spite of decentralization, advocates of decentralization are probably correct in concluding that significant decentralization, in terms of power shifts, has not occurred. Similarly, the advocates are also correct in noting, in light of the low participation rates and voter turnouts, that decentralization has not led to mass parental participation. At the same time, of course, neither have there been significant educational outcomes, and thus decentralization has been disappointing on that score as well.

What this means for the future is that the expectations for decentralization are likely to be reduced and the type of innovations similarly diminished in scale. Decentralization will no longer be viewed as a major reform effort or as a panacea for the problems of inner-city education. Instead, minor changes of a decentralizing nature may occur wherever there is a desire to increase parent participation (even at levels less than mass participation) or to institutionalize a local school board structure (even where the board's functions are limited). In short, future prospects for decentralization are unclear. However, future innovations are likely to be less grandiose in scale—and less grandiose in expectation—than in the past.[f]

References

Bell, Daniel and Virginia Held. 1969. "The Community Revolution." *The Public Interest* 16 (Summer), pp. 142-77.

Berube, Maurice R. and Marilyn Gittell. 1969. *Confrontation at Ocean Hill-Brownsville*. Praeger, New York.

Buskin, Martin. 1969. "Can Local Boards Really Run Ghetto Schools?" *School Management* 13 (March), pp. 31-36.

Coleman, James S. et al. 1966. *Equality of Educational Opportunity*. U.S. Government Printing Office, Washington, D.C.

Cronin, Joseph. 1973. *The Control of Urban Schools*. The Free Press, New York.

Decentralization and Community Involvement: A Status Report. 1969. Educational Research Service, Washington, D.C.

Fantini, Mario. 1969. "Participation, Decentralization, Community Control, and Quality Education." *Teachers College Record* 71 (September), pp. 93-107.

Fantini, Mario and Marilyn Gittell. 1973. *Decentralization: Achieving Reform*. Praeger, New York.

Fantini, Mario et al., 1970. *Community Control and the Urban School*. Praeger, New York.

Gittell, Marilyn et al. 1972. *Local Control in Education: Three Demonstration School Districts in New York City*. Praeger, New York.

_____. 1973. *School Boards and School Policy: An Evaluation of Decentralization in New York City*. Praeger, New York.

Glazer, Nathan. 1972. "Is Busing Necessary?" *Commentary* (March), pp. 39-52.

Kaestle, Carl F. 1973. *The Evolution of an Urban School System*. Harvard University Press, Cambridge, Mass.

---

[f]One exception to this may be in Boston, where continued racial segregation and political conflict may lead to major decentralization efforts. The Boston situation, however, may be unique because of the state Racial Imbalance Act that was passed in 1965 (see Reinhold, 1973).

Kelley, Jonathan. 1974. "The Politics of School Busing." *Public Opinion Quarterly* 38 (Spring), pp. 23-39.

LaNoue, George R. and Bruce L.R. Smith. 1973. *The Politics of School Decentralization*. Lexington Books, D.C. Heath, Lexington, Mass.

Lauter, Paul. 1968. "The Short Happy Life of the Adams-Morgan Community School Project." *Harvard Educational Review* 38 (Spring), pp. 235-62.

Lazerson, Marvin. 1971. *Origins of the Urban School*. Harvard University Press, Cambridge, Mass.

Lopate, Carol et al. 1970. "Decentralization and Community Participation in Public Education." *Review of Educational Research* (February), pp. 135-50.

Meranto, Philip. 1970. *School Politics in the Metropolis*. Merrill Publishing Co., Columbus. O.

The New York Times, 1972a. "Clark Asks a Curb on Decentralization." November 30, p. 2.

The New York Times. 1972b. "18 of 31 District School Superintendents Have Left Jobs Since Decentralization Began." May 21, p. 64.

Ornstein, Allan C. 1971. "Decentralizing Urban Schools." *Journal of Secondary Education* (February), pp. 83-91.

Ravitch, Diane. 1972. "Community Control Revisited." *Commentary* (February), pp. 69-74.

_____. 1974. *The Great School Wars*. Basic Books, New York.

Reconnection for Learning: A Community School System for New York City. 1967. Mayor's Advisory Panel on Decentralization of the New York City Schools, New York.

Reinhold, Robert. 1973. "More Segregated than Ever." *The New York Times Magazine*, September 30.

Report of the National Advisory Commission on Civil Disorders. 1968. Bantam Books, New York.

Rogers, David. 1968. *110 Livingston Street: Politics and Bureaucracy in the New York Public School System*. Random House, New York.

Rubin, Lillian B. 1972. *Busing and Backlash*. University of California Press, Berkeley.

Stein, Annie. 1971. "Strategies for Failure." *Harvard Educational Review* 41 (May), pp. 158-204.

U.S. Commission on Civil Rights. 1967. *Racial Isolation in the Public Schools*, Vol. 2. U.S. Government Printing Office, Washington, D.C.

Zimet, Melvin. 1973. *Decentralization and School Effectiveness*. Teachers College Press, New York.

8

Economic Development

Prelude to Decentralization

The preceding chapters focused on the decentralization of service delivery systems; the present chapter examines a somewhat contrasting approach to decentralization. This approach emphasizes what might be called "capacity-building"—the direct decentralization of resources to neighborhoods so they can increase their own economic situation and thereby solve their own problems. Although economic development involves little direct restructuring of existing service bureaucracies, the topic is of considerable interest for two reasons: First, the economic development innovations have involved the creation of new neighborhood institutions, with aspirations for a high degree of citizen participation and control (Kotler, 1971). Second, some advocates consider an economic development organization to be a prelude to political decentralization of major state and municipal functions:[a]

As its local authority increases in such fields as recreation, education, day care, and job development, the neighborhood corporation will build a public territorial jurisdiction. Eventually, this jurisdiction will become formalized and the private neighborhood corporation will become a public corporation [*Georgetown Law Journal* (1969), "From Private Enterprise to Public Entity"].

The Community Development Corporation

As in the previous chapters, the dominant scene for economic development efforts has been the inner-city, low-income neighborhood. The main instrument of economic development has been a new neighborhood institution, the *community development corporation* (CDC). A CDC has no simple definition, but several characteristics are present in almost all such organizations.[b] First, the scope of activities is territorially defined, as a CDC generally focuses on a particular neighborhood and uses "pride of place" as a major organizing force. In some cases, the CDC involves a

---

[a] In addition to the *Georgetown Law Journal* article cited in the text, see Hallman (1970); Kotler (1969); and Hallman (1973).

[b] Most of the literature on CDCs is composed of advocate statements and speculations on what CDCs might eventually accomplish. Works that are worth referring to include: Kotler (1969); Perry (1971); Ackerson and Sharf (1970); and Ford Foundation (1973).

coalition of neighborhoods, but the geographic area remains the organizing base. For example, in Durham, North Carolina, United Organizations for Community Improvement is made up of 21 different neighborhood groups representing residents of well-defined areas, but all of the areas are parts of the same region of the city. The feature that often defines a territory is a church, but boundaries are also set by geographic markers such as railroad tracks, arterial highways, and similar physical structures.

Second, the organizational structure of the CDC offers residents shares or memberships (depending on whether it has a profit or not-for-profit status) that carry voting rights on policy issues. When such shares or memberships are sold outside the neighborhood, as is sometimes necessary to obtain additional capital, they do not carry the right to influence the priorities of the corporation through voting, which thus preserves the territorial basis of formal control.[c]

Third, the CDC is an organization with multiple goals, which is a significant divergence from the standard corporate model, as well as a point of vulnerability in the eyes of CDC critics (Sturdivant, 1971). Every CDC has *economic* objectives and pursues these by a number of tactics that usually occur in combination. CDCs may develop and control their own businesses, which range from mattress manufacturing in the case of the East Los Angeles Community Union to data processing and management services in the case of Harlem Commonwealth Council. CDCs may also develop businesses and spin them off to individuals or local entrepreneurial groups. In Chicago, the West Side Community Development Corporation involves five constituent community organizations, which have become legal entities and operate businesses. One, formerly a delinquent gang, now operates two frozen custard franchises, a pool hall, and a fashion shop (Brower, 1971). CDCs also provide technical assistance to management and make loans for local entrepreneurs and other residents. The Bedford-Stuyvesant Restoration Corporation, through its prestigious board, formed a mortgage pool that made $65 million in FHA-insured loans available for the purchase and remodeling of housing stock. The availability of long-term FHA financing has reduced monthly payments to the size where purchase and proper maintenance are now feasible.

In addition, a CDC also has *social* objectives that are reflected in the criteria by which local governing boards set the priorities for their organiza-

---

[c] In Durham, North Carolina, neighborhood stockholders of the CDC elected two classes of directors to its board. Class A members were residents of the neighborhoods—the black, low-income target community—and held two-thirds of the seats on the board. The remaining one-third was held by owners of Class B stock, which had been offered for the purposes of obtaining more venture capital and establishing necessary links to key community groups. The stockholder's meetings came to be dominated by the Class B stockholders. To counteract this domination, formal training programs and special meetings of Class A directors were initiated (see Stein, 1972).

tions. In other words, the CDC has a political constituency to which it is responsible—that is, the residents of the neighborhood. Many of the activities engaged in by the CDC must therefore not only reflect economic objectives but also serve the priorities of the residents and their felt needs (Perry, 1973). The economic and social objectives need not clash, as some activities can satisfy both objectives simultaneously. For instance, one of the most prevalent large-scale activities undertaken by urban CDCs has been physical asset development, in both housing and commercial property. This type of program has highly desirable features for a CDC. The project is attractive to potential investors because it provides long-range neighborhood improvement and gives immediate service in the form of employment to neighborhood residents. Other ventures, however, may require tradeoffs between the economic and social objectives. In some instances, a CDC may have to forgo an economically profitable venture in favor of a more labor-intensive industry that will provide a job training "greenhouse" for neighborhood residents, which calls for a socialization as well as an employment experience, by attempting, for instance, to instill pride of work accomplished, good work habits, and a sense of the importance of one's place in the organization (Vietorisz and Harrison, 1970; and Harrison, 1972).

The point about CDCs in terms of decentralization is that they are based on strong commitments to both territorial and client-oriented decentralization. In addition, since the CDC is a new institution, there is no strong server group to resist innovations that give clients substantial control.

The Evolution of the CDC Strategy

Initial Attempts at Reform. The development of CDCs was not an original part of the federal antipoverty program. On the contrary, the early Community Action Programs focused on improving services for low-income neighborhoods, both by delivering rehabilitative services to the poor and by exerting political pressure on city governments on behalf of the poor. The major emphasis was a *service* strategy: developing new service programs and increasing new employment opportunities. However, the antipoverty programs often produced political conflicts with the municipal bureaucracy. These conflicts suggested that the service strategy was merely further institutionalizing a donor-recipient relationship; meaningful participation, in other words, was dependent upon having one's role validated by officials outside the neighborhood. According to the advocates of citizen power, a real redistribution of services is produced only when (1) a deprived group is self-sufficient enough to articulate and protect its own interests, independent of the will of the service-providing bureaucracy, and

(2) residents are able to participate in political decisionmaking rather than merely acting as recipients of services (Hamilton, 1970).

The employment programs of the early antipoverty projects also did not work as expected. Typically, paraprofessional opportunities in the target neighborhood were taken by nonresidents (Harrison, 1973). In addition, many employment programs relied heavily on education and training, on the assumption that people could expect future wage gains in proportion to the investment made in education and job-related training. However, for the inner-city black worker, there appear to be at least two identifiable sectors of the labor market, the core and the periphery, each of which is almost entirely self-contained (Bluestone, 1965; and Doeringer and Piore, 1971). The core, with its primary labor market, is characterized by high productivity, nonpoverty wages, and job stability. The periphery, with a secondary market, contains what Bennett Harrison (1972) terms the "training economy," with the hallmarks of low productivity, low wages, and high turnover, and no mechanisms for linking a worker to satisfactory employment opportunities. Enrollment in training programs, in effect, becomes an employment opportunity in and of itself, rather than a means to improved opportunities.

The early antipoverty approach therefore failed to provide either dramatically improved services or a route for economic integration and mobility. Moreover, there was little assurance that any new economic resources developed in the neighborhood would not immediately leave in the form of payments for goods and services outside the neighborhood. What the Community Action Program did accomplish was to expose black neighborhood leaders to the management of large amounts of money and the operations of federal and local government. In addition, the CAPs accelerated the growth of territorial awareness and established client boards as the organizing concept for citizen participation. In fact, the CAPs may be seen as laying important groundwork for a capacity-building approach.

Development of CDCs. The first Community Development Corporations actually emerged independently of the federal antipoverty programs mainly in neighborhoods where strong leadership stemmed from an existing organization, usually a church. The first CDCs were therefore not the result of a federal policy but were a genuinely local initiative (Faux, 1971). The oldest CDC is Zion Non-Profit Charitable Trust, established in 1962 by Rev. Leon Sullivan as a profit-making corporation. It is based on a "10-36" plan where individuals contribute $10 per month for 36 months to provide development capital for the CDC. In contrast, Cleveland Hough Area Development Corporation, organized by another minister, De Forest Brown, is a nonprofit venture. A third early CDC was founded in Rochester, where the Board for Urban Ministry invited Saul Alinsky to organize FIGHT.

Several models for CDCs therefore already existed in 1966, when Senator Robert Kennedy visited Bedford-Stuyvesant and subsequently helped to organize the Restoration and Development Corporation, with an impressive coalition of outside backers (Gifford, 1970). The initiation of the CDC was combined with expanded federal support for CDCs, provided by the Special Impact Program under Title I-D of the Economic Opportunity Act of 1967. With the rise of federal involvement and a concomitant increase in interest by private foundations, many new CDCs were organized. Since 1967, approximately 100 CDCs have been created across the country, in both urban and rural areas. The Special Impact Program had granted $132.5 million to individual CDCs by June 30, 1973. Although some CDCs have sought resources from foundations and others have received loans from industry, the primary source of support remains the federal government. This unfortunately has limited the CDC growth potential, as federal support usually comes in the form of debt rather than equity financing (Harrison, 1974).

Strategies for Change

In terms of the present study, the CDCs have followed three major strategies for decentralization: (1) the development of new neighborhood institutions; (2) the employment of neighborhood residents; and (3) political decentralization in the sense of giving control over the CDC to residents.

As a deviation from the rest of the study, the case survey also examined the effectiveness of the four *corporate* strategies commonly pursued by CDCs: business acquisitions; technical or financial assistance to neighborhood businesses; the development and divestment of new ventures; and the development and operation of new ventures. In acquiring businesses, a CDC buys out a local business and continues to operate it with neighborhood residents as staff. In Columbus, Ohio, for instance, a CDC purchases a tie factory, which provided jobs for 30 local persons. An example of providing technical or financial assistance is the Harlem Commonwealth Council's loans to pharmacies that have trouble collecting Medicaid funds; similarly, the Inner City Business Improvement Forum assists local entrepreneurs through the provision of technical assistance on management problems. In generating new enterprises and divesting them, a CDC may develop large manufacturing ventures that it will sell to local investors once the ventures are economically viable. Finally, Progress Plaza (a large shopping center development in Philadelphia) and Martin Luther King

Table 8-1
Major Economic Development Innovations

Start Date	Location	Area of Coverage	Main Innovation	Major Reported Outcomes[a]
1965	Columbus	East Central Citizens Organization and ECCO Development Corp. (non-profit/profit; 20,000 target population).	Housing rehabilitation; retail ventures; operation of social services.	About 20 jobs created by mid-1971.
1965	Rochester	FIGHT, Inc. (nonprofit 62,000 target population).	Manufacturing ventures; housing management and training; construction of housing project.	About 100 jobs created by mid-1971; profits realized and projected.
1967	New York	Bedford-Stuyvesant Restoration Corp. (nonprofit; 450,000 target population).	Scatter-site rehabilitation; mortgage loans; loans to local businesses; construction of commercial center of housing units.	Over 400 jobs created by mid-1971; profits realized and projected.

Year	City	Organization	Activities	Results
1967	Cleveland	Hough Area Development Corp. (nonprofit; 60,000 target population).	Construction of shopping center; franchises and established credit union.	Over 200 jobs created by mid-1971; no profits projected.
1968	Chicago	North Lawndale Economic Development Corp. (for profit; 87,000 target population).	Construction of shopping center; urban industrial park.	Unknown.
1968	New York	Harlem Commonwealth Council (nonprofit; 36,000 target population).	Office rental; operation of retail outlets; real estate development planned; technical assistance to small businesses.	Over 50 jobs created by mid-1971; no profits projected.
1968	Durham, N.C.	United Durham (for profit; 100,000 target population).	Operation of retail services.	Over 25 jobs created by mid-1971; internal managerial conflict.
1969	St. Louis	Union Sarah Economic Development Corp. (for profit; 41,000 target population).	Support of health center; technical assistance to small businesses; loan packaging.	Over 50 jobs created by mid-1971; no profits projected.

[a]Source: Abt Associates (1972).

Plaza (in Cleveland) are examples of business ventures that the CDC develops and operates under its own auspices.

The following section describes the results of the case survey, in terms of both the decentralization and the corporate strategies.

Results of the Case Survey

The survey covered 54 case studies of CDCs. Although these studies dealt only with 26 discrete innovations, these 26 represent all of the important urban CDCs, including those funded by private foundations and local donations as well as those supported primarily by the federal government. Table 8-1 lists the prominent CDCs, their characteristics, and the major outcomes that have been found.

Strategies Attempted

The majority of the seven decentralization strategies were not relevant to neighborhood economic development. Table 8-2 indicates that four strategies were found rarely or not at all: community relations, grievance mechanisms, physical redeployment, and administrative decentralization. These strategies are more appropriate where decentralization involves existing service delivery institutions. In the few studies that these strategies were tried in the economic development approach, they were related to the services being provided by the CDC. For example, a CDC might have used a community relations program to inform neighborhood residents of the existence of certain services. As to grievance procedures, a few CDCs serve as communication channels for information from the neighborhood to the municipal bureaucracies. For example, FIGHT, Inc., of Rochester, New York, attempts to confront the city government on behalf of individuals who have complaints.

In contrast to these infrequently tried decentralization strategies, the dominant economic development innovation involves a single combination of three strategies: employment of neighborhood residents, new neighborhood institutions, and political decentralization. This combination occurred as a multiple strategy in 36 of the 54 case studies. As a result of this distribution of strategies, the economic development studies were categorized as involving *no* cases of weak decentralization, 10 cases of moderate decentralization, and 42 cases of strong decentralization. Of the four corporate strategies, the development and operation of new ventures

Table 8-2
Decentralization Strategies Found among Economic Development Studies

Strategy	Number of Studies[a]
Community Relations	3
Physical Redeployment	0
Grievance Mechanisms	4
Administrative Decentralization	0
Employment of Neighborhood Residents	48
New Neighborhood Institutions	54
Political Decentralization	42

Note: N = 54.

[a]Total is greater than the total number of studies because of multiple occurrences of strategies within single studies.

Table 8-3
Corporate Strategies Found among Economic Development Studies

Strategy	Number of Studies[a]
Acquire Business through Purchases	22
Provide Technical or Financial Assistance to Neighborhood Business	27
Develop and Divest New Ventures	13
Develop and Operate New Ventures	43

Note: N = 54.

[a]Total is greater than the total number of studies because of multiple occurrences of strategies within single studies.

occurred most frequently. (Table 8-3 shows the frequency with which all the corporate strategies were found in the case studies.)

Outcomes

The outcomes in economic development were assessed in the same way as in previous chapters. As for the frequency of outcomes found, the economic development studies showed a somewhat different pattern than expected (see Table 8-4). First, increased client control occurred in only 25.9 percent of the studies, which ranks high compared with the other service areas (except for education) but is disappointing in relation to both the expectations for CDCs and the fact that the operational definition for "increased client control" was merely that residents had to implement some of their own ideas. Second, improved services occurred with greater frequency than any other service area or in 90.7 percent of the studies. Moreover, the high rate must be interpreted somewhat differently from the analysis in previous chapters, since the service outcomes were dominantly an increase in jobs (with the other public services in the previous chapters, service improvements were frequently based on actual changes in service outputs, not just inputs). Third, the economic development studies showed a distinctively low frequency of improved flow of information. CDCs apparently put great emphasis on producing service outcomes but play a very minor role in getting information about public services to residents.

Since so many of the economic development studies involved strong decentralization, no further analysis was possible in comparing the outcomes for the different types of decentralization strategies. However, a further examination was made of the correlates of the four corporate strategies. Table 8-5 shows the simple success rates for each of these strategies. No single strategy is associated with consistently high outcomes relative to the other strategies, but there is a tendency among the corporate strategies to be associated with an apparent tradeoff between two important outcomes, improved services and increased client control. Strategies that are high on one outcome tend to be low on the other. This contrast in outcomes can be pursued further if the corporate strategies are grouped into *mutually exclusive categories* according to whether the CDC pursued only the development and operation of new ventures (the most common corporate strategy) or whether that strategy was used in combination with one or more of the other corporate strategies. However, when these categories are compared with the two outcomes of improved services and increased client control, the results produce no statistically significant differences (see Table 8-5).

In summary, the case survey revealed the following results concerning the economic development studies:

1. The overwhelmingly dominant decentralization strategy was a combination of the employment, new neighborhood institutions, and political decentralization strategies, so that the vast majority of studies involved strong decentralization.
2. The outcomes for all studies were a surprisingly low rate of increased client control but a high rate of improved services (primarily an increase in jobs).
3. Because of the limited variety of decentralization strategies, no comparisons could be made among the strategies and their relationship to the five outcomes.
4. Among *corporate* strategies pursued by the CDCs, the development and operation of new ventures was more frequently reported than any of the three other strategies; but none of the corporate strategies appeared to be associated with distinctively different rates of outcomes.

151

Table 8-4
Decentralization Outcomes Found among Economic Development Studies

| | | Number of Studies | | |
Outcome	Yes	No	No Information	Percent Yes
More Information	10	44	0	18.5
Improved Agency Attitudes	4	49	1	7.4
Improved Client Attitudes	10	42	2	18.5
Improved Services	49	5	0	90.7
Increased Client Control	14	36	4	25.9

Note: N = 54.

Table 8-5
Outcomes for Corporate Strategies

| | Percentage Occurrence of Outcome | | | | |
Corporate Strategy[a]	More Information	Improved Agency Attitudes	Improved Client Attitudes	Improved Services	More Client Control
Acquire Businesses (n = 22)	27.3	9.1	22.7	86.3	18.2
Provide Technical or Financial Assistance (n = 27)	22.2	7.4	18.5	96.3	11.1
Develop and Divest New Ventures (n = 13)	30.8	23.1	7.7	84.7	30.8
Develop and Operate New Ventures (n = 43)	18.6	7.0	20.9	93.1	27.9
All Economic Development Studies (n = 54)	18.5	7.4	18.5	90.7	25.9

Note: N = 54.
[a]Total number of strategies is greater than the number of studies because of multiple occurrences of strategies within single studies.

Citizen Participation

Of the 54 studies, 50 reported citizen participation, with four having paraprofessional programs only, 24 having a board only, and 22 having both a

Table 8-6
Outcomes for Multiple Corporate Strategies

| | | Percentage Occurrence of Outcome[a] | |
Strategy	Number of Studies	Improved Services	Increased Client Control
Develop and Operate New Ventures Only	11	100.0	54.5
Develop and Operate (plus any other single strategy)	19	84.2	21.1
Develop and Operate (plus two or more of the other strategies)	13	100.0	15.4
All Other	11	81.8	18.2
Total	54	90.7	25.9

Note: N = 54.
[a]None of the differences is statistically significant.

board and a paraprofessional program.[d] The economic development studies thus reflected a high frequency both of participation and of boards. Variations in the type of citizen participation appear to be associated with one distinctive difference in outcomes. Unlike the overall trend for all service areas, the board-paraprofessional combination was associated with *lower* rates of increased client control than boards alone (see Table 8-7). The boards-paraprofessional outcome was in fact similar to the combined outcome for no citizen participation and paraprofessionals only.

There is no apparent explanation for this finding. One possibility may be that within CDCs, paraprofessional staff are less closely monitored by the board, which results in the paraprofessionals being more responsive to pressures from funding sources rather than neighborhood residents' own ideas.

Decentralization and Economic Development

Comparing Case Survey Results with Other Findings

There are few evaluations of CDCs with which to compare these case

[d]Paraprofessional programs were defined as situations in which the neighborhood residents worked within the structure of the CDC itself not in an auxiliary project developed by the CDC. For example, hiring neighborhood residents to work on a housing rehabilitation project was not considered as a paraprofessional program, but hiring residents to identify businesses in need of technical assistance was.

Table 8-7
Outcomes for Citizen Participation, Economic Development Studies

Citizen Participation	Total Number of Studies	Percentage Occurrence of Outcome				
		More Infor- mation	Improved Agency Attitudes	Improved Client Attitudes	Improved Services	More Client Control[a]
Boards Only	24	20.8	4.2	16.6	82.6	41.6
Boards and Paraprofessionals	22	13.6	13.6	27.2	100.0	13.6
No Citizen Participation or Paraprofessionals Only	8	25.0	0.0	0.0	87.5	12.3
All Economic Development Studies	54	18.5	7.4	18.5	90.7	25.9

Note: N = 54.
[a]$\chi^2 = 8.00$, $df = 2$, $p < .05$; none of the other differences is significant.

survey results. In general, even the case study literature is dominated by descriptions of the cases rather than by any attempt to analyze or compare the cases. More comprehensive reviews of ghetto economic development include narrative descriptions of CDCs, but only as illustrations and not as innovations to be evaluated.

Among the few relevant studies, Faux (1972) suggests that CDC leaders have had real problems with the issue of board representation and with the powers that the board should exercise; he states, "In a large number of cases, CDC boards represent a reaction to the often aimless bickering of elected neighborhood boards under the antipoverty program," and as a result, where boards exist, they do *not* dominate the operation of the CDC, in spite of the rhetoric of community participation. The findings from the 54 studies just surveyed tend to agree with Faux's conclusion, in that boards were found to exist in 46 of the 54 case studies, but throughout all of the economic development studies, increased client control occurred in only 14, or 25.9 percent, of the studies. This result is thus in marked contrast to the central goal envisioned by the planners of the CDC movement, who saw local control as the essential feature of the capacity-building approach. One possible remedy for increasing community control was recommended in an evaluation study of 16 CDCs (Abt Associates, 1972). This was to increase resident control through the distribution of stock, which is a mechanism of control uniquely available to the CDC, but not necessarily to innovations in the other four service areas of safety, education, health, or multiservice programs. Whether such a form of corporate control suffices as community control, however, depends heavily on the working relationship between the shareholders and the managers of a CDC; obviously, under most organizational procedures the managers still exercise almost complete autonomy from the shareholders (Alchian and Demsetz, 1972).

Two major evaluation studies have attempted to identify the market effects of CDCs more closely. The results may shed additional light on our own findings. Whereas nearly every CDC has had some success in providing new jobs, the overall profit picture has been bleak (in one study, 47 for-profit ventures had a net loss of $1.6 million after four years from the beginning of the venture), and the amount of employment, especially of the hardcore unemployed, has been small relative to the neighborhood's overall needs (Abt Associates, 1972; and Garn et al., 1973).

The Role of CDCs in the Future

Most of the studies of CDCs, including those in the case survey, have focused on problems of citizen participation and control. Although this aspect of CDCs is obviously important, its emphasis has possibly been at the expense of two other topics. The first deals with the nature of the services delivered by CDCs—that is, there are few indications of the amount, quality, or usefulness of the CDCs' output as a service to the neighborhood. The second topic is even more important; it deals with the economics of CDCs and the question of whether they are viable corporate entities. Here, the literature is grossly inadequate, and yet for the near-term future, the continuation of CDCs with possibly minimal amounts of federal support will be determined largely by the degree to which CDCs have become self-sufficient.

The case survey yielded no information about the economics of CDC operations, or which of the corporate strategies are economically most feasible under what market conditions. Moreover, the impression one gets from the literature is that, except for rare occasions, CDCs have not been notable successes in any economic sense, as they still rely heavily on outside sources of funds, such as the federal government; nor is this to be unexpected, for CDCs are operating under clearly disadvantageous conditions in coping with the economic problems of the ghetto. However, some recognition is needed that outside support may be required on a permanent basis, and we should have some estimate of the amount of such support. In other words, we may have to relinquish the myth that CDCs can eventually become self-supporting.

The economic shortcoming would not be so crucial if CDCs were visibly moving toward neighborhood government, which is yet another major long-term goal. In fact, as discussed in the multiservice programs, movement toward neighborhood government in general may be slowly increasing, but most of the impetus has not been based on CDCs. Given these developments, the future of CDCs remains quite uncertain. A few of the more prominent and successful CDCs, for example, the Bedford-Stuyvesant Restoration Corporation, will undoubtedly continue to operate in much the same fashion as in the past. Other CDCs may find consolidation and merger with other private enterprises to be the only viable economic alternative. Yet other CDCs will not be able to operate at all unless substantial outside funding is continued.

The economic development of the inner-city neighborhood may fare better than any particular CDC, because the neighborhood residents will continue to receive some transfer payments, either in welfare assistance or other voucher programs, and because the CDCs may have helped to continue the earlier antipoverty efforts in providing more effective job training and opportunities for employment. The CDCs may also have played a significant role in furthering the development of new business administrators in that a new cadre of potential leaders have been exposed to venture development experiences. These improvements in neighborhood capabilities, combined with an apparent decline in costly conflicts such as the urban riots, may mean that some inner-city neighborhoods will experience limited economic improvement.

Whatever the economic health of the CDCs or improvements for the inner-city neighborhoods, one must remember that any success should also be gauged by comparison with progress in white, middle-class enterprises. Even the most successful black enterprises are still failing to close the economic gap between themselves as a group and white-dominated enterprises as a group. A recent survey of the top 100 black-controlled enterprises in the country showed not only that the top enterprise had sales of about one-fifth that of the 500th company in the Fortune 500 listing, but also that the top 100 black enterprises had an average increase in revenues of 17.7 percent over fiscal 1974, whereas the Fortune 500 grew by about 20 percent (Holsendolph, 1974; a similarly less optimistic picture for black enterprises is also drawn in Brimmer, 1974). If progress is slow for these top 100 companies, then it is easy to imagine the continued nature of the problem for neighborhood-based enterprises where the neighborhood has a poverty-level economy.

References

Abt Associates. 1972. *Special Impact Program: Phase I Report,* 4 volumes. Cambridge, Mass.

Ackerson, Nels and Lawrence H. Sharf. 1970. "Community Development

Corporations: Operations and Financing." *Harvard Law Review* 83 (March), pp. 1558-671.

Alchian, Armen and Harold Demsetz. 1972. "Production Information Costs, and Economic Organization." *American Economic Review* 62 (December), pp. 777-95.

Bluestone, Barry. 1965. "Lower-Income Workers in Marginal Industries," in Louis Ferman et al., eds., *Poverty in America*. University of Michigan Press, Ann Arbor.

Brimmer, Andrew F. 1974. "Economic Developments in the Black Community." *The Public Interest* 34 (Winter), pp. 146-63.

Brower, Michael. 1971. "The Emergence of Community Development Corporations in Urban Neighborhoods." *American Journal of Orthopsychiatry* 41 (July), pp. 646-58.

Doeringer, Peter and Michael Piore. 1971. *Internal Labor Markets and Manpower Analysis*. Lexington Books, D.C. Heath, Lexington, Mass.

Faux, Geoffrey. 1972. *CDCs: New Hope for the Inner City*. Twentieth Century Fund, New York.

_____. "Politics and Bureaucracy in Community Controlled Economic Development." *Law and Contemporary Problems* 36 (Spring), pp. 277-96.

Ford Foundation. 1973. "CDCs: A Strategy for Depressed Urban and Rural Areas," unpublished manuscript. New York.

Garn, Harvey A. et al. 1973. "CDC Evaluation," discussion paper. The Urban Institute, Washington, D.C.

Georgetown Law Journal. 1969. "From Private Enterprise to Public Entity: The Role of the Community Development Corporation." Vol. 57 (May), pp. 956-90.

Gifford, Kilbert Dun. "Neighborhood Development Corporations: The Bedford-Stuyvesant Experiment," in Lyle C. Fitch and Annmarie H. Walsh, eds., *Agenda for a City*. Sage Publications, Beverly Hills, Calif.

Hallman, Howard W. 1973. *Government by Neighborhoods*. Center for Governmental Studies, Washington, D.C.

_____. 1970. *Neighborhood Control of Public Programs: Case Studies of Community Corporations and Neighborhood Boards*. Praeger, New York.

Hamilton, Charles V. 1970. "The Politics of Race Relations," in Charles V. Daley, ed., *Urban Violence*. University of Chicago Press, Chicago.

Harrison, Bennett. 1972. *Education, Training, and the Urban Ghetto*. Johns Hopkins Press, Baltimore.

_____. 1974. "Ghetto Economic Development: A Survey." *Journal of Economic Literature* 12 (March), pp. 1-38.

Harrison, Bennett. 1973. "The Participation of Ghetto Residents in a Model Cities Program." *Journal of the American Institute of Planners* 39 (January), pp. 43-55.

Holsendolph, Ernest. 1974. "Strong Growth in a Tough Year." *Black Enterprise* 4 (June), pp. 31-45.

Kotler, Milton. 1969. *Neighborhood Government: The Local Foundations of Political Life. Bobbs-Merrill, Indianapolis.*

_____. 1971. "The Politics of Community Economic Development." *Law and Contemporary Problems* 36 (Winter), pp. 3-12.

Perry, Stuart. 1973. "Federal Support for CDCs: Some of the History and Issues of Community Centers." Center for Community Economic Development, Cambridge, Mass.

_____. 1971. "National Policy and the Community Development Corporation." *Law and Contemporary Problems* 36 (Spring), pp. 297-308.

Stein, Barry. 1972. "United Durham, Inc.: A Case Study in Community Control." Center for Community Economic Development, Cambridge, Mass.

Sturdivant, Frederick D. 1971. "Community Development Corporations: The Problem of Mixed Objectives." *Law and Contemporary Problems* 36 (Winter), pp. 35-50.

Vietorisz, Thomas and Bennett Harrison. 1970. *The Economic Development of Harlem.* Praeger, New York.

9

Decentralization: A Summary Account

The five preceding chapters reported the overall rates of positive outcomes in each of five service areas and also discussed the peculiar patterns of strategies and outcomes in each. The highest rates of positive outcomes for each service area were the following:

1. For increased flow of information, 95 percent of multiservice studies and 87 percent of safety studies reported positive outcomes.
2. For improved agency attitudes, 26 percent of safety studies and 24 percent of education studies reported positive outcomes.
3. For improved client attitudes, 42 percent of safety studies and 23 percent of education studies reported positive outcomes.
4. For improved services, 91 percent of economic development studies and 66 percent of multiservice studies reported positive outcomes.
5. For increased client control, 59 percent of education studies and 26 percent of economic development studies reported positive outcomes.

Throughout the chapters we have emphasized the importance of service characteristics in accounting for these results. Here we summarize the argument and then present evidence to test the alternative view that non-service-specific factors can account for the decentralization outcomes.

The Significance of Service Differences

Decentralization Strategies and Outcomes

The service chapters have shown that each of the five services was marked by characteristically different strategies and outcomes. In particular, the safety, health, and multiservice areas had high occurrences of weak decentralization strategies, whereas the education and economic development areas had high occurrences of strong strategies. Table 9-1 summarizes the frequency of occurrence of weak, moderate, and strong strategies for each service area and shows that the relationship between services and types of strategy is indeed highly significant. Thus, the main effect of the service area is to condition the likely types of decentralization strategies that are to be attempted: The more open the service in terms of the degree of profes-

159

sional and bureaucratic control, the more frequently strong decentralization strategies have been tried; conversely, the more closed the bureaucracy, the more frequently weak strategies have been tried.

Because of these service variations in strategies attempted, it is not surprising that the five services also vary significantly in the frequency of positive outcomes. Table 9-2 shows the success rates for each outcome in each service area. The safety and multiservice areas tend to show high rates of increased flow of information but low rates of increased client control. Education and economic development, however, show distinctively higher rates of increased client control. Health appears throughout to have moderate outcome levels in comparison with the other service areas. For each outcome, the service variation is statistically significant.

We can now construct a single general explanation for the decentralization outcomes. The first part of the explanation is that stronger decentralization strategies are more successful than weak ones in improving services and increasing client control, an overall relationship that was shown in Chapter 3. This is because the strong and moderate strategies (new institutions, employment, and political decentralization) put greater political and economic resources in the hands of service deliverers and clients and constitute potent instruments for reshaping the service relationship. By contrast, the resources and administrative leverage provided by the weak strategies (community relations, grievance mechanisms, physical redeployment, and administrative decentralization) are less substantial. Thus, we would simply conclude that the stronger the decentralization strategy, the more successful it will be for improving services and increasing client control.

The second part of the explanation concerns the service conditions for decentralization. We have shown that the server-served relationship varies substantially among different service areas, and the attempt to create strong decentralization strategies also varies. Here our thesis is that there is an obstacle to decentralization that hinges on the openness or closedness of the service bureaucracy. Any decentralization strategy will encounter opposition in the more bureaucratic and professionalized (and hence closed) services. Closed bureaucracies will tend to permit only weak strategies to emerge. Conversely, strong strategies are likely to emerge and be successful in such open bureaucracies as education and economic development. In sum, the success of decentralization depends on *two* factors:

1. *Successful decentralization is directly related to the strength of the decentralization strategy.*
2. *Successful decentralization is inversely related to the degree of professional and bureaucratic control over service policies.*

Table 9-1

Weak, Moderate, and Strong Decentralization Strategies, by Service Area

Service Area	Total Number of Studies	Studies for Each Type of Decentralization Strategy		
		Strong	Moderate	Weak
Safety	38	4	10	24
Health	48	13	21	14
Multiservice	41	8	10	23
Education	34	26	3	5
Economic Development	54	42	12	0
Total	215	93	56	66

$\chi^2 = 92.08$, $df = 8$, $p < .001$.

Table 9-2

Decentralization Outcomes for Each Service Area

Type of Decentralization Strategy	Total Number of Studies	Percentage Occurrence of Outcome[a]				
		More Information	Improved Agency Attitudes	Improved Client Attitudes	Improved Services	More Client Control
Safety	38	86.8	26.3	42.1	39.5	5.3
Health	48	54.2	6.2	22.9	62.5	16.7
Multiservice	41	95.1	4.8	19.5	65.9	9.8
Education	34	70.6	23.5	23.3	61.8	58.8
Economic Development	54	18.5	7.4	18.5	90.7	25.9

[a]The χ^2 for the differences among service areas is significant at the $p < .01$ level for each of the five outcomes.

The relative importance of these two factors is different for the two important outcomes of improved services and increased client control. For improved services, the nature of the service organization is more important; for increased client control, the type of decentralization strategy is more important. This is shown in Table 9-3, which clusters the safety, health, and multiservice areas into a *closed* category and the education and economic development areas into an *open* category, and then presents the combinations of closed and open categories with the three types of decentralization. For improved services, the open categories have higher rates of success than their closed counterparts, but the strength of strategy within open or closed categories does not appear to matter.[a] This suggests that decentralization will especially result in improved services when there is an open service bureaucracy in which servers and served share influence over policymaking. In contrast, for increased control, the rates of success consistently decrease with weaker types of strategies, but differences between open and closed categories do not appear to matter.[b] This suggests that decentralization will especially result in increased client control when strong strategies are used. However, these relative comparisons should not obscure our major conclusion: For improved services or increased client control, *both* the type of service and the type of decentralization strategy are important.

Citizen Participation

Types of Participation. A similar interpretation is applicable to the summary findings on the types of citizen participation. The service chapters emphasized that different services created citizen boards to varying degrees. Table 9-4 summarizes this relationship, with the safety, health, and multiservice areas showing fewer attempts at any citizen participation and the education and economic development areas showing more attempts at boards. In other words, closed bureaucracies are also less likely to attempt strong forms of citizen participation, with either no participation or paraprofessionals-only being found more frequently. However, the relationship between the type of participation and the five decentralization outcomes is not as significant as the relationship between the weak, moderate, and strong strategies and the outcomes. Table 9-5 shows that on only one outcome, increased client control, does the type of participation appear to make a statistically significant difference. On this outcome, studies with no citizen participation produce increased client control none of the time; studies with paraprofessionals-only produce client control 10 percent of the time; and *client control increases substantially when either a board or the board-paraprofessional combination is present.*

Functions of Citizen Boards. As an attempt to elaborate the key functions of citizen boards, the case survey also examined six different board functions:

---

[a] Statistically, the open versus closed comparison is significant at the $p < .10$ level for strong strategies, at the $p < .05$ level for moderate strategies, and not significant for the weak strategies. The differences among strategies *within* open or closed are not significant.

[b] Statistically, the strength of strategies comparison is significant at the $p < .05$ level for open services, and $p < .001$ level for closed services. None of the open versus closed comparisons is significant.

Table 9-3
Type of Service and Type of Strategy Compared for Two Decentralization Outcomes

Service/Strategy Combination	Total Number of Studies	Studies with Improved Services		Studies with Increased Control	
		Number	Percent	Number	Percent
Open/Strong	68	54	79.4	31	45.9
Open/Moderate	15	13	86.7	3	20.0
Open/Weak	5	3	60.0	0	0.0
Closed/Strong	25	15	60.0	11	44.0
Closed/Moderate	41	24	58.5	2	4.9
Closed/Weak	61	33	54.1	1	1.6

Note: N = 215.

Table 9-4
Type of Citizen Participation, by Service Area

Service Area	Number of Studies for Each Type of Citizen Participation			
	No Citizen Participation	Paraprofessionals Only	Boards Only	Boards and Paraprofessionals
Safety	22	4	7	5
Health	12	12	11	13
Multiservice	16	8	14	3
Education	0	2	16	16
Economic Development	4	4	24	22
Total	54	30	72	59

$\chi^2 = 69.00$, $df = 12$, $p < .001$.
Note: N = 215.

1. Signoff authority over grant applications or service decisions;
2. Planning for new programs or facilities;
3. Grievance investigation;
4. Budget review of requests or expenditures;
5. Personnel review for hiring, firing, or promoting; and
6. Supervision over some paid staff.

A previous study had found that four of these functions were important board characteristics for increasing client control: grievance investigation, budget review, personnel review, and supervision over paid staff. Of these four functions, the last was found to be the most important in the earlier study (Yin et al., 1973).

Table 9-5
Type of Citizen Participation and Decentralization Outcomes

Type of Participation	Total Number of Studies	More Infor- mation	Percentage Occurrence of Outcome			
			Improved Agency Attitudes	Improved Client Attitudes	Improved Services	More Client Control[a]
No citizen Participation	54	70.4	14.8	30.0	59.3	0.0
Paraprofessionals Only	30	83.3	20.0	26.7	66.7	10.0
Boards Only	72	52.8	5.6	15.3	57.0	30.6
Boards and Paraprofessionals	59	52.5	15.3	30.5	83.1	39.0

Note: N = 215.
[a]Differences are significant at the $p < .001$ level; differences for the other four outcomes are not statistically significant.

With the exception of the grievance function, the case survey tended to confirm this pattern. Table 9-6 shows the six functions (not in mutually exclusive categories since there was heavy overlap among the functions) and their frequency in producing the five outcomes. Although the differences are small, the budget, personnel, and supervision over paid staff functions all had higher rates of increased client control than did the other three functions. This pattern is reinforced when we examine the relationship between the six board functions and the occurrence of post-implementation conflict, which is another variable that has been frequently associated with client power (see Table 9-7). Supervision over paid staff shows the highest rate of conflict, with the budget and personnel review functions having the next highest rates. In summary, the results suggest that supervision over paid staff is the most important board function in increasing client control, and the budget and personnel review functions are also important. The three remaining functions of signoff authority, grievance investigations, and planning for new programs are of lesser importance.

The Non-Service View

In contrast to our interpretation that successful decentralization is determined in part by the strategy and in part by the service, other analysts of citizen participation have frequently cited exogenous, non-service-specific factors as being most highly associated with success. These factors deal primarily with the preconditions for decentralization. Four preconditions

Table 9-6
Functions of Citizen Boards and Decentralization Outcomes

	Percentage Occurrence of Outcome				
Function[a]	More Information	Improved Agency Attitudes	Improved Client Attitudes	Improved Services	More Client Control
Signoff Authority (n = 37)	35.1	8.1	29.7	86.4	48.6
Planning (n = 93)	55.9	11.8	21.5	73.1	41.9
Grievance Investigation (n = 29)	72.4	10.3	31.0	51.6	41.4
Budget Review (n = 44)	65.9	13.6	27.3	71.8	54.5
Personnel Review (n = 44)	61.4	18.1	31.8	72.7	56.8
Supervision over Paid Staff (n = 39)	76.9	15.4	25.7	69.3	61.5

[a]The frequency of functions exceeds the total number of studies because of the multiple occurrence of functions within single studies.

Table 9-7
Functions of Citizen Boards and Occurrence of Post-Implementation Conflict

	Percent Post-Implementation Conflict		
Function[a]	Yes	No	No Information
Signoff Authority (n = 37)	48.6	51.4	0.0
Planning (n = 93)	45.2	50.5	4.3
Grievance Investigation (n = 29)	41.3	51.7	6.9
Budget Review (n = 44)	59.0	40.9	0.0
Personnel Review (n = 44)	54.6	50.9	4.5
Supervision over Paid Staff (n = 39)	74.3	23.1	2.6

[a]The frequency of functions exceeds the total number of studies because of the multiple occurrence of functions within single studies.

in particular have been thought to be related to successful decentralization experiences:

1. Financial support of the innovation by the federal government;
2. The support of the innovation by the mayor or municipal executive;
3. A moderate-sized (approximately 50,000) target population;

4. The avoidance of conflict during the pre-implementation stage of the innovation.

Of these four, the first two have been considered to be more critical than the last two. The case survey results show that most of these factors, when examined individually, do not account fully for the pattern of decentralization outcomes and hence cannot be used to negate our strategy/service interpretation.

Financial Support by the Federal Government

The availability of federal funds for an innovation is usually assumed to be advantageous because the funds allow an innovation to operate somewhat freely of local constraints. Moreover, the federal government is credited with having stimulated citizen participation and encouraged client control over a project, at least to a greater degree than has local government. For these reasons, it has usually been assumed that the availability of federal funds has been associated with more successful cases of decentralization, especially in increasing client control. In particular, a major recent study found that the proportion of federal funding was by far the most important correlate of a high degree of citizen participation (Cole, 1974, pp. 73-74).

Table 9-8 shows the decentralization outcomes associated with the presence of federal support. The results indicate that there are no significant differences for any of the five outcomes, and hence *the presence of federal support makes little difference for decentralization outcomes;* if anything, federal support may be associated with a lower frequency of increased client control. Similarly, when the relationship between federal funds and the type of citizen participation is examined, federal funds make no difference in the frequency with which citizen boards occur (see Table 9-9).

These results differ considerably from those reported by others, but the explanation of the difference is quite simple. Previous studies have focused primarily on CAP and Model Cities efforts, whereas our study has focused on decentralization in specific urban services. Thus, although the proportion of federal funds may be an important factor in building citizen participation in new programs such as CAPs and Model Cities, the presence of such funds does not, and should not be expected to, influence the outcomes of decentralization in existing service bureaucracies.

Mayoral Support

A second factor that has been considered very important to successful

Table 9-8
Relationship of Federal Financial Support to Decentralization Outcomes

Federal Financial Support for the Innovation	Total Number of Studies[a]	Percentage Occurrence of Outcome[b]				
		More Infor- mation	Improved Agency Attitudes	Improved Client Attitudes	Improved Services	More Client Control
Dominant	126	56.3	12.6	24.6	71.4	18.3
Negligible	85	67.1	12.9	25.9	60.0	28.2

Note: N = 215.
[a]Four "no information" studies not shown.
[b]None of the differences for the five outcomes is statistically significant.

Table 9-9
Relationship of Federal Financial Support to Occurrence of Citizen Boards

Federal Financial Support for the Innovation	Number of Studies[a]	Occurrence of Boards[b]	
		Yes	No
Dominant	126	61.1	38.9
Negligible	85	60.0	40.0

Note: N = 215.
[a]Four "no information" studies not shown.
[b]The differences are not statistically significant.

decentralization is the active participation of the mayor or municipal executive in the innovation. Previous studies of Model Cities programs in particular have identified mayoral support for an innovation as a major component for success (U.S. Department of Housing and Urban Development, 1973; and Washnis, 1974). The interpretation has been that a mayor's commitment to an innovation may mean the availability of more local resources; but at a minimum, his support means that city hall will probably not try to undermine the implementation of the innovation.

The case survey included a question regarding the role of the mayor or municipal executive in the implementation of the innovation. For analysis, the answers to this question were clustered into two categories: The mayor or municipal executive was active in or aware of the implementation, or there was no involvement. Of course, the answers were quite sensitive to the completeness or focus of the original case study; there were 89 studies, or over 40 percent of the caseload, in which "no information" was given as the answer to this question. This "no reponse" rate was much higher than that of any other question reported throughout this entire study, and the results should therefore be interpreted with extreme caution.

The only decentralization outcomes for which mayoral or municipal executive activity appeared to make a difference were for increased flow of information and improved services (see Table 9-10). Mayoral activity was *not* related to increased client control. The interesting aspect of these findings, however, is that the mayoral activity was *inversely* related to improved services and positively related to increased information, which suggests that mayoral participation was associated with the weak decentralization strategies. In addition, when mayoral activity is compared with the occurrence of citizen boards, the results show no relationship between the two (see Table 9-11). In general, *the case survey, with a high "no response" rate on this question, showed no positive relationships between mayoral activity and either the service or control outcomes or the occurrence of citizen boards*. These results are again at variance with those of other studies and imply that once decentralization has been examined in the context of specific services, the mayoral or municipal executive role may not be important.

Moderate-Sized Target Population

Two other exogenous factors have been cited as possibly related to decentralization outcomes, though not with as much emphasis as the federal and mayoral roles. First, the size of the target population for a decentralization innovation is believed to have an effect on the outcome of the innovation. Moderate-sized target populations are believed to create better opportunities for client control and for improved services (Austin, 1972).

Table 9-12 compares the relationships between target populations of different sizes and the major decentralization outcomes. The results show that client control tends to increase as the target size decreases. The frequency of improved services is highest for target populations of about 10,000-50,000 and is lowest for the largest target population. In short, the evidence suggests that *smaller-sized populations (under 10,000) are associated with the highest frequency of increased client control, whereas moderate-sized populations (10,000 to 50,000) are associated with the highest frequency of improved services*. The relationship between target size and the different types of citizen participation was also examined. However, there were no consistent differences in the type of participation that was attributable to increases or decreases of target size.

These results lend some support to the potential importance of moderate to small target populations for successful outcomes. Target population size should therefore be considered an additional factor besides the strategy/service conditions.

Table 9-10

Relationship of Mayor's Role to Decentralization Outcomes

		Percentage Occurrence of Outcome				
Mayor's Role	Total Number of Studies	More Information[a]	Improved Agency Attitudes	Improved Client Attitudes	Improved Services[a]	More Client Control
Active or Aware	71	76.1	12.6	26.8	60.6	25.4
No Involvement	55	52.7	12.8	20.0	80.1	30.9
No Information	89	55.1	12.3	25.8	61.8	14.6

Note: N = 215.

[a]The differences for both outcomes are significant at the $p < .01$ and $p < .05$ levels, respectively.

Table 9-11

Relationship of Mayor's Role to Occurrence of Citizen Boards

		Occurrence of Boards[b]	
Mayor's Role	Total Number of Studies[a]	Yes	No
Active or aware	71	63.4	36.6
No involvement	55	72.7	27.3

Note: N = 215.

[a]89 "no information" studies not shown.

[b]The differences are not statistically significant.

Pre-Implementation Conflict

The occurrence of conflict within the community before the start of an innovation is thought to reduce the likely success of the innovation. In the case survey, conflict or confrontation was assumed whenever a study mentioned an employees' strike, delays due to resignations or excessive turnover of staff during the planning stage, difficulties among service agencies (often between the municipal executive and a line agency), or other incidents stemming from a lack of consensus that seriously threatened the implementation of the innovation. When a study described the pre-implementation events but made no mention of any conflict, none was assumed; and when a study failed to describe the pre-implementation process at all, this led to a judgment of "no information" regarding conflict.

An analysis of the relationship between the occurrence of conflict and the decentralization outcomes revealed that, as might be expected, *conflict*

Table 9-12
Relationship of Target Size to Decentralization Outcomes

		Percentage Occurrence of Outcome			
Size of Target Population	More Information	Improved Client Attitudes	Improved Client Attitudes	Improved Services[a]	More Client Control[a]
100,000 or More (n = 81)	61.7	12.3	21.0	50.7	16.0
50,000 to 100,000 (n = 26)	50.0	19.2	23.1	76.9	15.4
10,000 to 50,000 (n = 38)	63.2	13.1	26.3	86.8	21.1
Less than 10,000 (n = 36)	80.6	8.4	30.6	72.2	52.8
No Information (n = 34)	47.1	11.7	26.4	64.8	11.8

Note: N = 215.
[a]The differences for both outcomes are significant at the $p < .01$ and $p < .001$ levels, respectively.

tended to occur more frequently when increased client control was the outcome (see Table 9-13). However, the occurrence of pre-implementation conflict was not associated with any other outcome, especially improved services, which seemed to be reported at about the same rate whether conflict had occurred or not. Pre-implementation conflict also, not surprisingly, occurred with greater frequency when citizen boards were the type of citizen participation than when they were not (see Table 9-14).

If pre-implementation conflict is considered one of the "costs" of citizen participation, then the overall pattern of results suggests that stronger forms of participation may incur greater costs, with the main apparent benefit an increase in client control. Although improvements in services do not occur less frequently if conflict occurs, neither do they occur with any greater frequency that might justify the higher costs. Finally, because of the lack of relationship to service improvements, these results do not support the interpretation that the occurrence of pre-implementation conflict can account for the decentralization outcomes.

Summary

The findings on these four non-service factors do not provide overall support for the interpretation that such factors can account for the decentralization outcomes. Of the four factors, only a moderate- to small-sized target population appeared to have any relationship to both the improved

Table 9-13

Relationship of Pre-Implementation Conflict to Decentralization Outcomes

Pre-implementation Conflict	Percentage Occurrence of Outcome				
	More Imformation	Improved Agency Attitudes	Improved Client Attitudes	Improved Services	More Client Control[a]
Yes (n = 43)	62.8	9.3	23.3	69.8	46.5
No (n = 146)	63.0	15.0	27.4	65.1	17.8
No Information (n = 26)	42.3	3.8	11.5	65.4	7.7

Note: N = 215.

[a]Differences are significant at the $p < .001$ level.

Table 9-14

Relationship of Pre-Implementation Conflict to Occurrence of Citizen Boards

Pre-Implementation Conflict	Total Number of Studies[a]	Occurrence of Boards[b]	
		Yes	No
Yes	43	95.3	4.7
No	146	55.5	44.5

Note: N = 215.

[a]26 "no information" studies not shown.

[b]$\chi^2 = 22.94$, $df = 1$, $p < .001$.

services and increased control outcomes. The availability of federal funds, the active participation of the mayor, and the occurrence of pre-implementation conflict were shown not to have the requisite relationships to the outcomes. As a result, our interpretation of the importance of strategy and service factors remains as the main conclusion regarding urban decentralization.

References

Austin, David M. 1972. "Resident Participation: Political Mobilization or Organizational Co-optation?" *Public Administration Review* 32 (September), pp. 409-20.

Cole, Richard L. 1974. *Citizen Participation and the Urban Policy Process.* Lexington Books, D.C. Heath, Lexington, Mass.

U.S. Department of Housing and Urban Development. 1973. *The Model Cities Program: A Comparative Analysis of Participating Cities—*

Process, Product, Performance, and Prediction. U.S. Government Printing Office, Washington, D.C.

Washnis, George J. 1974. *Community Development Strategies: Case Studies of Major Model Cities.* Praeger, New York.

Yin, R. K., W. A. Lucas, P. L. Szanton, and J. A. Spindler. 1973. *Citizen Organizations: Increasing Client Control over Services.* The Rand Corporation, Santa Monica, Cal., R-1196-HEW.

10 Decentralization and Urban Policy

The previous chapter presented the basic findings from our study and our interpretation of those findings. Our study also bears certain implications for future urban policy, and this chapter attempts to deal with several facets of this policy. First, we comment on the problem of interpreting the decentralization experience in terms of success or failure. Second, we discuss the implications of the problem of evaluating street-level innovations; and third, we present our views on the lasting effects of decentralization.

The Success and Failure of Decentralization

Our survey of decentralization research revealed that the major outcomes of decentralization innovations were increased information between servers and served, and improved services being delivered. Increases in client control or improvements in service officials' or clients' attitudes were reported only infrequently. We interpreted these outcomes as being reflections of the types of decentralization strategies attempted, with strong decentralization (in which clients are intended to have some policymaking authority) being associated with the highest rates of both improved service and increased control. Furthermore, we sought to explain the variations in strategies attempted in terms of the traditional server-served relationship in various public services. Where the relationship entailed a large status gap (as in health and safety) between servers and served in overseeing policymaking, weak decentralization strategies were predominant. Where the relationship was based on some mutual influence over policymaking (as in education and community development), strong decentralization strategies were predominant. As one result, it came as little surprise that increased control occurred in the majority of cases in education, but a major disappointment was in economic development, where a strong mandate for control over a new neighborhood institution, presumably easy to accomplish, resulted only in a 25 percent rate of increased control.

Where we have attempted to explain decentralization outcomes in terms of the traditional patterns of server-served relationships, others have viewed decentralization as a general change in public organizations. And where our findings provide room for viewing decentralization innovations

173

as a partial success given the nature of the server-served relationship, the general view held by *reformers, participants,* and *the majority culture* is that decentralization has failed to produce the desired changes. An attempt to reconcile this seeming contradiction between the apparent success and failure of decentralization provides the best opportunity for summarizing the major lessons to be learned from the urban decentralization experience. Each lesson contains both policy and research conclusions.

The Reformist Critique: More Power to the People

The reformist critique is straightforward: Except for a very few cases, decentralization innovations have not given clients substantial authority (Fantini and Gittell, 1973; Gittell, 1972; Hallman, 1973; Katznelson, 1972; Lipsky, 1969; and Perry, 1973). Neither has substantial client control occurred; and thus, for the reformists, decentralization has simply not yet been put to a full test (Gittell, 1972). This view of the decentralization experience is certainly a valid one. A significant shift in power from servers to served, for instance, would result not only in the emergence of new and powerful client-dominated organizations but also in the waning of existing provider-dominated organizations; and such changes in the institutional balance of power have not occurred. What the reformers have themselves failed to demonstrate, however, is (1) whether there are any viable means of achieving their goals, and (2) how a successful experience can be assessed and recognized.

The first problem varies considerably by service area, and only in education has there been any evidence of frequent (though not necessarily substantial) increases in client control. Even in education, however, no successful reform strategy has emerged; the current guidelines still do not adequately assure that new decentralization attempts will not also be accompanied by a more than compensatory surge of union or centrist power and that the new attempts will not ultimately result in the same sort of abortive (from the reformers' view) decentralization as currently exists in New York City's school system. For other service areas, the lack of a viable strategy is an even greater deficiency. There are no demonstrable mechanisms for substantially increasing client control over such closed bureaucracies as the police or fire departments. The only alternative would appear to be the establishment of new organizations that provide the same services and are client-controlled. However, this alternative must be discarded on the basis of the experience with another new organization, the community development corporation. The reformers have failed to address the question of why substantial community control did not emerge even here, but one suspects that the development of a new institution may not be the phase during which client control can work effectively.

In short, the reformers have not developed a strategy for creating client-controlled urban services in the variety of organizational circumstances in which such services are delivered. Such open bureaucracies as education may be amenable to some change, but the paths to success are unproved; for either closed bureaucracies (for example, public safety) or the development of new neighborhood institutions, the reform strategy is simply nonexistent. Given the lack of such strategies, the reformists' critique of the decentralization experience becomes somewhat utopian, rather than a matter of pragmatic public policy. For the reformists, the failure of decentralization is a judgment based on the failure to attain unachievable goals.

The second problem is related to the shortcomings of the reformers as researchers and relates to the *measurement* of citizen control. Here, what is lacking is some assurance that the reformers would all agree on the same operational definition for when "power to the people" had been achieved in any given situation. In none of the case studies reviewed was any serious attempt made to measure the degree of client power and to indicate at what point "control" took place. Of course, the problem of assessing such power is difficult even in the setting of traditional organizations and communities. The strange fact remains, however, that few of the case studies even attempted to apply the well-developed (even if controversial) positional, reputational, or decisionmaking approaches in community power studies to the problem of decentralization.[a] Ironically, urban decentralization was occurring at the height of intellectual interest in the measurement of community power and would presumably have been an excellent opportunity for further empirical testing of the latest theoretical developments.

Because of the failure either to develop new measures or to use old ones when dealing with the issue of client control, the reformers have been constantly forced to use highly subjective terms. It is no wonder that the resulting ambiguity creates frustrations between service officials and researchers as well as among clients. In the absence of external guidelines, successful client control at the local level is likely to be defined by each individual as the fulfillment of a self-interest, a natural characteristic of localism[b] that may lead to internal dissension and not necessarily to institution building. Moreover, without external guidelines, participants are likely to consider client control a sham unless a way of serving their own self-interest has been found; actions favoring a more collective community interest, which presumably cover the reformists' main objectives, are just unlikely to occur.

---

[a] The extended debate on the use of these three approaches and the more general elitist versus pluralist controversy have produced numerous contributions to the literature. For an excellent collection of relevant articles, see Aiken and Mott (1970, pp. 193-358).

[b] The difference between local and cosmopolitan interests and activities in urban politics has been the topic of considerable research. For an excellent example, see Wilson and Banfield (1971).

In summary, the reformers' critique of urban decentralization, while valid, is not a sufficient commentary on the decentralization experience. It stems primarily from a utopian perspective and may be discarded as it does not provide a practical assessment of the actual decentralization experience in relation to the range of viable alternatives.

The Participants' Critique: The "Costs" of Decentralization

Ask most urban officials and they will still shy away from any significant attempt to develop client participation, much less control, over an urban service activity. Most people who have participated in decentralization innovations as client representatives also tend to have negative feelings toward their experiences. In effect, those who have been participants in the decentralization process, whether servers or served, generally feel that decentralization has been a failure. Their judgment is based primarily on an implicit benefit-to-cost calculus:[c] The personal or collective benefits from decentralization have failed to justify the heavy personal "costs" of participation—that is, the endless hours, emotions, and conflicts and frustrations that all of us have experienced in participating in any community affair whether we have been the servers or the served.

The participants' critique cannot be discarded. Aside from increased control, an outcome already plagued by a lack of any objective measures by which to judge success, the other possible benefits from decentralization that were uncovered by our study were all minor and certainly were not likely to justify heavy participant "costs." So while in our terms decentralization may have succeeded, in the participants' terms it did not succeed nearly enough. And future decentralization efforts must keep this implicit calculus in mind: Whatever the projected benefits, they must outweigh the costs of participation; more precisely, it is the incremental benefit derived as a result of participation that must outweigh the costs of participation. The research problem that must be solved to implement such a policy is again one of measurement. We need to know the terms in which participant "costs" can be assessed to make any prediction concerning the likely benefit-cost calculus.

The Majority Critique: Improving the Quality of Urban Life

The majority critique is also straightforward, though it does not appear in

[c] A more detailed discussion of the importance of such an implicit benefit-to-cost calculus in decentralization is found in Yates (1973, pp. 111-23) .

one coherent statement anywhere. Rather, it is captured by the declining public interest in decentralization. The critique is implicitly based on a certain view of the 1960s, which was that the city was burdened with urban problems such as increased crime and drug addiction, declining quality of inner-city education and health, high rates of unemployment and welfare dependency, and residential abandonment and decay. The survival problems of living in the inner-city ghetto are described in a wide range of literature. Who can forget the Harlem portrayed by Claude Brown (1965) and the problem Brown poses when New York fails to provide the promised land that had been the vision of many Southern black migrants? Our urban condition has been correctly interpreted not in terms of the administration of government but in terms of the quality of urban life, with safety, health, and economic opportunity perhaps its key elements.

The proposals for decentralization, as described in the previous chapters on each service area, generally stemmed from a desire to deal with these urban problems and the quality of life. Federal initiatives like the Model Cities Program also had this flavor. Decentralization today is still associated with vague but important expectations that one's city or neighborhood will become a more pleasant place in which to live.[d] The extent of this association is dramatically seen if one realizes the lack of such an association with other governmental reforms: program budgeting, changes in city charters from weak to strong mayors, and even the civil service reform movement. All of these have generally been associated with such objectives as the development of "good" government or the increase in governmental efficiency, but *not* with any direct improvements in the quality of urban life.

The majority critique of decentralization is that it has failed to produce visible changes in the quality of urban life. Obviously, our own results have not dealt with this level of outcome but have focused on less visible and less important service changes. Once again, the statement that decentralization has failed is valid but does not contradict our results. However, the majority critique makes two assumptions that must be examined before the next round of governmental reform begins.

The two assumptions underlie the main conclusion that many people may draw from the majority critique: Decentralization failed to produce changes in the quality of life, not because of some major fallacy of design but because the nation did not try hard enough (spend enough money). An impassioned and well-intended statement by an evaluator of the Model Cities Program continually points out that the country committed $575 million each year (about 5 percent of New York City's budget) during 1970 and 1971 for use by 150 cities, a remarkably low amount of money from

---

[d] Most decentralization proposals assert something like the following: Decentralization can "provide a framework for the solution of the City's serious and pressing problems." For but one example, see Farr et al. (1972, p. 183).

which visible neighborhood changes were expected; and the low expenditure levels appear as one of the main culprits in the failure to produce results (Warren, 1971). Similar arguments have been made concerning the level of effort of other decentralization innovations: Except for the new citywide innovations in education, the innovations have usually involved meager amounts of money and focused on single neighborhoods; decentralization might produce more substantial results if it occurred simultaneously in many neighborhoods and affected a dominant portion of the existing service delivery effort.

The two assumptions upon which this line of thinking is based are first, that indeed more money and greater resources can be spent through decentralization innovations; and second, that changes in governmental *organization* of any sort, regardless of the level of effort, can be related to changes in the quality of urban life. As for the first assumption, the most comprehensive evaluation of the Model Cities Program used *the ability of a given project to spend resources already allocated by Washington*, and not any assessment of achievements, as the main measure of success, and most of the projects were unable to spend anywhere near their whole allocation (U.S. Department of Housing and Urban Development, 1973). Although this experience has been recorded in only one federal program and the bureaucratic obstacles in that program may have been atypical, this observation strongly suggests that the level of effort that goes into many types of decentralization innovations may be restricted as much by deficiencies in the ability to spend as by the unwillingness to allocate. In essence, the common model of billions of dollars being poured into decentralization might not be a realistic one even if billions of dollars were available.

For future research on this first assumption, the message again is clear. We need to know what level of effort is possible for different institutional innovations and whether there are limits other than the availability of funds in developing large-scale decentralization. In other words, creating organizational change may not be as amenable to large expenditures as is going to the moon or building new highways. The experience in our present study suggests that research has a long way to go on this topic, for nowhere in our case survey did we find suitable documentation on the level of effort of existing innovations. Few of the case studies had dollar or staffing figures, and no other proxies were available. For this reason, the level of effort could not be taken into account even in examining the existing innovations, much less in speculating about new ones; nor is this a trivial problem, for in a decentralized school system, for instance, how are the financial costs of decentralization to be calculated?

As for the second assumption, we have already hinted that decentralization may be unique in that expectations concerning quality of life changes have been associated with changes in the organization of government.

There is some evidence that the *business* of both the federal government (a highway program, an urban renewal project, or a welfare payments program) and local governments (a public school, a sanitation cleanup, or normal police operations) can affect the quality of urban life, but we know of little evidence suggesting that the *organization* of government can have such effects. Decentralization, after all, has to do with the reorganization of political procedure, whether entirely within the bureaucracy or involving external citizen control mechanisms. Such reorganization can rightly be expected to have administrative effects (shifts in power, greater efficiency, more pluralistic decisionmaking, or changed physical location of governmental offices), but one has to withhold judgment about its potential effects on the quality of life (increased safety, health, and economic opportunity).

The relationship between the organization of government and effects on the quality of life is a topic for further research, and it ought to be carried out before the next round of centralization or decentralization is proposed in the name of changing the conditions under which urban residents live. Whether a municipal executive is building superagencies, inducing massive horizontal integration and services coordination, or decentralizing offices, there is a need for some evidence that any such organizational changes make a difference beyond purely operational effects.

If organizational changes were unlikely to influence the quality of urban life and thereby to attack the urban problems of the 1960s, there remains the question of what, if anything, government could have done either in lieu of or along with decentralizing. This question touches upon the current debate between services versus income-supplementing strategies, where the general disappointment with the service-oriented Great Society programs has led to experimentation with various forms of income supplements, such as education or housing vouchers. Although decentralization is actually an *organizational* change, it has been associated in the past with *service* strategies because of the simultaneous development of the service-oriented programs like CAPs and Model Cities. It is possible that neither organizational nor service strategies could really work alone in dealing with the city in the 1960s. Whether *income-supplementing* strategies would have done better is an open question, but if the effects of diferentials in welfare assistance payments among cities and states are taken as any guide, the chances are slim that income-supplementing strategies would have made a difference. If they did, one would expect that those cities and states with higher levels of payments would have shown at least a slightly better quality of urban life, but this has not necessarily been the case.

Rather than organizational, service, or income-supplementing strategies, within political constraints, government might have pursued a *regulatory* strategy. The obvious (though politically sensitive) focus might have been to explicitly address the rate of migration into the city in the 1950s and 1960s, possibly as foreign immigration had been regulated 30 years before.[e] A more evenly distributed population influx by blacks, Spanish-speaking, and rural families into various cities might have affected the quality of urban life. Lest this suggestion appear inflammatory, it should immediately be noted that federal housing and taxation policies certainly worked to facilitate the massive migration to the suburbs that generally *preceded* the migration into the city. Government policies actually encouraged the rapid and often exclusionary growth of metropolitan areas following World War II, thereby setting the stage for an enormous and selective turnover rate in the central city. A second suggested focus for a regulatory strategy might have been pursued by city governments. If we return to the problem of the social asymmetry between the servers and the served, for instance, urban governments might have insisted on residence requirements for civil service positions (if not residence in the neighborhood, at least residence in the city). The quality of services might have changed, but the mutual trust between the servers and served might not have been lost and thus the service crisis of the 1960s might have taken a different and possibly less severe form.

This discussion of the success and failure of decentralization does not give a full sense of the effects of decentralization or its implications for future urban policymaking. To begin with, the problem of evaluating street-level innovations has important implications for such policymaking.

The Problem of Evaluating Street-Level Innovations

In describing the case survey and the decentralization literature, we repeatedly pointed out that by strictly scientific standards it is for several reasons an unarguably weak literature. The studies rarely contain careful experimental designs and procedures. Often the evaluators were themselves active participants in the innovations. In addition, the criteria for success and failure varied and were vague and ambiguous. Many of the studies covered brief time periods and therefore did not present a persuasive account of the innovation's changing character over time. In spite of these shortcomings, the case survey was used to elicit the characteristics of each case study so that systematic aggregation and analysis could be carried out. The resulting case survey information has been our main source of evidence, and there are no doubt methodological improvements that can be made in future applications of the case survey method.

---

[e] For a discussion of the role of foreign immigration and the attempt to control it, see Yin (1973, pp. ix-xx).

The Problem of Evaluation

Beyond the scholarly problem of how to treat an unscientific literature, there is a far more serious problem for public policy—that is, how can government possibly decide whether to expand, contract, replicate, or terminate particular decentralization innovations when the evidence about their performance is so limited and ambiguous? How can adequate policy evaluations be made under these conditions? The traditional answer to this kind of dilemma given by policy analysts is that techniques of evaluation should be improved and that more careful and systematic evaluation should be undertaken.[f]

In many areas of public policy, there is indeed a strong need to increase the rigor and competence of program evaluation. In particular, policy decisions concerning weapons systems, transportation systems, housing programs, air pollution control, and of course, the construction of dams and bridges should be subject to more rigorous systems analysis, benefit-cost analysis, and similar techniques. These areas of public policy are characterized by technical considerations, by clear engineering tradeoffs, and, in general, by a concern with bricks and mortar. Important problems of social cost and externalities are involved in these policy decisions, but the decisionmaking framework is highly structured. Similarly, in designing a new national income policy through the introduction of a negative income tax, or in contemplating the use of vouchers for such a specific purpose as improved housing, or even in experimenting with new national health insurance alternatives, it is feasible and useful to see what happens to household economic behavior when family income is raised by federal policy. In these situations, large-scale social experiments can actually be carried out with evaluations following appropriate quasi-experimental designs.

But there is a large and important realm of public policy where scientific policy evaluation is vastly more difficult. Various writers have already commented on the difficulty of applying the techniques of systems analysis, originally designed for military decisions, to the domestic policy areas of education, public safety, and urban management (Weiss and Rein, 1970). The problem is that organizational or community changes may be the main focus of such public programs, and it may be difficult to identify and distinguish the strands of public purpose, to find out exactly what happened as a result of the program, and to isolate the effects of the program from other forces and interactions in the social environment.

Street-level innovations contain all of these difficulties for evaluation and present a whole range of new difficulties as well. Quite simply, street-

---

[f] Several recent books on policy evaluation review the state of evaluation methodology and call for more rigorous evaluation research. See Rossi and Williams (1972), Caporaso and Roos (1973), and Weiss (1972).

level innovations are difficult to evaluate because they tend to be diffuse and multi-faceted, they are loosely controlled administratively, and they are characterized by a trial-and-error and occasionally erratic pattern of problem solving. But, most important, the decentralization innovations we have considered address the delicate, highly personal relationship between the servers and the served and seek improvements in the elusive realm of mutual trust and communication. This is an intricate relationship. It raises questions of social symmetry and social distance, accessibility and communication, and learned behavior and attitudes. We would therefore not expect the service relationship to be "fixed" in the same straightforward way a pothole is fixed or a new school is built. Rather, the forging of a new service relationship is likely to take time and to follow a developmental process about which little is known. Other decentralization innovations involve a deliberate attempt at neighborhood institution building, an inherently complex enterprise. It means creating, maintaining, and developing institutions in communities that lack experience with enduring service organizations and that either provide few foundations for institution building or contain a tangle of competing and fragmented neighborhood groups. In these cases, even the basic administrative capacity has to be developed and requires a learning process in which community participants and district-level officials build up their own administrative abilities as a central element of institution building.

In short, because of the nature of the street-level service relationship and because of the requirements of institution building, we would expect decentralization innovations to undergo a long and uncertain process of development. And this means that any evaluation of these innovations, as its essential condition of success, must have the ability to chart and assess over time the development of institutions and the relationship between the servers and the served. This is not the way program evaluation is normally conducted. Such evaluation is typically based either on economic notions of allocative efficiency (and benefit-cost measurement) or on notions of experimental design (and the use of control groups and the manipulation of single variables). But street-level innovations defy these evaluative paradigms. Given the multi-faceted quality of most decentralization innovations and the multiplicity of goals and costs, it is very difficult to mount anything like a satisfactory benefit-cost analysis. Similarly, for a controlled experimental evaluation to work, the innovation would require a precise objective to be pursued consistently. But street-level innovations tend to lack such fixity and clarity of purpose and operation.

The Costs of Evaluation

Because of these difficulties, attempts to apply rigorous, scientific evaluation techniques to street-level innovations are not only likely to be unsuccessful but also will produce negative side-effects. Where elaborate formal evaluations are undertaken, various problems of deception and self-deception, false perceptions, and misplaced concreteness are likely to result. Formal evaluations will be deceptive because they will tend to capture some facets of the innovation but not others; or they will emphasize certain tangible standards of measurement and assessment such as attendance rates or "number of persons served" that offer a very superficial insight into the workings of the innovations; or, as is often the case, they will look at the most explicit effects (and especially economic benefits and costs) and will ignore the more elusive latent effects (and especially political and social benefits and costs). Similarly, there may be significant false perceptions in the evaluation if, as is likely, evaluators attempt to assess the innovation according to the originally stated goals of the innovation or by any other fixed set of goals (which are, of course, essential to evaluation but are rarely found in a rapidly evolving innovation). False perceptions also often arise if evaluators talk only to the administrators of the experiment, if they make announced visits that the street-level administrators or residents can prepare for, and if they fail to devise a strategy to gain a street-level perspective on the innovation. Finally, formal evaluation will produce misplaced concreteness if the available hard evidence in the experiment is taken to constitute anything like a full and adequate record. All of these problems will reduce the chances of the evaluation being successful.[g]

The potentially negative side-effects of the formal evaluation on the street-level innovation may occur in at least three other ways. First, formal evaluation may undermine the fragile incentives for citizens and public employers to cooperate and communicate in new street-level innovations—that is, if a new relationship between the servers and the served requires an extended learning experience and if the willingness to undertake the new relationship depends on the good will and hopefulness of the participants, then external evaluation, which implies criticism of the innovation if only in a constructive vein, may create a reverse "Hawthorne" effect. If the experiment at first does not succeed and is critically evaluated, what incentives are there for the participants to "keep trying" or to try another approach? Faced with early critical evaluation, participants may well say, "Well, we tried and it apparently didn't work and what's more, no one appreciates our efforts anyway. Why should we take this constant inspection and criticism? Here we're trying to do something new and untried, and all we hear about is what we're doing wrong and what we should be doing."

Second and related to the first point, formal external evaluation inevita-

---

[g] For discussions of the problems of applying the traditional evaluation paradigms, see, for example, Weiss and Rein (1970); Campbell (1970); Harrar and Bawden (1972); Wholey (1972); and Cook and Sciolo (1972).

bly undermines the basic premise and understanding of street-level innovations that local participants will be given new authority and autonomy in dealing with their service problems. In principle, this delegation of authority should mean that street-level participants have the discretion and responsibility to experiment, to use their own judgment, and indeed to make and learn from their own mistakes. In this context, then, formal evaluation represents a hedge against local responsibility and keeps local participants dependent on central government advice and approval. Local reaction to the continued watchful presence of higher-level government may vary, but several typical reactions are clearly damaging to street-level innovations and experimentation. Local administrators may deal with only the simplest problems and may mount only safe, no-risk initiatives so as to avoid any unfavorable evaluation. Similarly, they may emphasize programs with easily measured outputs in order to take advantage of evaluations rather than be injured by them. Also, they may set strict objectives and stick to them (even when a change in strategy is desirable) so as to avoid giving the impression to evaluators that they were unable to follow through on their stated goals. Finally, they may be so responsive to the tastes and reactions of evaluators, as they hear them and as they anticipate them, that they make the evaluators the de facto architects of the innovations.

This last "reaction" is perhaps the most widespread and worrisome. For not only does it mean that street-level administrators yield much of their authority and flexibility to evaluators, but they also spend a disproportionate amount of their time and energy trying to please central government evaluators so as to insure continued funding and support. In the extreme case, this pattern produces a vicious cycle. Central government creates street-level innovations in order to stimulate experimentation and local decisionmaking. But local participants, worried about continued funding and organizational survival, avoid risky experimentation and tailor their decisions to satisfy the perceived tastes and preferences of central government. The practical result in this extreme and somewhat caricatured case is thus to create a new institution, at substantial cost, that may replicate the perspectives of central government. This is not decentralization, but an extension of centralized administration by other means.

Third, it is often the case that the practical effect of formal evaluation is to provide political ammunition for supporters and critics of the innovation. This is a well known pattern, but it has special significance for most street-level experiments because expectations of these experiments tend to vary widely and because there is great uncertainty about how the experiment will actually work. Many decentralization experiments were launched in a context of inflated hopes and fears. Advocates often argued that decentralization would prove a miracle cure and would have a dramatic, immediate effect in bringing government closer to the neighborhoods.

By contrast, critics believed that decentralization would open up a Pandora's box of corruption, inequity, inefficiency, and fragmentation. In this context, formal evaluations are likely to operate less as narrow program reviews than as highly interpretable Rorschach tests for interested observers. Even in laboratory experiments, a single study is rarely sufficient to establish an unequivocal "fact." Specific findings must be replicated under different conditions and in different laboratories before a scientific fact is produced. If this is so, then any evaluation will almost certainly leave room for some criticism. As a result, the innovation is likely to experience a dramatic crash in confidence and support, as anything less than a glowing evaluation will produce disappointment and very often intense disillusionment among the most enthusiastic advocates.

Put simply, central government officials and the public want from evaluation a clear answer to the question: "Does decentralization work?" But our contention is that no simple answer can be given in the short run and that it is a serious mistake to seek such an answer through evaluation. If this is true, street-level innovations such as decentralization experiments require a strategy of evaluation that will avoid the various analytical problems described above and that will be sensitive to the special characteristics of these innovations.[h]

A Strategy of Street-Level Evaluation

The strategy for evaluating street-level innovations presented below is based on four general principles: (1) Evaluation should be multifaceted and eclectic by making use of narrative history, participant observation, surveys of consumers, and "hard" benefit-cost analyses; (2) evaluation should primarily be concerned with discovering and weighing many assessments of the experiment from different vantage points rather than rendering single, global judgments about the success or failure of the innovation; (3) as far as possible, street-level participants should conduct evaluations, and, as a corollary, the aloof "sitting in judgment" function of higher-level evaluators should be reduced to a minimum; (4) the fundamental purpose of evaluation should be to increase the capacity of innovations to adjust to pressures and shortcomings so they may move with increased awareness and dexterity through the uncertain process of development. The strategy of evaluation that grows out of these principles has seven main elements.

---

[h] There is a desperate need to develop alternative evaluation paradigms. Unfortunately, existing discussions of alternatives have not produced any detailed expositions of the alternatives. See, for example, Guttentag (1971); and, for a more speculative discussion, Mitroff and Blankenship (1973).

1. Evaluation should follow an adversary method of discussion and debate with local evaluators assigned to take advocate and critic roles in assessing the experiment. The same practice should be followed by higher-level evaluators to the extent that they are involved in evaluation. This method is chosen because we expect that many opposing views will inevitably arise from the experiments and these disagreements are best dealt with openly.

2. Evaluation should be an ongoing process rather than a sporadic threat—that is, evaluators (be they from the street-level or city hall) should closely follow the experiment for several years. In so doing, they should write narrative histories of the innovation's development and report regularly on participants' perceptions of the experiment's major problems and accomplishments.

3. The primary thrust of evaluation should be toward self-evaluation by the main participants in the experiment. We expect that a street-level innovation will make mistakes, undergo periods of drift, and face unexpected developments. Seen in this light, the purpose of evaluation is to prepare local participants for uncertainty and to guide their adjustment to the inevitable problems that arise.

4. Higher-level evaluators should work closely with local administrators and evaluators in a consultative relationship. Local participants should have guaranteed access to all reports and critiques made by higher-level evaluators. Higher-level evaluators should therefore conceive their role as limited partners in the enterprise rather than as circuit judges or traveling executioners.

5. Community participants, including clients, should be involved as evaluators. In particular, community participants should be used to help assess the effects of the innovation on the neighborhood.

6. The innovation should hold regular "town meetings" in which general issues and problems are discussed. To the extent that it is possible, the emphasis in these meetings should be on considering solutions to problems rather than to criticizing the shortcomings of programs and personnel.

7. Audits should be the main instrument for insuring that the innovation is adhering to acceptable and honest budgeting and accounting practices.

In sum, this strategy of evaluation seeks to make evaluation's primary role that of a positive steering mechanism rather than an instrument of critical review. The hope is that street-level innovations will become more flexible and less insecure. At the same time, central administrators who feel that they require a critical review should rely not so much on formal evaluations as on the continued reactions of the servers and the served in the innovation.

The Lasting Effects of Decentralization

It is important not only to see what decentralization has achieved to date, but also to consider, albeit in a more speculative way, decentralization's potential future effect. As with other attempts at forecasting social policy, this analysis is based both on inferences from present experience and on an admittedly rough sense of the potentialities of decentralization. We believe the urban decentralization experience may influence urban and national policymaking in four ways: (1) Strengthening the neighborhood approach to policy analysis; (2) understanding neighborhood institutions and citizen participation; (3) sustaining a human service orientation; and (4) maintaining server-served accountability.

Strengthening the Neighborhood Approach to Policy
Analysis

One of the most significant implications of decentralization is that it brings the analysis of service problems down to the street-level—that is, decentralization entails a view of urban problems that is unusually sensitive to block-by-block and neighborhood-by-neighborhood needs and problems. Such a street-level analysis of service problems is a rare element in public planning and policy analysis. Typically, the dominant concern in public policymaking has been to increase the planning and analytical capacities of city hall or of the federal government. Policy innovations such as master planning, systems analysis, program budgeting, management information systems, and administrative consolidation have sought to give central policymakers better knowledge about and control over the city as a whole. These approaches naturally seek to understand how the system as a whole is working, and, being committed to the discovery of general patterns, the approaches must give far less attention to the particularities of neighborhood problems.

By contrast, decentralized service delivery makes the particularity of neighborhood services its central concern, and it highlights the important variations in the supply of and demand for services between neighborhoods. These variations spring from differences in the physical structure, geography, composition, economic resources, racial and ethnic composition, age distribution, and patterns of stability and change in urban neighborhoods. The variations touch upon such abstract concerns as the equitable distribution of services and more concrete service delivery problems. For instance, police or garbage problems become a series of highly particular (and not simply additive) problems in particular neighborhoods. This analytic treatment seems to match the reality of urban residents, for when they call for greater responsiveness in municipal service delivery, they are calling for a greater sensitivity in government to particular vacant lots, abandoned buildings, gaping potholes, broken stoplights, vandalized park equipment, and rowdy after-hours bars. Seen from this perspective, for a policy analyst to know that there is a "problem" concerning abandoned buildings or after-hours bars is to know very little. There is no way to act on the problem until someone has determined the nature *and* location of the problem. It is this kind of street-level detective work that decentralization experiments have fostered, and we believe that decentralization strategies have the potential to strengthen the neighborhood approach to problem solving in the future.

Understanding Neighborhood Institutions and Citizen Participation

A second important effect of decentralization lies in the improved understanding of neighborhood institutions and citizen participation. Decentralization has shown that intricate and dynamic political forces continually operate in the neighborhood and between neighborhoods and city government and that attempts to install major organizational changes inevitably lead to secondary effects that may more than compensate for the initial changes. Nowhere is the "balance of power" notion more relevant than in local politicals, and nowhere are the competition and turnover of social institutions more in evidence than at the neighborhood level.

An improved understanding is essential and may ultimately lead to more effective plans for neighborhood institution building. And neighborhood institutions are extremely important because they provide a persistent opportunity and point of entry for citizen participation. To move beyond erratic protest efforts, citizens need ongoing institutional structures through which they can channel their energies and in which they can find a ready vehicle for expressing their views. In other words, although the town hall scale of governance may be a misleading myth, citizen participation in democratic states must occur first and foremost through neighborhood institutions. Such institutions must be durable and be capable of accommodating mass local participation while dealing with specific neighborhood problems. Building new institutions or replacing old ones will be of continuing concern whether government is involved in the building process or not.

Sustaining a Human Service Orientation

A third potential effect of urban decentralization is that it may sustain a strong, human service orientation in urban policy. Only in recent years has the quality of municipal service delivery in general received more than sporadic attention from policymakers both in the city and in national government. Decentralization, along with other managerial innovations, has helped to call attention to the intricacies of service delivery. But the distinctive contribution of decentralization is to emphasize the street-level relationship between the servers and the served. Since this human relationship, if our thesis is correct, lies at the heart of urban services, a solidification of the service focus through decentralization will perform the useful function of anchoring urban administration to specific social relationships. They require considerable time and energy to be influenced, as the adoption of new attitudes on the part of both citizens and public officials occurs only gradually and involves sustained experimentation and trial-and-error adjustment.

Maintaining Server-Served Accountability

A fourth effect of decentralization bears directly on the relationship of the servers and the served in urban services. Although one would probably not go so far as to claim that client participation has been institutionalized in the sense that formal mechanisms for participation will always be provided, the decentralization experience has probably counteracted the previous trend in which servers and service bureaucracies were becoming increasingly accountable to themselves alone. And what may have become institutionalized is the notion that clients have a right to significant influence over service delivery as well as the ever present threat that client power can be called upon to act as a curb whenever service bureaucracies become unresponsive.

In the neighborhood, we would expect to find a larger number of block or other resident or client associations—for example, the parents of children in a given school—to remain active than if there had been no decentralization experience, and we would expect mayors and other politicians to use client participation mechanisms to help make service agencies more accountable. Similarly, local chapters of such client organizations as the National Welfare Rights Organization should act as the basis for the formation of a continuing series of formal client organizations. Whatever public programs are designed in the future, there should by now be an automatic concern for considering the desires of those to be served as well as a somewhat diminished arrogance by servers that they have all the answers. In this broad sense, then, the servers-served relationship may have struck a new balance. In some cases, as in a local board's relationship to a teachers' union, or a beneficiary group's relationship to a medical staff, there may even be some bargaining as part of the revised relationship.

Alternative Policies for Decentralization

These four effects suggest certain policy choices and alternatives that may be important in future decentralization efforts and policymaking. First, given a choice between a federally initiated or a locally initiated policy, we would opt for locally based policies reflecting the diversity of neighborhood characteristics and service characteristics. This is because we have found that federal support was not a major condition of success on the one hand, and, on the other hand, that the complexity of the neighborhood service setting calls for a hand-tailoring of an innovation to its environment. Second, given the choice between comprehensive and service-specific strategies, our findings indicate that decentralization strategies must be tailored to fit particular services. Decentralization should not be thought of as a single policy instrument but as an array of instruments, some of which are better suited than others to particular services. Finally, given a choice between strong and weak strategies, we cannot give a decisive answer or policy recommendation. Strong strategies produce a higher rate of positive outcomes, but they may also meet intensive resistance in "closed" service environments. This does not mean that strong strategies should not be tried in closed environments, but rather that the probabilities of their working are low and the cost of making them work high. A more confident conclusion is that both strong and weak strategies do work, albeit in different ways, and therefore a combination of strategies might be tried in most neighborhoods and service areas.

References

Aiken, Michael and Paul E. Mott, eds. 1970. *The Structure of Community Power*. Random House, New York.

Brown, Claude. 1965. *Manchild in the Promised Land*. Macmillan, New York.

Campbell, Donald T. 1970. "Considering the Case against Experimental Evaluations of Social Innovations." *Administrative Science Quarterly* (March), pp. 110-13.

Caporaso, James A. and L. L. Roos, eds. 1973. *Quasi-Experimental Approaches*. Northwestern University Press, Evanston, Ill.

Cook, Thomas J. and Frank P. Scioli, Jr. 1972. "Research Strategy for analyzing the Impact of Public Policy." *Administrative Science Quarterly* (September), pp. 328-39.

Fantini, Mario and Marilyn Gittell. 1973. *Decentralization: Achieving Reform*. Praeger, New York.

Farr, Walter G., Jr. et al. 1972. *Decentralizing City Government: A Practical Study of a Radical Proposal for New York City.* Praeger, New York.

Gittell, Marilyn. "Decentralization and Citizen Participation in Education." *Public Administration Review* (October), pp. 670-86.

Guttentag, Marcia. 1971. "Models and Methods in Evaluation Research." *Journal of Theory and Social Behavior* (April), pp. 75-95.

Hallman, Howard. 1973. *Government by Neighborhoods.* Center for Government Studies, Washington, D.C.

Harrar, William and D. Lee Bawden. 1972. "The Use of Experimentation in Policy Formulation and Evaluation." *Urban Affairs Quarterly* (June), pp. 419-30.

Katznelson, Ira. 1972. "Antagonistic Ambiguity: Notes on Reformation and Decentralization." *Politics and Society* (Spring), pp. 323-36.

Lipsky, Michael. 1969. "Radical Decentralization: A Response to American Planning Dilemmas," unpublished paper. Institute for Research on Poverty, University of Wisconsin, Madison.

Mitroff, Ian I. and L. Vaughan Blankenship. 1973. "On the Methodology of the Wholistic Experiment." *Technological Forecasting and Social Change* 4, pp. 339-53.

Perry, Stuart. 1973. "Federal Support for CDCs: Some of the History and Issues of Community Centers," unpublished paper. Center for Communication Economic Development, Cambridge, Mass.

Rossi, Peter and Walter Williams, eds. 1972. *Evaluating Social Programs.* Seminar Press, New York.

U.S. Department of Housing and Urban Development. 1973. *The Model Cities Program: A Comparative Analysis of Participating Cities Process, Product, Performance, and Prediction.* U.S. Government Printing Office, Washington, D.C.

Warren, Roland L. 1971. "The Model Cities Program: An assessment," unpublished paper. Brandeis University, Waltham, Mass.

Weiss, Carol H., ed. 1972. *Evaluating Action Programs.* Allyn and Bacon, Boston.

Weiss, Robert and Martin Rein. 1970. "The Evaluation of Broad-Aim Programs: Experimental Design, Its Difficulties, and an Alternative." *Administrative Science Quarterly* (March), pp. 97-109.

Wholey, Joseph. 1972. "What Can We Actually Get from Program Evaluation?" *Policy Sciences* 3 (September), pp. 361-9.

Wilson, James W. and Edward C. Banfield. 1971. "Political Ethos Revisited." *American Political Science Review* 65 (December), pp. 1048-62.

Yates, Douglas. 1973. *Neighborhood Democracy.* D.C. Heath, Lexington, Mass.

Yin, Robert K. 1973. "Introduction," in R. K. Yin, ed., *Race, Creed, or National Origin: A Reader on Racial and Ethnic Identities in American Society*. Peacock, Itasca, Ill.

Appendixes

Appendix A
Sources Searched and List of Case Studies

Sources Searched

Bibliographic Services

Cumulated Index Medicus
Educational Resources Information Center
National Criminal Justice Reference Service
National Institute of Mental Health Clearinghouse
National Technical Information Service
Public Affairs Information Service

Libraries

Boston Public Library
Cambridge Public Library
Columbia University Library
Department of Health, Education, and Welfare Library
Department of Housing and Urban Development Library
The George Washington University Medical School Library
Harvard Graduate School of Education Library
Harvard Medical School Library
Massachusetts Institute of Technology Library
National Institute of Law Enforcement and Criminal Justice Library
National League of Cities Library
National Library of Medicine
New School for Social Research Library
New York City Public Library
New York University Library
Office of Economic Opportunity Library
Office of Education Library
Rand Library
Urban Institute Library

Journals

	Volume No.		Year	
	Start	*Finish*	*Start*	*Finish*
Administrative Science Quarterly	8	18	1964	1973
American Behavioral Scientist	4	16	1961	1973
American Journal of Orthopsychiatry	37	43	1967	1973
American Journal of Public Health	55	63	1965	1973
American Journal of Sociology	66	79	1960	1973
American Political Science Review	54	67	1960	1973
American Sociological Review	25	38	1960	1973
City Magazine	1	6	1967	1972
Crime and Delinquency	6	19	1960	1973
Current Municipal Problems	8	14	1966	1972
Education and Urban Society	1	6	1968	1973
Harvard Education Review	30	42	1960	1972
Inquiry	5	10	1968	1973
Journal of Criminal Law, Criminology, and Police Science	52	64	1960	1972
Journal of Law and Education	1	2	1972	1973
Journal of the American Institute of Planners	26	39	1960	1973
Journal of Urban Law	44	50	1966	1972
Law and Contemporary Problems	25	37	1960	1972
Law and Society Review	1	7	1967	1973
Medical Care	1	10	1963	1972
Nation's Cities	7	11	1969	1973
Police Chief	32	40	1965	1973
Politics and Society	1	3	1971	1973
Public Administration Review	20	33	1960	1973
Public Health Reports	81	88	1966	1973
Public Interest	1	32	1966	1973
Review of Educational Research	30	42	1960	1972
Social Casework	44	54	1963	1973
Social Forces	43	51	1965	1973
Social Policy	1	3	1970	1973
Social Problems	10	20	1963	1973
Social Research	34	40	1967	1973
Social Science Quarterly	49	53	1969	1973
Social Service Review	37	47	1963	1973
Social Work	5	18	1960	1973
Urban Affairs Quarterly	1	9	1965	1973

	Volume No.		Year	
	Start	Finish	Start	Finish
Urban Education	1	6	1968	1973
Urban Lawyer	1	4	1969	1973
Welfare in Review	5	10	1967	1972

List of Case Studies

Safety

Allen, Robert F. et al. 1969. "Conflict Resolution: Team Building for Police and Ghetto Residents," *Journal of Criminal Law, Criminology and Police Science* 60 (June), pp. 251-55 (Grand Rapids).*

Bard, Morton. 1969. "Family Intervention Police Teams as a Community Mental Health Resource." *Journal of Criminal Law, Criminology and Police Science* 60 (June) pp. 247-50 (New York).

Bell, Robert L. et al. 1969. "Small Group Dialogue and Discussion: An Approach to Police-Community Relationships." *Journal of Criminal Law, Criminology and Police Science* 60 (June), pp. 242-6 (Houston).

Black, Algernon D. 1968. *The People and the Police*. McGraw-Hill, New York (New York).

Blackmore, J.R. and Lee P. Brown. 1967. *Development of a Police-Community Relations Program*. Law Enforcement Assistance Administration, U.S. Department of Justice, Washington, D.C. (San Jose).*

Blatt, Stephen J. and Thomas R. Tortoriello. 1973. *An Evaluation of the Neighborhood Assistance Officer Program*. Communication Research Associates, Dayton, O. (Dayton).

Bloch, Peter B. 1972. *Preliminary Evaluation of Operation Neighborhood*. The Urban Institute, Washington, D.C. (New York).

———— and David Specht. 1973. *Neighborhood Team Policing*. The Urban Institute, Washington, D.C. (Oxnard, Calif;* Los Angeles; Holyoke, Mass.;* Albany;* St. Petersburg;* Cincinnati;* Detroit*).

Bouma, Donald H. et al. 1970. *An Evaluation of a Police-School Liaison Program*. Michigan Department of State Police, East Lansing, Mich. (Muskegon-Saginaw, Mich.).

---

*An asterisk indicates that the study was eliminated by the initial screening for internal validity (see text for further discussion). This list thus shows the total number of cases found (n = 269) and the number of cases discarded (n = 54). All subsequent analysis was carried out using the remaining 215 cases.

Bray, Raymond. 1968. *Community Relations Program*. Philadelphia Police Department, Philadelphia (Philadelphia).

Butler, Edgar W. et al. *Winston-Salem Police Department Community Services Unit: First Report and Preliminary Evaluation*. Department of Sociology, University of North Carolina, Chapel Hill (Winston-Salem).

Coxe, Spencer. 1961. "Police Advisory Board: The Philadelphia Story." *Connecticut Bar Journal* 35, pp. 138-55 (Philadelphia).

Eagan, John G. 1972. "Pilot 100: An Innovative Approach to Improving Police-Student Relations." *Police Chief* 39 (March), pp. 42-43 (Buffalo).

Erikson, James M. 1973. "Community Service Officer." *Police Chief* 40 (June), pp. 40-46 (New York).

Fink, Joseph. 1968. "Police in a Community: Improving a Deteriorated Image." *Journal of Criminal Law, Criminology and Police Science* 59 (December), pp. 624-31 (New York).*

Furstenberg, Frank F., Jr. and Charles F. Wellford. 1973. "Calling the Police: The Evaluation of Police Service." *Law and Society Review* 7 (Spring), pp. 393-406 (Baltimore).

Gabriel, Walter et al. 1971. *Milwaukee Fire and Police Commission Community Relations Mobile Unit*. Report to Law Enforcement Assistance Administration. U.S. Department of Justice, Washington, D.C. (Milwaukee).

Goode, John E. 1970. "Police Youth Patrol Pilot Program." *Law and Order*. 18 (March), pp. 34-41 (Jacksonville, Fla.).*

Howland, John T. 1967. "Police-Community Relations. Boston Police Department, Boston (Boston).*

Hudson, James R. 1972. "Organizational Aspects of Internal and External Review of the Police." *Journal of Criminal Law, Criminology and Police Science* 63 (September), pp. 427-33 (Philadelphia).

Jacob, John E. 1967. *Police Community Alert Council*. Office of Law Enforcement Assistance, U.S. Department of Justice, Washington, D.C. (Washington, D.C.).

Kelly, Rita M. et al. 1972. *The Pilot Police Project: A Description and Assessment of a Police-Community Relations Experiment in Washington, D.C.* American Institute for Research, Kensington, Md. (Washington, D.C.).

Kreins, Edward S. 1972. "A Community Resource Program for Youth." *Police Chief* 39 (March), pp. 36-41 (Pleasant Hills, Calif.).

Lohman, Joseph D. et al. 1966. *The Police and the Community: The Dynamics of Their Relationship in a Changing Society*, Volumes I and

II. U.S. Government Printing Office, Washington, D.C. (San Diego;* Philadelphia: Civilian Review Board, Community Relations).

Marx, Gary. 1973. "Riverview CSO Project," unpublished paper. Department of Urban Studies and Planning, M.I.T., Cambridge, Mass. (Riverview, Mass.).*

Marx, Gary. 1973. "Fall River CSO Project," unpublished paper. Department of Urban Studies and Planning, M.I.T., Cambridge, Mass. (Fall River, Mass.).

_____. 1973. "Worcester CSO Project," unpublished paper. Department of Urban Studies, M.I.T., Cambridge, Mass. (Worcester, Mass.).

McCrory, James T. 1968. "The St. Louis Story." in A.F. Brandstatter and L.A. Radelet, eds., *Police and Community Relations: A Source Book.* Glencoe Press, Beverly Hills, Calif. (St. Louis).

McLaughlin, Wendell W. 1968. *Police-Community Relations.* Office of Law Enforcement Assistance, U.S. Department of Justice, Washington, D.C. (Des Moines).*

Norris, Donald F. 1973. *Police-Community Relations: A Program That Failed.* D.C. Heath, Lexington, Mass. (Richmond, Va.).

Oliver, John P. 1973. "Paraprofessionals: The Precinct Receptionist Program." *Police Chief* 40 (January), pp. 40-41 (New York).

Phelps, Lourn and Robert Murphy. 1969. "The Team Patrol System in Richmond, California." *Police Chief* 36 (June), pp. 48-51 (Richmond, Calif.).

Police Community Council. 1968. Office of Law Enforcement Assistance, U.S. Department of Justice, Washington, D.C. (Charlotte, N.C.).

Portune, Robert. 1968. *The Cincinnati Police-Juvenile Attitude Project.* Law Enforcement Assistance Administration, U.S. Department of Justice, Washington, D.C. (Cincinnati).

Rogowsky, Edward T. et al. 1971. "Police: The Civilian Review Board Controversy," in Jewel Bellush and Stephen David, eds., *Race and Politics in New York City.* Praeger, New York (New York).

Schonnesen, William. 1968. *Police-School Liaison Program.* Office of Law Enforcement Assistance, U.S. Department of Justice, Washington, D.C. (Minneapolis).

Sherman, Lawrence W. et al. 1973. *Team Policing.* Police Foundation, Washington, D.C. (Dayton; Detroit; New York;* Syracuse, New York; Holyoke Mass.; Los Angeles).

Skolnick, Jerome H. 1972. "The Police and the Urban Ghetto," in Charles E. Reasons and Jack L. Kuykendall, eds., *Race, Crime, and Justice.* Goodyear Publishing Co., Pacific Palisades, Calif. (San Francisco).

Smith, William R. 1967. *Police-Community Relations Aides in Richmond, California.* Survey Research Center, University of California, Berkeley (Richmond, Calif.).

Wichita Police Department. 1967. *Police-Community Relations Section: Final Report*, Grant No. 109. Office of Law Enforcement Assistance, U.S. Department of Justice, Washington, D.C. (Wichita, Kan.).

Education Case Studies

Aberbach, Joel D. and Jack L. Walker. 1972. "Citizen Desires, Policy Outcomes, and Community Control." *Urban Affairs Quarterly* 8 (September), pp. 55-75 (Detroit).

Bard, Bernard. 1972. "Is Decentralization Working?" *Phi Delta Kappan* 54 (December), pp. 238-43 (New York).

Bauer, Raymond et al. 1969. *Urban Education: Eight Experiments in Community Control.* Arthur D. Little, Inc., Cambridge, Mass. (New York: Ocean Hill-Brownsville, Harlem, Two Bridges; Washington, D.C.: Anacostia, Adams-Morgan; Chicago; Boston).

Congreve, Willard J. 1969. "Collaborating for Urban Education in Chicago." *Education and Urban Society* 1 (February), pp. 177-91 (Chicago).

Gittell, Marilyn. 1971. "Education: The Decentralization-Community Control Controversy," in Jewel Bellush and Stephen David, eds., *Race and Politics in New York City.* Praeger, New York (New York).

———— et al. 1972. *Local Control in Education: Three Demonstration School Districts in New York City.* Praeger, New York (New York).

————. *School Boards and School Policy: An Evaluation of Decentralization in New York City.* Praeger, New York (New York).

Gottfried, Frances. 1970. "A Survey of Parental Views of the Ocean Hill-Brownsville Experiment." *Community Issues* 2, no. 5 (October) (New York: Ocean Hill-Brownsville).

Grant, William R. 1971. "Community Control versus School Integration: The Case of Detroit." *The Public Interest*, no. 24 (Summer), pp. 62-79 (Detroit).

Guttentag, Marcia. 1972. "Children in Harlem's Community Controlled Schools." *Journal of Social Issues* 28 (December), pp. 1-20 (New York: Harlem).

Jacoby, Susan. 1973. "Community Control, Six Years Later." *The Washington Post*, May 13, p. C3 (Washington, D.C.: Adams-Morgan).*

Karp, Richard. 1968. "School Decentralization in New York: A Case

201

Study." *Interplay* 2 (August-September), pp. 9-14 (New York: Ocean Hill-Brownsville).

La Noue, George R. and Bruce L.R. Smith. 1973. *The Politics of School Decentralization*. D.C. Heath, Lexington, Mass. (Washington, D.C.: Adams-Morgan, Anacostia; St. Louis; Los Angeles; Detroit; New York).

Lauter, Paul. 1968. "The Short, Happy Life of the Adams-Morgan Community School Project." *Harvard Educational Review* 38 (Spring), pp. 83-110 (Washington, D.C.).*

Levin, Betsy. 1969. "Decentralization/Community Control of Philadelphia Schools," Working Paper 701-4. The Urban Institute, Washington, D.C. (Philadelphia).*

McCoy, Rhody. 1970. "The Formation of a Community-Controlled School District," in Henry M. Levin, ed., *Community Control of Schools*. Brookings Institution, Washington, D.C. (New York: Ocean Hill-Brownsville).*

Moore, Charles H. and Ray E. Johnston. 1971. "School Decentralization, Community Control, and the Politics of Public Education." *Urban Affairs Quarterly* 6 (June), pp. 421-46 (Detroit).

Natzke, John H. and William S. Bennett, Jr. 1970. "Teacher Aide Use and Role Satisfaction of Inner-City Teachers." *Education and Urban Society* 2 (May), pp. 295-314 (unnamed site).

Ports, Suki. 1970. "Racism, Rejection, and Retardation," in Annette T. Rubenstein, ed., *Schools against Children*. Monthly Review Press, New York (New York: Harlem).*

Ravitch, Diane. 1972. "Community Control Revisited." *Commentary* 54 (February), pp. 69-74 (New York).

Rebell, Michael A. 1973. "New York's School Decentralization Law." *Journal of Law Education* 2 (January), pp. 1-38 (New York).

Rubin, Morton. 1971. *Organized Citizen Participation in Boston*. The Urban Institute, Boston University, Boston (Boston).*

Sakolsky, R. 1973. "The Myth of Government-Sponsored Revolution." *Education and Urban Society* 5 (May), pp. 321-43 (New York).*

Surkin, Marvin. 1971. "The Myth of Community Control," in Peter Orleans and W. Ellis, Jr., eds., *Race, Change, and Urban Society*. Sage, Beverly Hills, Calif. (New York: Ocean Hill-Brownsville).*

Sussman, Leila and Gayle Speck. "The Community Participation in Schools: The Boston Case." *Urban Education* 7 (January), pp. 341-56 (Boston).*

Swanson, Burt E. et al. 1968. *An Evaluation Study of the Process of School Decentralization in New York*. Final report of the Advisory Committee on Decentralization to the Board of Education of the City of New York (New York: Two Bridges, Harlem, Ocean Hill-Brownsville).

Ward, Agee. 1970. "Ocean Hill," in Hans Spiegel, ed., *Citizen Participation in Urban Development: Vol. II*. Center for Community Affairs, New York (New York).*

Wasserman, Miriam. 1970. *The School Fix, NYC, USA*. Outerbridge and Dienstfrey, New York (New York: Harlem).

Wilson, Charles E. 1970. "First Steps toward Community Control," in Annette T. Rubenstein, ed., *Schools against Children*. Monthly Review Press, New York (New York).

Zimet, Melvin. 1973. *Decentralization and School Effectiveness*. Teachers College Press, New York (New York).

Health Case Studies

Bellin, Seymour and H. Jack Geiger. 1972. "The Impact of a Neighborhood Health Center on Patients' Behavior and Attitudes Relating to Health Care: A Study of a Low-Income Housing Project." *Medical Care* 10 (May-June), pp. 224-39 (Boston).

Bellin, Seymour et al. 1969. "Impact of Ambulatory Health Care Services on the Demand for Hospital Beds." *New England Journal of Medicine* 280 (April 10), pp. 808-12 (Boston).

Berger, David G. and Elmer A. Gardner. 1971. "Use of Community Surveys in Mental Health Planning." *American Journal of Public Health* 61 (January), pp. 110-18 (Philadelphia).

Bradshaw, B.R. and C.B. Mapp. 1972. "Consumer Participation in a Family Planning Program." *American Journal of Public Health* 62 (July), pp. 969-72 (Atlanta).

Branch, Geraldine B. and Natalie Felix. 1971. "A Model Neighborhood Program at a Los Angeles Health Center." *HSMHA Health Reports* 86 (August), pp. 684-91 (Los Angeles).

Brickman, Harry R. 1967. "Community Mental Health: The Metropolitan View." *American Journal of Public Health* 57 (April), pp. 641-50 (Los Angeles).*

Campbell, John. 1971. "Working Relationships between Providers and Consumers in a Neighborhood Health Center." *American Journal of Public Health* 61 (January), pp. 97-103 (Cleveland).*

Chu, Franklin D. and Sharland Trotter. 1972. *The Mental Health Complex, Part I: Community Mental Health Centers*. Task Force Report on the National Institute of Mental Health. Center for Responsive Law, Washington, D.C. (Washington, D.C.; Pontiac, Mich.).

Cowen, David L. 1969. "Denver's Neighborhood Health Program." *Public Health Reports* 84 (December), pp. 1027-31 (Denver).

Davis, Milton S. and Robert E. Tranquada. 1969. "A Sociological Evaluation of the Watts Neighborhood Health Center." *Medical Care* 7 (March-April), pp. 105-17 (Los Angeles).

Domke, Herbert. 1966. "The Neighborhood-Based Public Health Worker." *American Journal of Public Health* 56 (April), pp. 603-8 (Pittsburgh).

Drummond, David W. and Eric W. Mood. 1973. "Actions of Residents in Response to Environmental Hazards in the Innter City." *American Journal of Public Health* 63 (April), pp. 335-40 (Philadelphia).

Fink, R. et al. 1969. "Change in Family Doctors' Services for Emotional Disorders after Addition of Psychiatric Treatment to Prepaid Group Practice Program." *Medical Care* 7 (May-June), pp. 209-24 (New York).

Freed, Harvey. 1972. "Promoting Accountability in Mental Health Services." *American Journal of Orthopsychiatry* 42 (October), pp. 761-70 (Chicago).

Gales, Harriet. 1970. "The Community Health Education Project." *American Journal of Public Health* 60 (February), pp. 322-27 (Detroit).

Gottschalk, Louis A. et al. 1970. "The Laguna Beach Experiment." *Comprehensive Psychiatry* 11 (May), pp. 226-34 (Los Angeles).

Hallowitz, Emanuel and Frank Riessman. 1967. "The Role of the Indigenous Nonprofessional in a Community Mental Health Neighborhood Service Center Program." *American Journal of Orthopsychiatry* 37, pp. 766-78 (New York).

Health Policy Advisory Center, Inc. 1971. *Evaluation of Community Involvement in Community Mental Health Centers*. New York (Pontiac, Mich.; San Francisco).

Hillman, Bruce and Evan Charney. 1972. "A Neighborhood Health Center." *Medical Care* 10 (July-August), pp. 336-44 (Rochester, N.Y.).

Hochheiser, Louis I. et al. 1971. "Effect of the Neighborhood Health Center on the Use of Pediatric Emergency Departments in Rochester, New York." *New England Journal of Medicine* Vol 285 (July 15), pp. 148-52 (Rochester, N.Y.).

Hollister, Robert M. 1971. "From Consumer Participation to Community Control of Neighborhood Health Centers," Ph. D. dissertation. M.I.T., Cambridge, Mass. (St. Louis;* Denver).

Hospital and Community Psychiatry. "A Community Mental Health Consortium." Vol. 21 (October), pp. 329-32 (San Francisco).

Kaplan, Seymour R. and Melvin Roman. 1973. *The Organization and Delivery of Mental Health Services in the Ghetto: The Lincoln Hospital Experience*. Praeger, New York (New York).

Kent, James A. and C. Harvey Smith. 1967. "Involving the Urban Poor in Health Services through Accommodation." *American Journal of Public Health* 57 (June), pp. 997-1003 (Denver).

Klein, Michael et al. 1973. "The Impact of the Rochester Neighborhood Health Center on Hospitalization of Children, 1968 to 1970." *Pediatrics* 51 (May), pp. 833-9 (Rochester, N.Y.).

Lashof, Joyce C. 1969. "Chicago Project Provides Health Care and Career Opportunities." *Hospitals* 43 (July), pp. 105-8 (Chicago).

Lawrence, Leonard E. 1972. "On the Role of the Black Mental Health Professional." *American Journal of Public Health* 62 (January), pp. 57-59 (San Antonio).

Leyhe, D.L. et al. 1973. "Medi-Cal Patient Satisfaction in Watts." *Health Services Report* 88 (April), pp. 351-9 (Los Angeles)

Lindaman, Francis C. and Marjorie A. Costa. 1972. "The Voice of the Community." *American Journal of Public Health* 62 (September), pp. 1245-8 (New York).*

Luckham, Jane and David W. Swift. 1969. "Community Health Aides in the Ghetto: The Contra Costa Project." *Medical Care* 7 (July-August), pp. 332-9 (Richmond Calif.).

Milio, Nancy. 1967. "A Neighborhood Approach to Maternal and Child Health in the Negro Ghetto." *American Journal of Public Health* 57 (April), pp. 618-24 (Detroit).

Minkowski, William L. et al. 1971. "The County of Los Angeles Health Department Youth Clinics." *American Journal of Public Health* 57 (April), pp. 757-62 (Los Angeles).

New, Peter K. et al. 1972. *Citizen Participation and Interagency Relations*. Tufts University School of Medicine, Boston (unnamed sites: Uptown;* Southeast; Cactus City).

Nobel, Milton. 1972. "Community Organization in Hospital Social Services." *Social Casework* 53 (October), pp. 494-501 (New York).

Orden, Susan A. and Carol B. Stocking. 1971. *Relationships between Community Mental Health Centers and Other Caregiving Agencies*. National Opinion Research Center, Chicago (Rochester, N.Y.; New Orleans; Philadelphia: Hahnemann,* Psychiatric Center*).

Parker, Alberta W. 1970. "The Consumer as Policy Maker: Issues of Training." *American Journal of Public Health* 60 (November), pp. 2139-53 (Berkeley, Calif.).

Partridge, Kay B. 1973. "Community and Professional Participation in Decision Making at a Health Center." *Health Services Reports* 88 (June-July), pp. 527-34 (unnamed site).

Philippus, M.J. 1971. "Successful and Unsuccessful Approaches to Mental

Health Services for an Urban Hispano American Population." *American Journal of Public Health* 61 (April), pp. 820-830 (Denver).

Salber, Eva J. et al. 1972. "Health Practices and Attitudes of Consumers at a Neighborhood Health Center." *Inquiry* 9 (March), pp. 55-61 (Boston).

Schonfeld, Hyman K. and Charles L. Milone. 1972. "The Utilization of Dental Services by Families at the Hill Health Center." *American Journal of Public Health* 62 (July), pp. 942-52 (New Haven, Conn.).

Sellers, Rudolph V. 1970. "The Black Health Worker and the Black Health Consumer." *American Journal of Public Health* 60 (November), pp. 2154-70 (New Haven, Conn.).

Shneidman, Edwin S. and Norman L. Farberow. 1965. "The Los Angeles Suicide Prevention Center." *American Journal of Public Health* 55 (January), pp. 21-26 (Los Angeles).

Whittington, H.G. and Charles Steenbarger. 1970. "Preliminary Evaluation of a Decentralized Community Mental Health Clinic." *American Journal of Public Health* 60 (January), pp. 64-77 (Denver).

Wise, Harold B. et al. 1968. "The Family Health Worker." *American Journal of Public Health* 58 (October), pp. 1828-38 (New York).

_____. 1968. "Community Development and Health Education: I." *Milbank Memorial Fund Quarterly* 46 (July), pp. 329-39 (New York).

Wood, Eugene C. 1969. "Indigenous Workers as Health Care Expediters." *Hospital Progress* 49 (September), pp. 64-68 (Pittsburgh).*

Young, M.M. 1970. "Chattanooga's Experience with Reorganization for Delivery of Health Services." *American Journal of Public Health* 60 (September), pp. 1739-48 (Chattanooga, Tenn.).

Young, M.M. and Genevieve P. Hamlin. 1969. "People Workers: A Local Health Department's Experience with Health Education Aides." *American Journal of Public Health* 59 (October), pp. 1845-50 (Chattanooga, Tenn.).

Zukin, P. et al. 1973. "Evaluating a Primary Care Clinic in a Local Health Department," *Health Services Reports* 88 (January), pp. 65-76 (Los Angeles).

Multiservice Case Studies

Abt Associates. 1969. *A Study of the Neighborhood Center Pilot Program*, Vol. 2. Cambridge, Mass. (Boston; Chattanooga; Chicago; Minneapolis).

Adams, James. 1972. "Cincinnati's Hub Center." *City* 6 (March-April), pp. 58-59 (Cincinnati).*

Ayres, Alice. 1973. "Neighborhood Services: People Caring for People." *Social Casework* 54 (April), pp. 195-215 (Chicago).

Bernard, Sydney E. et al. 1968. "The Neighborhood Service Organization." *Social Work* 13 (January), pp. 76-84 (Detroit).*

Birnbaum, Martin L. and Chester H. Jones. 1967. "Activities of the Social Work Aides." *Social Casework* 48 (December), pp. 626-32 (New York).

Booz, Allen, Public Administration Services, Inc. 1972. *A Study of the Seattle Unicenter*. Community Development Evaluation Series No. 4. U.S. Department of Housing and Urban Development, Washington, D.C. (Seattle).

Brager, George. 1965. "The Indigenous Worker." *Social Work* 10 (April), pp. 33-40 (New York).

Brody, Stanley J. et al. 1972. "Benefit Alert: Outreach Program for the Aged." *Social Work* 17 (January), pp. 14-24 (Philadelphia).

Budner, Stanley et al. 1973. "The Indigenous Nonprofessional in a Multiservice Center." *Social Casework* 54 (June), pp. 354-9 (New York).

Burgess, Philip M. et al. 1973. "Puerto Rico's Citizen Feedback Program" in Alan J. Wyner, ed., *Executive Ombudsmen in the United States*. Institute of Governmental Studies, University of California, Berkeley (Puerto Rico).

Caplovitz, David and Steven Cohen. 1972. "The Neighborhood Offices of the Law Enforcement Division of the Department of Consumer Affairs," unpublished paper. Law Enforcement Assistance Administration, U.S. Department of Justice, Washington, D.C. (New York).

Coggs, Pauline R. and Vivian R. Robinson. 1967. "Training Indigenous Community Leaders for Employment in Social Work." *Social Casework* 48 (May), pp. 278-81 (Milwaukee).*

Cudaback, Dorothea. 1969. "Case-Sharing in AFDC Program." *Social Work* 14 (July), pp. 93-99 (Alameda County, Calif.).

Davison, John and Robert D. Rippeto. 1964. "A Public Agency Project to Strengthen Client and Community." *Social Casework* 45 (July), pp. 398-403 (San Mateo County, Calif.).

Goodstein, Leonard D. 1972. *An Evaluation of the Dayton Ombudsman*. University of Cincinnati, (Dayton).

Murphy, Joseph B. et al. 1971. *Evaluation of Social Services to the Elderly in the Pilot City Area of Minneapolis*. Institute for Interdisciplinary Studies, Minneapolis (Minneapolis).

Nordlinger, Eric A. 1972. *Decentralizing the City: A Study of Boston's Little City Halls*. M.I.T. Press, Cambridge, Mass. (Boston).

Puerto Rico's Citizen Feedback System. 1970. U.S. Department of Housing and Urban Development, Washington, D.C. (San Juan).

Rabagliati, Mary and Ezra Birnbaum. 1959. "Organizations of Welfare Clients," in Harold Weissman, ed., *Community Development in the Mobilization for Youth Experience*. Association Press, New York (New York).

Rodgers, William H., Jr. 1970. "When Seattle Citizens Complain." *Urban Lawyers* 2 (Summer), pp. 386-97 (Seattle).*

Steinbacher, Roberta and Phyllis Solomon. 1971. *Client Participation in Service. Organizations*. Cleveland Urban Observatory, Cleveland (Cleveland).

Sterzer, Earl E. 1971. "Neighborhood Grant Program Lets Citizens Decide." *Public Management* 53 (January), pp. 10-11 (Dayton).*

Tibbles, Lance. 1970. "Ombudsmen for Local Government?" *Urban Lawyer* 2 (Summer), pp. 364-85 (Buffalo).

U.S. Department of Housing and Urban Development. 1971. "Neighborhood Facility Site Visits," regional office memoranda. Washington, D.C. (Erie, Pa.; Minneapolis; Colorado Springs; St. Paul; Hutchinson, Kan.; Ontario, Calif.; Passaic, N.J.; San Bernadino, Calif.; Seattle).

Washnis, George J. 1972. *Municipal Decentralization and Neighborhood Resources*. Praeger, New York (Kansas City, Mo.; Chicago; New York; Atlanta; Houston; Boston; Baltimore; Columbus, O.; San Antonio).

Weissman, Harold H. 1970. *Community Councils and Community Control*. University of Pittsburgh Press, Pittsburgh (New York).

Yates, Douglas. 1970. "More Notes from the Small Area Studies: The Mayor's Urban Action Task Force," unpublished paper. New York City-Rand Institute, (New York).*

Yin, Robert K. et al. 1972. "Neighborhood Government in New York City," unpublished paper. The Rand Corporation, Santa Monica, Calif. (New York).

Economic Development Case Studies

Abt Associates. 1972. *An Evaluation of the Special Impact Program*, Vol. III-IV. Cambridge, Mass. (St. Louis;Durham, N.C.; Roanoke, Va.; Washington, D.C.; Chicago; Detroit; New York: Harlem Bedford-Stuyvesant; Rochester, N.Y.; Columbus, O.).

Ackerson, Nels and Lawrence H. Sharf. 1970. "Community Development Corporations: Operations and Financing." *Harvard Law Review* 83 (May), pp. 1558-1671 (Los Angeles; Columbus, O.; Cleveland; Philadelphia).

Berkeley, Ellen P. 1971. "The New Process in Hartford's North End." *City* 5 (Summer), pp. 36-37 (Hartford, Conn.).*

Brower, Michael. 1971. "The Emergence of Community Development Corporations in Urban Neighborhoods." *American Journal of Orthopsychiatry* 41 (July), pp. 646-58 (Chicago; New York; Columbus, O.; Cleveland).

Campbell, Louise. 1968. "Communities: Bedford-Stuyvesant." *City* 2, nos. 2 and 3 (March), pp. 20-27; (May), pp. 22-33 (New York).

Fathergill, Alfred. 1972. *Citizen Participation in Denver*, Vol. IV. Denver Urban Observatory, Denver (Denver).

Faux, Geoffrey. 1971. *CDCs: New Hope for the Inner City*. Twentieth Century Fund, New York (New York; Rochester, N.Y.; Cleveland; Durham, N.C.;* Los Angeles: Operation Bootstrap, TELACU; Philadelphia).

Ford Foundation. 1973. "Community Development Corporations: A Strategy for Depressed Urban and Rural Areas," Ford Foundation policy paper. New York (New York: Bedford-Stuyvesant, Harlem; Los Angeles; Chicago).

Gifford, D. 1970. "Neighborhood Development Corporations: The Bedford-Stuyvesant Experiment," in Lyle Fitch and Annmarie Walsh, eds., *Agenda for a City*. Sage, Beverly Hills, Calif. (New York).

Money, James L. and Mel Epstein. 1971. *Housing Development*. Center for Economic Development, Cambridge, Mass. (Boston).

Owen, Raymond. 1971. "Community Organization and Participatory Democracy," unpublished Ph.D. dissertation. State University of New York at Buffalo (Buffalo).

Puryear, Alvin, N. and Charles A. West. 1973. *Black Enterprise, Inc.* Doubleday, Garden City, New York (New York).

Stein, Barry. 1973. "Harlem Commonwealth Council," unpublished report. Center for Community Economic Development, Cambridge, Mass. (New York).*

_____. 1973. "Rebuilding the Ghetto: Community Economic Development in Bedford-Stuyvesant," unpublished report. Center for Community Economic Development, Cambridge, Mass. (New York).

_____. 1972. *United Durham, Inc.* Center for Community Economic Development, Cambridge, Mass. (Durham, N.C.).

Urich, Helen and Nancy Lyons. 1973. *Profiles in Community Development*, Center for Community Economic Development, Cambridge, Mass. (Denver;* Seattle; Racine, Wisc;* Memphis;* Kansas City, Mo; Boston: Circle, Inc., East Boston;* Buffalo; Roanoke, Va; Los Angeles: Watts, Action, Operation Bootstrap; Durham, N.C.; St. Louis; Chicago: North Lawndale, FPPD Corp.;* Phildelphia; Newark,

N.J.; Detroit;* Cleveland; New York: Harlem, Bedford-Stuyvesant; Rochester, N.Y.; Camden, N.J.; Portland, Ore.).

Westinghouse Learning Corporation. 1970. *An Evaluation of FY 1968 Special Impact Programs: Vol. V.* Cleveland (Cleveland; New York).

Appendix B
Percent Responses for Cases Analyzed

Case Study Characteristics	*Percent Responses for Cases Analyzed* (N = 215)
A. Dominant service area covered by case:	
(1) Public Safety	17.7
(2) Education	15.8
(3) Health	22.3
(4) Multiservice Programs	19.1
(5) Economic Development	25.1
B. Did the author have any affiliation at any time with the innovation?	
(1) Yes	29.8
(2) No	70.2
C. What was the city in which this case took place? [a]	
D. Has this innovation also been reported in another case study?	
(1) Yes	50.2
(2) No	49.8
E. Was this case an evaluation of the innovation?	
(1) Yes	58.6
(2) No	41.4
F. Is this one of several cases reported by the same author?	
(1) Yes	53.0
(2) No	47.0

Nature of the Case Study	*Percent Responses for Cases Analyzed*
1. The first author of the study:	
(1) Has an academic affiliation only	28.8
(2) Is employed by the relevant local service (even if also academic)	25.1

[a] See list of sites at the end of this appendix

211

(3) Is employed by government, but not in the
    relevant local service ⎤
(4) Is a beneficiary of the local service   ⎦ 10.2
(5) Is employed by an independent research or-
    ganization   33.5
(8) Other (specify)_____
(9) Absolutely no information   2.3

2. The study appears in:
  (1) An academic journal (university editor)   34.4
  (2) A trade journal
  (3) A newspaper or popular magazine   1.9
  (4) A book   20.5
  (5) A report   43.3
  (8) Other (specify)_____
  (9) Absolutely no information   —

3. The main sponsor of the study was:
  (1) A federal government agency   53.0
  (2) A state or local government agency   7.9
  (3) A private source (e.g., foundations)   21.9
  (4) A university   15.3
  (5) Self-support
  (9) Absolutely no information   1.9

4. The study was published in:
  (1) 1970-73   74.9
  (2) 1966-69   21.9
  (3) 1962-65   1.4
  (4) 1961 or earlier   1.9
  (9) Absolutely no information   —

5-11. As evidence, the study uses:

	Yes	No	No Info
5. A sample survey	20.0	80.0	—
6. Public service records (e.g., crime rates, school tests, utilization rates, etc.)	35.8	63.7	0.5
7. Interviews or questionnaires of a non-systematic sample	28.4	71.6	—
8. Fieldwork or observations	45.6	54.4	—
9. The author's own experiences	23.7	76.3	—
10. Previously published reports	39.1	60.9	—
11. Other (specify)_____	2.8	96.7	0.5

	Percent
	Responses for
	Cases Analyzed

12. As measures, the study has:
    (1) Operational outcome[b] measures — 32.6
    (2) A mixture of operational outcome measures and other measures — 11.2
    (3) No operational measures, but other measures or observations that were used informally — 56.3
    (4) No explicitly cited measures or observations — Excluded
    (9) Absolutely no information — —

13. The research design of the study uses:
    (1) Experimental and comparison groups, with pre- and post-observations — 4.2
    (2) Experimental and comparison groups, but with only a single observation period — 11.2
    (3) An experimental group with pre- and post-observations — 8.8
    (4) An experimental group, with only a single observation period — 75.8
    (5) No specific experimental group or no clear observation period — Excluded
    (9) Absolutely no information — —

14. Many studies are flawed because of faults such as "creaming," "Hawthorne" effects, different pre- and post-tests, or a high dropout rate within the groups studied. The present study appears to have:
    (1) No obvious faults — 3.3
    (2) A few minor faults — 7.0
    (3) A few questionable faults — 18.6
    (4) A few serious faults — 70.7
    (9) Absolutely no information — 0.5

15. What (implicit or explicit) grounds does the author have for generalizing his results to other cities?
    (1) The services are similar to those of other cities — 25.6
    (2) The client population shares similar characteristics (e.g., race or income) as those of other cities — 26.5
    (3) The nature of the "social problem" is similar to other cities — 27.4

[b] Described in sufficient detail that a new investigator could repeat the investigation. The "outcome" may be any category of measure (e.g., attitude, input, or output).

(4) None of the above   20.5
(8) Other (specify)_____   —
(9) Absolutely no information   —

16-21. Many studies cannot be generalized to other cities because of unique factors. The present study explicitly cites (check each line):

	Yes	No	No Info
16. A unique client group	3.7	96.3	—
17. A unique set of personalities and individuals	15.8	84.2	—
18. A unique historical or political situation	16.3	83.7	—
19. A unique innovation or organizational change	6.0	94.0	
20. Other (specify)_____	5.1	94.9	—
21. No unique factors	67.4	32.6	—

Percent Responses for Cases Analyzed

22. The case being studied is described as:
    (1) A specific intervention program that has already ended   11.2
    (2) A specific intervention program that is still in progress   83.3
    (3) Organizational changes that are well defined but not part of a discrete intervention program   3.7
    (4) Organizational changes that are poorly defined   0.5
    (5) An intervention program or organizational changes that are still being planned   1.4
    (6) A time period, with no focus on a deliberate intervention or organizational changes   —
    (9) Absolutely no information   —

23. The difference between the publication date and the beginning of the program innovation was:
    (1) Less than one year   5.1
    (2) One to less than three years   40.5
    (3) Three to five years   33.0
    (4) More than five years   16.7
    (9) Absolutely no information   4.7

Background Factors

24. The study took place in a:
    (1) City, 500,000 persons or more   69.8
    (2) City, 100,000-500,000 persons   20.5
    (3) City, fewer than 100,000 persons   4.7
    (4) County or township   3.3
    (9) Absolutely no information   1.9

25. The study took place in the following region:
    (1) Conn., Me., Mass., N.H., R.I., Vt.
    (2) Del., Md., N.Y., N.J., Pa., P.R., D.C.   } 48.4
    (3) Ala., Fla., Ga., Ky., Miss., N.C., S.C.,
        Tenn., Va., W. Va.
    (4) Ark., La., Okla., Tex.   } 7.9
    (5) Ill., Ind., Mich., Minn., Ohio, Wisc.
    (6) Iowa, Kans., Mo., Neb., N.D., S.D.   } 24.2
    (7) Colo., Idaho, Mont., Nev., Utah, Wyo.
    (8) Alaska, Ariz., Cal., Haw., N.M., Ore.,
        Wash.   } 17.7
    (9) Absolutely no information   1.9

26. The area of study included:
    (1) An entire city, township, or county   24.2
    (2) A district or neighborhood
    (3) An area within a district or neighborhood   } 59.5
    (4) A group of districts or neighborhoods   16.3
    (9) Absolutely no information   —

	Yes	No	No Info
27-33. The target population was:			
27. Dominantly low-income	73.5	25.1	1.4
28. Dominantly black	57.2	38.6	4.2
29. Dominantly a Spanish-speaking or other ethnic group	12.6	81.9	5.6
30. Dominantly a special age group	10.2	87.4	2.3
31. Dominantly a special role group (e.g., students, unemployed persons, or unwed mothers)	19.1	79.1	1.9
32. None of the above	14.9	84.2	0.9
33. Other (specify)	5.6	93.5	0.9

34. During the pre-implementation state, the innovation involved a serious conflict (defined as involving major delays, strikes, hostilities, or confrontations) between:
    (1) Two or more citizen or neighborhood groups
    (2) The municipal executive (e.g., mayor) and a community
    (3) Service officials and the community   20.0
    (4) Service officials and the municipal executive
    (5) Federal or state officials and any of the above
    (6) None of the above because there was no serious conflict   67.9
    (8) Other (specify)_____   1.4
    (9) Absolutely no information   10.7

35. How much unanticipated delay was there simply in implementing the innovation?
    (1) One year or more   7.9
    (2) Three months to one year   17.7
    (3) Up to three months
    (4) Minimal or no delay   60.0
    (9) Absolutely no information   14.4

36. The one who was responsible for implementing the innovation was:
    (1) The mayor's office   6.5
    (2) A state or local agency   43.7
    (3) A local group or coalition (client, provider, or nonprofit)   40.5
    (4) A federal agency   1.4
    (5) A university   7.4
    (9) Absolutely no information   0.5

37. In the implementation process, the mayor or municipal executive:
    (1) Was an active participant
    (2) Was aware or spoke of the innovation, but did not participate   33.0
    (3) Played no role, and no municipal agency was involved

(4) Played no role, but some municipal agency
was involved $\quad\rbrace$ 25.6
(9) Absolutely no information $\quad$ 41.4

38. The major impetus for the innovation came from:
    (1) The mayor or municipal executive $\quad$ 9.3
    (2) Union officials $\quad$ 1.4
    (3) A state or local agency $\quad$ 23.3
    (4) A university $\quad$ 7.0
    (5) The federal government $\quad$ 14.0
    (6) A foundation $\quad$ 2.8
    (7) Citizens or citizen groups $\quad$ 35.3
    (8) None of the above $\quad$ 3.3
    (9) Absolutely no information $\quad$ 3.7

39. The major resistance to the innovation came from:
    (1) The mayor or municipal executive $\quad$ 1.9
    (2) Union officials $\quad$ 10.7
    (3) A state or local agency $\quad$ 6.5
    (4) A university $\quad$ 0.5
    (5) The federal government $\quad$ —
    (6) A foundation $\quad$ —
    (7) Citizens or citizen groups $\quad$ 7.4
    (8) None of the above $\quad$ 60.0
    (9) Absolutely no information $\quad$ 13.0

Characteristics of the Innovation

40-47. The innovation concerned the following service:

	Yes	No	No Info
40. Education	21.4	78.6	—
41. Public safety	20.9	79.1	—
42. Health or sanitation	21.4	78.6	—
43. Social services or recreation	24.2	75.8	—
44. Housing, transportation, public works, or planning	19.1	80.0	—
45. "Helping" or access services[c]	24.2	75.3	0.5
46. Economic development	28.4	71.6	—
47. Mental health	13.0	86.5	0.5

---

[c] A service primarily aimed at making other services more responsive. The "helping" service itself is not to be considered a substantive service.

Percent
Responses for
Cases Analyzed

48. The innovation had a client population of roughly:
    (1) More than 100,000 persons — 37.7
    (2) 50,000-100,000 persons — 12.1
    (3) 10,000-50,000 persons — 17.7
    (4) Fewer than 10,000 persons — 16.7
    (9) Absolutely no information — 15.8

49. The innovation attempted to provide
    (1) Only a redistribution of service or of information
    (2) Expanded scheduling or other minor extensions of existing services — 42.3
    (3) Major new service of one type
    (4) Major new service of several types — 57.7
    (9) Absolutely no information — —

50. In relation to the relevant public service agency, the innovation was:
    (1) Entirely outside the agency — 54.0
    (2) Within a small part of the agency — 31.6
    (3) Within most of the agency but only to a minor extent (e.g., a summer program)
    (4) Within most of the agency and touched upon some basic personnel or organizational issues — 14.0
    (9) Absolutely no information — 0.5

51. The innovation was financially supported mainly by:
    (1) No new funds — 5.6
    (2) A federal agency (even if state is pass-through) — 58.6
    (3) A state or county agency
    (4) A municipal agency
    (5) Neighborhood residents — 34.0
    (6) Private sources
    (9) Absolutely no information — 1.9

52. The resources involved in the innovation were equivalent to:
    (1) A substantial part of the most directly related public agency budget — 10.2

    (2) A minor portion of the most directly related public agency budget, but able to support one or more major service facilities   53.5

    (3) A minor portion of the agency budget, and able to support some minor activities   29.3

    (9) Absolutely no information   7.0

53. The innovation was designed as a reaction to:

    (1) Certain types of events (e.g., riots)   8.8

    (2) The needs of certain target populations (e.g., juveniles)   20.0

    (3) The needs of certain neighborhood(s) (e.g., a low-income area)   57.2

    (4) No specific needs or events   13.0

    (9) Absolutely no information   0.9

54. The innovation called for the formation of:

    (1) A new outside organization   50.7

    (2) A new unit within the existing service organization   23.7

    (3) Only a new citizens' unit to oversee some aspect of the service organization   12.1

    (4) No new organizational structure   13.0

    (9) Absolutely no information   0.5

55-60. Citizen participation in the innovation occurred:

	Yes	No	No Info
55. In the actual receipt of services	96.7	2.8	0.5
56. Informally in the delivery of services	7.4	85.1	7.4
57. Via organized volunteer programs	6.0	84.7	9.3
58. Via paraprofessional or other service groups	41.4	50.2	8.4
59. Via a formal client group or board structure	60.9	32.1	7.0
60. Via special elections dealing with the service	29.3	60.0	10.7

Note: If 55 is the only affirmative answer, go to question 72.

(N = 169)[d]

61-65. The general characteristics for most of the leading citizen participants included:

61. Prior experience as community leaders	50.3	34.9	14.8

[d] 46 cases had only Q.55 affirmative in the 55-60 section.

62. Special training in leadership or service
    delivery   27.8 62.1 10.1
63. Payment for participation   21.3 66.9 11.8
64. Membership in a target population or
    area   81.7 13.0   5.3
65. Selection by existing public service offi-
    cials   25.4 67.5   7.1

66-71. The citizen participants had some influence over
   the following service functions:
66. Sign-off authority over grant applica-
    tions or other service decisions 21.9 63.9 14.2
67. Review of service budget requisitions or
    expenditures   26.0 59.2 14.8
68. Review of some service personnel hir-
    ing, firing, or promoting   26.0 63.3 10.7
67. Review or investigation of grievances 17.2 65.7 17.2
70. Planning for new programs or facilities 55.0 36.1   8.9
71. Supervision over some paid staff 23.1 63.9 13.0

Percent
Responses for
Cases Analyzed
(N = 215)

72. Participation in the innovation by officials of the
    existing public service agency:
    (1) Did not occur at all   24.2
    (2) Occurred in an informal manner   12.6
    (3) Occurred in a formal manner   57.2
    (9) Absolutely no information   6.0

73. In terms of control for service clients or their rep-
    resentatives, the innovation *was intended* to:
    (1) Provide direct control to client representa-
        tives chosen on some elective basis
    (2) Provide direct control to some client rep-
        resentatives (whether over minor or   43.3
        major matters)
    (3) Provide only indirect control (e.g., through
        grievance mechanisms, citizen polls,
        etc.)   11.6
    (4) Provide no new control over service delivery 41.4
    (9) Absolutely no information   3.7

74. For physical deployment of personnel or facilities, the innovation was intended to redeploy:
   (1) Both operating personnel and facilities to serve clients on a more local basis
   (2) Operating personnel only (e.g., team policing)   31.2
   (3) Facilities, but not operating personnel (e.g., storefronts to distribute leaflets)
   (4) No personnel or facilities   68.4
   (9) Ábsolutely no information   0.5

75. For the flow of information or contact between officials and clients, the innovation *specifically* intended:
   (1) No new flow of information   47.4
   (2) New information, primarily from service agents to clients   40.5
   (3) New information, primarily from clients to service agents   10.2
   (4) A new two-way flow of information between clients and service officials
   (9) Absolutely no information   1.9

76. As for procedural changes within the existing service organization, the innovation intended:
   (1) No such changes
   (2) A new organization unit, but no changes in the existing field or district command structure   79.5
   (3) Field or district commanders to have increased responsibilities, but no new organizational unit
   (4) Both a new organization unit and increased responsibilities by field or district commanders   20.0
   (9) Absolutely no information   0.5

77. As for the employment of clients in service, positions, the innovation was intended to provide:
   (1) Neither the training nor employment of clients or client-types   45.1
   (2) Training, but no employment   1.4
   (3) Employment, but no training   46.0
   (4) Training and employment
   (9) Absolutely no information   7.4

78. As for client feedback about services, the innovation was intended to create:
    (1) No new opportunities for complaints or comments   66.0
    (2) New complaint procedures, but no organizational changes
    (3) New organizational units or personnel to handle complaints   } 27.0
    (4) Some procedure other than a grievance process, in order to gain citizen feedback (e.g., a survey)   4.2
    (9) Absolutely no information   2.8

79. In your opinion, the main thrust of the innovation was to:
    (1) Reorganize the command structure within the service bureaucracy   4.2
    (2) Give clients greater control over service delivery   13.5
    (3) Provide improved information between service agents and clients   15.3
    (4) Provide training and employment opportunities for clients or client-types   2.3
    (5) Give clients a better opportunity for making complaints   7.4
    (6) Develop new service institutions   16.7
    (7) Bring services physically closer to clients   10.2
    (8) Other (specify)_____   29.8
    (9) Absolutely no information   0.5

Outcomes

80. The innovation survived until:
    (1) Its planned termination after an operational phase   4.7
    (2) The time of study, with a clear operational phase   87.9
    (3) The time of study, with only a planning phase evident   3.3
    (4) A premature termination after an operational phase   4.2
    (5) A premature termination after only a planning phase   —
    (9) Absolutely no information   —

Note: If answer is 80(1), (2), (3), or (9), skip next question.

81. If the innovation had terminated prematurely, it
    was because of:

    (N = 9)

    (1) Disagreement among citizen or client groups — —
    (2) Disagreement between citizens and service
        groups — 33.3
    (3) Disagreements among service groups — 11.1
    (4) A lack of funds — —
    (8) Other (specify) — 55.5
    (9) Absolutely no information — —

82. The period of survival was:

    (N = 215)

    (1) Less than one year — 6.0
    (2) One to less than three years — 43.7
    (3) Three to five years — 29.3
    (4) More than five years — 17.2
    (9) Absolutely no information — 3.7

83. During the period of innovation, the activity level
    within the innovation appeared to:

    (1) Stay at the same level — 14.4
    (2) Rise, in general, over the period — 56.7
    (3) Decline, in general, over the period — 1.4
    (4) Fluctuate over the period — 7.0
    (9) Absolutely no information — 20.5

84. During the period of innovation, public attention
    appeared to:

    (1) Stay the same — 21.9
    (2) Rise, in general, over the period — 30.7
    (3) Decline, in general, over the period — 1.9
    (4) Fluctuate over the period — 5.6
    (9) Absolutely no information — 40.0

85. During the period of innovation, the innovation
    actually reached, in one manner or another:

    (1) No service beneficiaries — 1.9
    (2) A small percentage of beneficiaries — 51.2
    (3) At least a near-majority of them — 29.8
    (4) Virtually all intended beneficiaries — 9.3
    (9) Absolutely no information — 7.9

86. The innovation produced serious conflict (defined as major delays, strikes, hostilities, or confrontations) between:
    (1) Two or more local groups   7.0
    (2) The municipal executive (e.g., mayor) and the community
    (3) Service officials and the community   } 14.4
    (4) Service officials and the municipal executive or among service officials   2.8
    (5) Federal or state officials and any of the above   7.4
    (6) None of the above because there was no serious conflict   58.6
    (8) Other (specify)_____
    (9) Absolutely no information   9.8

87. The innovation affected community cohesion by producing:
    (1) Increased unity within the target population or neighborhood   26.5
    (2) A fragmenting effect within the target population or neighborhood   14.4
    (3) No effect, though there might have been one
    (4) No effect, because there was no target population or neighborhood   } 36.7
    (9) Absolutely no information   22.3

88. The innovation affected public service cohesion by producing:
    (1) Increased unity among the public service employees   5.6
    (2) A fragmenting effect among public service employees   14.9
    (3) No effect, though there might have been one
    (4) No effect, because no public service employees were involved   } 64.7
    (9) Absolutely no information   14.9

89. The innovation resulted in increased client influence over services to the following extent:
    (1) Clients were able to implement some of their own ideas in service delivery   22.3
    (2) Services changed due to increased information about client needs   13.0
    (3) There was no appreciable influence   54.4
    (9) Absolutely no information   10.2

90. The innovation enhanced community leadership to
    the extent that clients or client representatives had:
    (1) Formal opportunities for leadership positions
        (e.g., boards)   52.6
    (2) Employment opportunities in service-related ⎤
        positions   ⎬   20.0
    (3) Informal exposure to service delivery   ⎦
    (4) No opportunities to learn about service de-
        livery   21.9
    (9) Absolutely no information   5.6

91. The innovation helped to change the influence of
    the client population in affairs beyond immediate
    service delivery to the extent that client groups:
    (1) Became more influential in other affairs ⎤
                                                  ⎬   34.9
    (2) Established an identity on the scene   ⎦
    (3) Had no increase in influence   37.7
    (4) Suffered losses in influence   0.9
    (9) Absolutely no information   26.5

92-98. The innovation produced an increased flow of
    information between clients and service officials
    by:

	Yes	No	No Info
92. Adding new communications channels (e.g., emergency phone numbers)	21.9	74.0	4.2
93. Increasing opportunities for informal contact between clients and officials	42.3	54.9	2.8
94. Disseminating written information to clients about services	34.9	57.2	7.9
95. Giving service officials client-oriented training	15.8	78.1	6.0
96. Adding communications specialists (e.g., paraprofessionals) to the service staff	27.9	68.4	3.7
97. Increasing the number of complaints received	15.3	71.2	13.5
98. None of the above since there was no increase in information flow	35.8	61.4	2.8

Percent
Responses for
Cases Analyzed

99. The innovation changed the service budget by creating:

   (1) Dollar savings — 0.9

   (2) More services at the same cost — 1.4

   (3) No change — 7.0

   (4) Fewer services at the same cost — —

   (5) More expenditures — 84.7

   (9) Absolutely no information — 6.0

100. The improved flow of information resulted mainly in:

   (1) Improved use of substantive, not merely "helping" services — 10.2

   (2) A general increase in understanding of client needs

   (3) A general increase in understanding of service problems — 21.4

   (4) A negative impact (e.g., increased frustration, more disrespect) — 2.8

   (5) None of the above — 58.6

   (9) Absolutely no information — 7.0

101. The innovation resulted in about twenty or more of the community or target population representatives having:

   (1) Gained permanent employment in professional or supervisory jobs — 0.9

   (2) Gained permanent employment in paraprofessional, clerical, or blue-collar jobs — 40.9

   (3) Held temporary or part-time jobs — 0.9

   (4) Had no substantial employment opportunities — 46.5

   (9) Absolutely no information — 10.7

102. As a result of the innovation, the attitudes of clients toward the service or officials appear to have:

   (1) Improved, because of actual changes in services or service officials — 16.3

   (2) Improved, because of greater empathy for the service of officials — 8.4

   (3) Remained unchanged — 44.7

(4) Deteriorated   7.4
(9) Absolutely no information   23.3

103. As a result of the innovation, the attitudes of service officials toward the service or clients appear to have:
  (1) Improved, because of actual changes in services or among the client population   5.6
  (2) Improved, because of greater empathy for the service or clients   7.0
  (3) Remained unchanged   54.0
  (4) Deteriorated   6.0
  (9) Absolutely no information   27.4

104. As a result of the innovation, there were substantive (not merely "helping") service improvements in the sense that:
  (1) Service output increased (e.g., improved reading scores, decreased crime, or decreased unemployment)   23.7
  (2) Service input increased (e.g., more office hours, more police, etc.)   34.0
  (3) Both of the above   8.4
  (4) Neither of the above   25.6
  (9) Absolutely no information   8.4

105. As a result of the innovation, client satisfaction with substantive services increased in that there was:
  (1) Increased use of the service   10.2
  (2) Expressed verbal satisfaction with the service (e.g., via a survey)   12.1
  (3) Both of the above   2.8
  (4) Neither of the above   56.3
  (9) Absolutely no information   18.6

106. As a result of the innovation, other innovations in the same service or organization were:
  (1) Started successfully   ⎱ 51.2
  (2) Planned or considered   ⎰
  (3) Not affected in any way   28.4
  (4) Slowed down or stopped   1.9
  (9) Absolutely no information   18.6

107. As a result of the innovation, other innovations in the municipal bureaucracy in general were:

(1) Started successfully   0.9
(2) Planned or considered   3.7
(3) Not affected in any way   66.0
(4) Slowed down or stopped   —
(9) Absolutely no information   29.3

108. As a result of the innovation, citizen participation (aside from service use):

(1) Increased, and involved many community members   19.5

(2) Increased, and involved a few community members ⎫
(3) Remained unchanged   ⎬ 73.0
(4) Declined   ⎭ —

(9) Absolutely no information   7.4

109-115. The study presents the following type of evidence in relation to each outcome:

	Service Records			Interviews or		No
	Auth. Rep.	Input	Output	Surveys	None	Info
109. The flow of information between clients and service officials	49.8	2.8	7.4	1.9	37.2	0.9
110. Actual service delivered	28.8	13.0	33.5	2.8	20.0	1.9
111. Attitudes of service officials toward the service or clients	21.9	—	0.9	9.8	65.6	1.9
112. Attitudes of clients toward the service or officials	25.6	—	0.9	19.5	53.0	0.9
113. Employment of clients in service positions	13.5	12.6	24.2	0.5	45.1	4.2
114. Increased control of clients over services	41.9	—	2.3	6.5	48.8	0.5
115. Amount of citizen participation	50.7	3.7	19.1	4.7	21.9	—

Percent Responses for Cases Analyzed

116. According to the author, the innovation appears to have been:

(1) A success	54.4
(2) A mixed bag of successes and failures	34.0
(3) A failure	11.2
(4) Not a notable success or failure	
(9) Absolutely no information	0.5

117. The author's judgment of success or failure is primarily based on:

(1) Conflict (or lack of it)	10.2
(2) Service changes (not "helping")	30.7
(3) Power changes (or lack)	13.5
(4) Popular support (or lack)	11.6
(5) Budgetary support (or lack)	12.6
(6) Information changes (or lack)	9.3
(7) Attitude changes (or lack)	7.9
(8) Production of other innovations	0.5
(9) Absolutely no information	3.7

118. According to the author, the factor most affecting the outcome was:

(1) The urban setting or background	2.8
(2) A unique individual(s)	13.5
(3) Money and resources	8.8
(4) Client-service relations	16.7
(5) Client attitudes or organization	9.8
(6) Service attitudes or organization	27.4
(8) Other (specify)_____	9.3
(9) Absolutely no information	11.6

List of Cities in Which Case Studies Occurred

City	Number of Case Studies
Alameda County, California	1
Atlanta, Georgia	2
Baltimore, Maryland	2
Berkeley, California	1
Boston, Massachusetts	8
Buffalo, New York	4
Camden, New Jersey	1
Charlotte, North Carolina	1
Chattanooga, Tennesse	3

Chicago, Illinois 11
Cincinnati, Ohio...1
Cleveland, Ohio 6
Colorado Springs, Colorado 1
Columbus, Ohio...4
Dayton, Ohio 3
Denver, Colorado..5
Detroit, Michigan 8
Durham, North Carolina.....................................2
Erie, Pennsylvania 1
Fall River, Massachusetts....................................1
Holyoke, Massachusetts......................................1
Houston, Texas 2
Hutchinson, Kansas 1
Kansas City, Missouri..2
Los Angeles, California 15
Los Angeles County, California 1
Milwaukee, Wisconsin 1
Minneapolis, Minnesota 4
Muskegon-Saginaw, Michigan 1
New Haven, Connecticut 2
New Orleans, Louisiana......................................1
New York, New York 52
Ontario, California 1
Passaic, New Jersey 1
Philadelphia, Pennsylvania 12
Pittsburgh, Pennsylvania 1
Pleasant Hills, California 1
Pontiac, Michigan 2
Portland, Oregon...1
Richmond, California 3
Richmond, Virginia 1
Roanoke, Virginia 2
Rochester, New York 7
St. Louis, Missouri..4
St. Paul, Minnesota 1
San Antonio, Texas..2
San Bernadino, California....................................1
San Francisco, California 3
San Juan, Puerto Rico...2
San Mateo County, California 1
Seattle, Washington..3
Syracuse, New York 1

Washington, D.C. 9
Wichita, Kansas...1
Winston-Salem, North Carolina 1
Worcester, Massachusetts 1

Unnamed site 4

Total (56 cities)..215 cases

Appendix C
Interanalyst Reliability

Reliability

Reliability is the self-consistency of a method of gathering evidence, or the degree to which separate, independent measurements or judgments of the same phenomenon agree with each other. When the method of judgment warrants, reliability is usually expressed by a correlation coefficient indicating the level of agreement among different observers. Use of a correlation, however, requires either interval or ordinal data. Where interval data are used, a Pearson product-moment correlation is generally employed; in the case of ordinal data, a Spearman rank correlation or a Kendall rank correlation is appropriate. In either case, the statistic has a known sampling distribution, and therefore the researcher knows the chance probability of the obtained occurrence and can reject the null hypothesis at a specified level of confidence.

The present study on decentralization relies primarily on nominal data in the checklist of 118 questions. For such data, in which observations are assigned to categories that are different from each other but not conceived to be equidistant along any dimension or capable of being ranked in an ordinal fashion, the available measures of interobserver agreement are not readily interpretable in terms of confidence levels and deviations from chance. For instance, the most common descriptive measure is to calculate the percent agreement among observers. But this measure does not take into account the amount of interobserver agreement that may result from chance guessing.

Previous investigators have dealt with this problem in a number of ways, none of which is adaptable to the current study. The most common nonparametric statistic for the degree of association between two nominal scales is the contingency coefficient.[a] This coefficient, however, is most applicable to the situation where there are numerous observations for the same question; the measure is less useful where only pairs or trios of observers have observed a whole series of questions, since the low number of observers means that the n will be very low.

Bennett has devised a second statistic that accounts for agreement as a function of the number of available categories, but this statistic is based on the assumption that all categories in the question have equal probability of

[a] Sidney Siegel, *Non-Parametric Statistics* (New York: McGraw-Hill, 1956).

233

use ($1/k$, where k = total categories available).[b] This is not a tenable assumption for coding when the phenomena being coded are likely to cluster in one or two categories. A third possible statistic, which expresses reliability as the ratio of the number of categories on which coders agree to the total of all category assignments by all coders, has been used in content analysis but makes the same faulty assumption that all categories are equally probable.[c]

Studies of small groups and interpersonal interaction, involving the categorization of observed behavior, suggest a fourth possibility. These studies define their categories in terms of ranks, so that judgments are made, for example, on which group members had the most task-oriented interactions.[d] This procedure is not readily adapted to the current study, where many of the questions simply do not imply any scalar dimension. Finally Scott has devised an index of reliability, π, that corrects for the number of categories in the category set and for the frequency distribution with which each category has been used.[e] The use of π, however, does not permit statements about confidence levels of agreement.

As a result of the difficulty in assessing confidence levels, Table C-1 merely gives the percent of agreement between two observers for 14 different case studies, along with the number of response categories for each question. For all questions, the average observed agreement was 67.0 percent.

---

[b] E.M. Bennett et al., "Communications through Limited Response Questioning," *Public Opinion Quarterly* 18 (Fall 1954), pp. 303-8.

[c] Robert North et al. *Content Analysis,* (Evanston, Ill.: Northwestern University Press, 1966); W.C. Shutz, "Reliability, Ambiguity, and Content Analysis," *Psychological Review* 59 (1952), pp. 119-29; and W.C. Shutz, "On Categorizing Quantitative Data in Content Analysis," *Public Opinion Quarterly* 22 (1958), pp. 502-15.

[d] Robert F. Bales and Philip Slater, "Role Differences in Small Decision Making Groups," in T. Parsons and R. Bales, eds., *Family, Socialization, and Interaction Process* (Glencoe, Ill.: The Free Press, 1955); and James A. Jones, "An Index of Consensus on Rankings in Small Groups," *American Sociological Review* 24 (August 1959), pp. 533-6.

[e] William Scott, "Reliability of Content Analysis: The Case of Nominal Scale Coding," *Public Opinion Quarterly* 19 (1955), pp. 321-5; and William Scott, "Empirical Assessment of Values and Ideologies," *American Sociological Review* 24 (June 1959), pp. 299-310.

Table C-1
Percent of Agreement between Two Observers, 14 Case Studies

Question	No. of Response Categories	Observed Agreement (%)	Question	No. of Response Categories	Observed Agreement (%)
1	6	78.5	49	4	42.8
2	6	100.0	50	4	71.4
3	5	64.2	51	6	78.5
4	4	92.8	52		questions
5	2	92.8	53		omitted
6	2	71.4	54	4	57.1
7	2	64.2	55	2	92.8
8	2	71.4	56	2	92.8
9	2	78.5	57	2	92.8
10	2	92.8	58	2	78.5
11	2	92.8	59	2	85.7
12	4	57.1	60	2	92.0
13	5	57.1	61	2	50.0
14		questions	62	2	60.0
15		omitted	63	2	40.0
16	2	92.8	64	2	40.0
17	2	92.8	65	2	40.0
18	2	85.7	66	2	50.0
19	2	85.7	67	2	50.0
20	2	85.7	68	2	70.0
21	2	50.0	69	2	60.0
22	6	92.8	70	2	60.0
23	4	78.5	71	2	60.0
24	4	92.8	72	3	85.7
25	8	100.0	73	4	71.4
26	4	85.7	74	4	78.5
27	2	78.5	75	4	78.5
28	2	71.4	76	4	57.1
29	2	78.5	77	4	78.5
30	2	92.8	78	4	35.7
31	2	78.5	79	8	42.8
32	2	71.4	80	5	85.7
33	2	92.8	81	5	no cases
34	7	71.4	82	4	64.2
35	4	42.8	83		questions
36	5	50.0	84		omitted
37	4	50.0	85	4	35.7
38	8	42.8	86	7	85.7
39	8	42.8	87	4	42.8
40	2	92.8	88	4	50.0
41	2	85.7	89	3	50.0
42	2	78.5	90	4	57.1
43	2	64.2	91	4	71.4
44	2	85.7	92	2	50.0
45	2	85.7	93	2	57.1
46	2	92.8	94	2	78.5
47	2	85.7	95	2	78.5
48	4	71.4	96	2	64.2

Table C-1 (continued)

Question	No. of Response Categories	Observed Agreement (%)	Question	No. of Response Categories	Observed Agreement (%)
97	2	71.4	108	4	71.4
98	2	78.5	109	5	64.2
99	5	50.0	110	5	35.7
100	5	35.7	111	5	50.0
101	4	71.4	112	5	71.4
102	4	21.4	113	5	71.4
103	4	28.5	114	5	50.0
104	4	42.8	115	5	35.7
105	4	35.7	116	4	85.7
106	4	35.7	117		questions
107	4	71.4	118		omitted

Appendix D
Comparison of Case Studies of Three Different Levels of Research Quality (Selected Questions Only)

	Cases Included in Study		Cases Excluded from Study
	High Quality Cases (N = 88)	Moderate Quality Cases (N = 127)	Poor Quality Cases (N = 54)

General Characteristics[a]

A. Service Area

	High Quality	Moderate Quality	Poor Quality
(1) Safety	27.3	11.0	27.8
(2) Education	9.1	20.5	18.5
(3) Health	20.5	23.6	16.7
(4) Multiservice Programs	19.3	18.9	11.1
(5) Economic Development	23.9	26.0	25.9

B. Did the author have any affiliation at any time with the innovation?

(1) Yes	28.4	30.7	33.3
(2) No	71.6	69.3	66.7

E. Was this case an evaluation of the innovation?

(1) Yes	77.3	45.7	33.3
(2) No	22.7	54.3	66.7

Nature of the Case Study

1. The first author of the study:

(1) Has an academic affiliation only	36.4	23.6	24.1
(2) Is employed by the relevant local service (even if also academic)	26.1	24.4	27.8
(3) Is employed by government, but not in the relevant local service			

[a] The letters and numbers refer to the original checklist (see Appendix B).

237

(4) Is a beneficiary of the local service	– 6.8	12.6	7.4
(5) Is employed by an independent research organization	28.4	37.0	40.7
(8) Other (specify)_____			
(9) Absolutely no information	2.3	2.4	—

3. The main sponsor of the study was:

(1) A federal government agency	61.4	47.2	35.2
(2) A state or local government agency	5.7	9.4	11.1
(3) A private source (e.g., foundations)	15.9	26.0	50.0
(4) A university	14.8	15.7	3.7
(5) Self-support			
(9) Absolutely no information	2.3	1.6	—

23. The difference between the publication date and the beginning of the program innovation was:

(1) Less than one year	5.7	4.7	14.8
(2) One to less than three years	39.8	40.9	46.3
(3) Three to five years	35.2	31.5	25.9
(4) More than five years	17.0	16.5	7.4
(9) Absolutely no information	2.3	6.3	5.6

Background Factors

24. The study took place in a:

(1) City, 500,000 persons or more	68.2	70.9	59.3
(2) City, 100,000-500,000 persons	21.6	19.7	29.6
(3) City, fewer than 100,000 persons	5.7	3.9	7.4
(4) County or township	2.3	3.9	1.9
(9) Absolutely no information	2.3	1.6	1.9

72. Participation in the innovation by officials of the existing public service agency:

(1) Did not occur at all	27.3	22.0	22.2
(2) Occurred in all informal manner	11.6	11.8	16.7
(3) Occurred in a formal manner	53.4	59.8	59.3
(9) Absolutely no information	5.7	6.3	1.9

Strategies

50. In relation to the relevant public service agency, the innovation was:
    (1) Entirely outside the agency — 55.7 · 52.8 · 50.0
    (2) Within a small part of the agency — 33.0 · 30.7 · 37.0
    (3) Within most of the agency but only to a minor extent (e.g., a summer program)
    (4) Within most of the agency and touched upon some basic personnel or organizational issues — 11.4 · 15.7 · 13.0
    (9) Absolutely no information — 1.1 · — · —

73. In terms of control for service clients or their representatives, the innovation *was intended* to:
    (1) Provide direct control to client representatives chosen on some elective basis
    (2) Provide direct control to some client representatives (whether over minor or major matters) — 36.4 · 48.0 · 42.6
    (3) Provide only indirect control (e.g., through grievance mechanisms, citizen polls, etc.) — 15.9 · 8.7 · 3.7
    (4) Provide no new control over service delivery — 42.0 · 40.9 · 53.7
    (9) Absolutely no information — 5.7 · 2.4 · —

74. For physical deployment of personnel or facilities, the innovation was intended to redeploy:
    (1) Both operating personnel and facilities to serve clients on a more local basis
    (2) Operating personnel only (e.g., team policing)
    (3) Facilities, but not operating personnel (e.g., storefronts to distribute leaflets) — 34.1 · 29.1 · 27.8

(4) No personnel or facilities   64.8   70.9   72.2
(9) Absolutely no information   1.1   —   —

75. For the flow of information or contact
between officials and clients, the innovation *specifically* intended:

(1) No new flow of information	46.6	48.0	44.4
(2) New information, primarily from service agents to clients	35.2	44.1	48.1
(3) New information, primarily from clients to service agents	15.9	6.3	7.4
(4) A new two-way flow of information between clients and service officials			
(9) Absolutely no information	2.3	1.6	—

76. As for precedural changes within the
existing service organization, the innovation intended:

(1) No such changes			
(2) A new organization unit, but no changes in the existing field or district command structure	81.8	78.0	64.8
(3) Field or district commanders to have increased responsibilities, but no new organizational unit			
(4) Both a new organization unit and increased responsibilities by field or district commanders	18.2	21.3	31.5
(9) Absolutely no information	—	0.8	3.7

77. As for the employment of clients in
service positions, the innovation was
intended to provide:

(1) Neither the training nor employment of clients or client-types	54.5	52.0	57.4
(2) Training, but no employment	—	2.4	1.9
(3) Employment, but no training			
(4) Training and employment	37.5	38.6	29.6
(9) Absolutely no information	8.0	7.1	11.1

78. As for client feedback about services, the innovation was intended to create:
  (1) No new opportunities for complaints or comments   61.4   69.3   79.6
  (2) New complaint procedures, but no organizational changes ⎤
  (3) New organizational units or personnel to handle complaints ⎦   26.1   27.6   16.7
  (4) Some procedure other than a grievance process, in order to gain citizen feedback (e.g., a survey)   8.0   1.6   1.9
  (9) Absolutely no information   4.5   1.6   1.9

Outcomes

82. The period of survival was:
  (1) Less than one year   9.1   3.9   16.7
  (2) One to less than three years   39.8   46.5   50.0
  (3) Three to five years   31.8   27.6   18.5
  (4) More than five years   17.0   17.3   9.3
  (9) Absolutely no information   2.3   4.7   5.6

89. The innovation resulted in increased client influence over services to the following extent:
  (1) Clients were able to implement some of their own ideas in service delivery   14.8   27.6   20.4
  (2) Services changed due to increased information about client needs   6.8   17.3   1.9
  (3) There was no appreciable influence   61.4   49.6   68.5
  (9) Absolutely no information   17.0   5.5   9.3

91. The innovation helped to change the influence of the client population in affairs beyond immediate service delivery to the extent that client groups:
  (1) Became more influential in other affairs ⎤
  (2) Established an identity on the scene ⎦   28.4   39.4   18.5

(3) Had no increase in influence	42.0	34.6	51.9
(4) Suffered losses in influence	2.3	—	3.7
(9) Absolutely no information	27.3	26.0	25.9

92-98. The innovation produced an increased flow of information between clients and service officials by:

98 None of the above since there was no increase in information

Yes	37.5	34.6	35.2
No	58.0	63.8	63.0
No Info	4.5	1.6	1.9

102. As a result of the innovation, the attitudes of clients toward the service or officials appear to have:

(1) Improved, because of actual changes in services or service officials	26.1	9.4	3.7
(2) Improved, because of greater empathy for the service or officials	11.4	6.3	3.7
(3) Remained unchanged	33.0	52.8	48.1
(4) Deteriorated	4.5	9.4	16.7
9) Absolutely no information	25.0	22.0	27.8

103. As a result of the innovation the attitudes of service officials toward the service or clients appear to have:

(1) Improved, because of actual changes in services or among the client population	9.1	3.1	—
(2) Improved, because of greater empathy for the service or clients	8.0	6.3	5.6
(3) Remained unchanged	51.1	55.9	57.4
(4) Deteriorated	4.5	7.1	7.4
(9) Absolutely no information	27.3	27.6	29.6

104. As a result of the innovation, there were substantive (not merely "helping") service improvements in the sense that:

(1) Service output increased (e.g., improved reading scores, decreased crime, or decreased unemployment)   36.4   15.0   3.7

(2) Service input increased (e.g., more office hours, more police, etc.)   17.0   45.7   33.3

(3) Both of the above   12.5   5.5   3.7

(4) Neither of the above   29.5   22.8   42.6

(9) Absolutely no information   4.5   11.0   16.7

105. As a result of the innovation, client satisfaction with substantive services increased in that there was:

(1) Increased use of the service   6.8   12.6   7.4

(2) Expressed verbal satisfaction with the service (e.g., via a survey)   27.3   1.6   3.7

(3) Both of the above   5.7   0.8   —

(4) Neither of the above   45.5   63.8   64.8

(9) Absolutely no information   14.8   21.3   24.1

116. According to the author, the innovation appears to have been:

(1) A success   55.7   53.5   31.5

(2) A mixed bag of successes and failures   ⎤
                                             ⎥
(3) A failure   ⎥ 33.0   34.6   51.9
                ⎥ 10.2   11.8   14.8
(4) Not a notable success or failure   ⎦

(9) Absolutely no information   1.1   —   1.9

Appendix E
Critiques of Twelve
Illustrative Decentralization
Studies

Study: Abt Associates, *An Evaluation of the Special Impact Program: Phase I Report*, 4 volumes, Cambridge, Massachusetts, March 1972.

This study is a comprehensive evaluation of 17 community development corporations in the Special Impact Program. The study provides an example of the multi-case study, usually carried out by a consulting organization and concerning a somewhat controversial or sensitive topic and meant to serve as a formal evaluation for the supporting federal agency.

The format and style of the report appear designed to preclude easy reading. Numerous tables and inquiries are scattered throughout all four volumes although the 17 case studies are all found in a single volume. The cases were by a few different authors, and even though the same research design and outline appear to have been executed, the cases vary widely in the degree of detail about the use of the data collected and their analysis. No attempt is made to compare the CDC experiences with those of other groups in the same neighborhood, and there is no cross-sectional or pre-post design.

The study relies on two types of evidence: responses to a questionnaire (e.g., the percentage of people who believe that the CDC created better jobs), and analysis of economic indicators (e.g., the amount of bank loans to CDCs and their ventures). The main virtue of the study is that it attempts to produce measures covering the three major goals of CDCs as implicitly reflected in the original OEO legislation: establishment of community control, mounting of a demonstration program, and stimulation of the flow of capital into a neighborhood. The main problem with the study is that there is little discussion of the research methods: the nature of the interview sample, sample sizes for specific tabular results, sources of data for economic indicators, discussion of operational definitions of variables, or methods for arriving at conclusions. Moreover, the study presents a regression model, which is then poorly explained and related to the rest of the study.

Each case study provides descriptions of the innovation, including documentation of the budget history and legal status of each CDC. The case study also includes general demographic characteristics of the target neighborhood and wisely notes the difficulty of defining such an area for a CDC. The cases do not include any notation about why some types of evidence were used and others ignored, nor any genuine attempt at evaluative comments other than some individual recommendations.

The overall conclusions for the 17 cases as a group are weak. Findings and recommendations are given on nine subject areas (venture profitability and other short-term goals, the role of OEO, the future of the program, and so forth), but the study does not address the key evaluative questions: Are CDCs a viable alternative, and have these 17 CDCs performed well or poorly? Similarly, no attempt is made to compare the 17 cases with each other according to some uniform criteria.

The published version of the study does contain a brief critique of the study by representatives of the CDCs studied. The critique does not challenge the overall validity of the report but notes some specific points and the difficulty of applying too much scientific evaluation to CDC activities. The report does not contain any review of the literature or bibliography and has one other deficiency that is unacceptable to the general reader: For definitions of some specific variables, the reader is referred to the project's quarterly reports, which are inaccessible to him. Finally, the poor editing of the entire report is most obviously reflected by differences in tone and emphasis between the general discussion of conclusions and the executive summary. The summary is written in such a way that the link between findings and conclusions is not very clear.

Validity of Methods. The study tries to develop objective measures of CDC performance based on interim data and economic indicators. There is no research design, other than the collection of these data in a similar fashion for each of 17 cases, and the measures themselves are poorly reported. Moreover, the cases have been written by different authors, so the case discussions vary considerably in their use of the available evidence. Given the poor state of the art of evaluating CDCs, the study stands as an acceptable piece of work; given any concern for research methods, the study must be considered quite deficient.

Author Bias. The study was carried out as a third-party evaluation of service innovations. Several portions of the study receive adequate self-criticism (e.g., the conclusions to be drawn from the rudimentary cost-benefit analysis). Others, like the trustworthiness of the sources of economic indicators, do not receive much critical attention. The critique of the study by the CDC officials does not raise any issues of author bias, other than the general inappropriateness of using any scientific evaluation methods. As outsiders, the authors may have had difficulties in gaining CDC cooperation during site visits or in gaining access to CDC data. Few such difficulties are reported.

Nature of Conclusions. For such an extensive effort, this study arrives at surprisingly few evaluative conclusions. Most of the conclusions are of the uncritical variety (e.g., the program needs more money, without evi-

dence of additional effectiveness) and clearly avoid any potentially controversial issues.

Study: Seymour S. Bellin et al., "Impact of Ambulatory-Health-Care Services on the Demand for Hospital Beds," *New England Journal of
Medicine* 280 (April 1969), pp. 808-12.

Among the case studies of health services, this study is one of the most
comprehensive yet straightforward in research methods. The study
analyzes hospital utilization records for 209 families (980 individuals) before the opening of a neighborhood health center and then two years
following the opening. The sample population was drawn from a randomly
selected group of residents, including all those who lived in the community
for the two-year period and who were not over 65.

A main feature of the research is its explicit focus on a highly measur-
able dependent variable: utilization of hospital beds at a specific hospital.
The basic finding is that utilization rates have declined sharply from 461
days to 66 days during the two-year interval. The authors then mention
three possible ways of accounting for this finding: patients make greater
use of other hospitals not monitored in the study, patients' health status has
improved spontaneously, or patients' medical care needs are now being
served by the new neighborhood health center. The analysis presents data
comparing these three alternatives and then arrives at the major conclusion
of the study, that hospital utilization rates appear to have declined because
of the opening of the new health center.

While the research design would have benefited from a control group,
the pre-post design, focusing on hospital utilization rates and the supplementary analysis of other possible causal factors, provides fairly strong
evidence regarding the effectiveness of the neighborhood health center. In
few other services has any attempt been made to assess service innovations
in terms of such actual outcomes. In addition, the study itself does not
appear to be the sort requiring a substantial level of research effort, so the
results have been obtained at minimal cost.

The study has several shortcomings. First, as a journal article rather
than a more extensive case study, there is little review of the previous
literature or any substantial description of the program innovation. These
are partially excusable because the authors do refer to several previous
publications of their own. Second, as with many of the other health case
studies, the authors were directly affiliated with the program innovation
and may have an unknown bias in favor of positive results.

Validity of Methods. The basic research inquiry is a pre-post comparison of hospital utilization records for a previously identified sample of
residents. The results are dramatic and simple and do not even require

statistical treatment. There is no control group, but supplementary analyses attempt to deal directly with alternative causal factors. The pre-post design, however, does not adequately resolve one of Campbell's threats to external validity that of not being able to generalize to other *unpretested* populations. Aside from this flaw, the research is more than adequate.

Author Bias. The case study appears in a prominent medical journal and contains no overtly admitted biases. However, the authors were directly involved in operating the service innovation, and the effects of this affiliation are not clear. As with most journal articles, there is no attempt to be self-critical in any of the discussion.

Nature of Conclusions. The theme of the article is openly evaluative. The authors conclude that their study "adds to the growing body of evidence that points to the value of ambulatory health-care services in preventing and effectively treating illnesses that otherwise might require hospital care."

Study: Leonard D. Goodstein, "An Evaluation of the Dayton Ombudsman," unpublished report, University of Cincinnati, Cincinnati, 1972.

This study represents one of the more data-rich studies of neighborhood multiservice programs. Though the research design called for only a post-innovation assessment and there was no control group, the assessment covers the reactions of a wide variety of audiences: The ombudsman and his staff, 43 line agency officials, a sample of 50 citizens who used the ombudsman's services, 111 community leaders, and a household sample of 502 residents in the Dayton area.

The major finding of the report—that the vast majority of people were pleased and satisfied with the ombudsman's role and services—is thus based on separate analyses of the interviews of these five different audiences. The results are reported both in the body of the text (22 tables) and in a thorough appendix of over 50 pages of interview instruments and tabulations, though no statistical inference techniques are used. The author frankly admits that the study must be regarded as a one-shot case study, with no attempt to make comparisons between Dayton and other cities or within the Dayton group of respondents (e.g., a sample of respondents who used the ombudsman to investigate some complaint versus a sample who complained but did not use the ombudsman). The study also makes no attempt to analyze the nature or rate of success in disposing of grievances by the ombudsman.

The study contains no real review of the literature, but it does include a thorough account of the genesis of the innovation and an item only occasionally found in any of our case studies, a tabular presentation of the ombudsman's operating budget and sources of income. These budget figures are usually missing from other reports. In terms of the three methodological concerns, the study may be described in the following manner:

Validity of Methods. The study presents a wide variety of survey data on existing attitudes toward the ombudsman. Since the responses were generally favorable, it is somewhat unfortunate that there was no control group or even comparison with other services (e.g., maybe Daytonians rate all their governmental services highly). The surveys themselves were satisfactorily conducted.

Author Bias. The author was not associated with the program and filled the role of an official evaluator. The author is candid about the study's methodological limitations and its reliance on impressionistic evidence as well as survey results. He also mentions at the outset his own positive disposition to the concept of the ombudsman. As one partial check on author bias, the final report also includes comments on the study by the ombudsman's office. Even though these comments were not very critical in reviewing the study or its conclusions, the idea of allowing program officials to respond to evaluation reports is an excellent one.

Nature of Conclusions. The author has no trouble in arriving at an evaluative conclusion, that the ombudsman was well received by all relevant audiences. This conclusion comes directly from the survey results but can be faulted for the lack of any control group and the lack of an analysis of the grievance data themselves to determine "objectively" whether complaints were satisfactorily handled or not.

Study: Marcia Guttentag, "Children in Harlem's Community Controlled Schools," *Journal of Social Issues* 28 (December 1972), pp. 1-20.

This study attempts to go beyond the standard field account by using seven separate measures to assess the effects of decentralization in a school district, with occasional comparisons to a neighboring nondecentralized school and to a suburban school. The measures were dominantly of the social-psychological variety: an organizational climate index, an activities index, parent utilization of the school building, administrators' use of time, teacher-pupil interaction, student achievement, and teacher self-image. Unfortunately, the study has several flaws that severely limit its usefulness.

First, the seven measures were not applied uniformly to all schools in the decentralized district. In fact, the author openly admits that the data should be considered as part of seven separate studies, none of which alone is adequate, but which collectively provide strong evidence about decentralization. Thus, some measures are applied to certain schools while other measures are applied to others; in some cases, the data compare a few decentralized schools with nondecentralized schools, but this comparison is not uniform. Since the study gives no strong rationale for the selection of schools for each substudy, one must question, at a minimum, how the effects of the seven substudies can be aggregated.

Second, the study does not report its findings fully. In most cases, the raw data, including notation of such basic facts as the sample size, are not reported. Only the results of statistical comparisons are given, but these are difficult to interpret without the descriptive data.

Third, the author consistently makes strong inferences about attitudes, even though most of the measures concern only behavior. For instance, the notation of a larger number of contacts between the principal and the parents is followed by the assertion that the parents must therefore perceive the school as less threatening. Similar inferences are made from other behavioral data, such as the parents' utilization of the school buildings.

These three flaws all raise doubts as to the author's intentions in carrying out the study, especially since the study begins not with an account of the decentralization program or of the general demographic characteristics of the school district, but with a highly polemical discussion of elitist versus egalitarian philosophies. Since the study was supported in part by the school board of the decentralized district, the study's conclusions may come as no surprise: Community control significantly improves school conditions and learning, and the two reasons for its effects are the small size of the district with its ensuing informal and strong social environment and the sheer ideological commitment of the community's members.

Validity of Methods. The study attempts to provide more than informal field evidence on the effects of decentralization in a school district by using seven measures of school conditions. These measures are not uniformly applied to all the schools of the district, and only in some cases is there a comparison made between decentralized and nondecentralized schools. Moreover, the data are not fully reported, so it is difficult to interpret the final results, even though the statistical differences appear significant. There is no attempt to describe the nature of the decentralization program or the demography of the community.

Author Bias. The study begins with a strong advocacy statement for the egalitarian view. While this has the advantage of making the author's values explicit and clear, the statement, along with the inadequate design and presentation of empirical results and the partial support of the study by the local school board, all lead to the suspicion that the conclusions preceded the analysis. The author herself, being affiliated with a local university, appears to have had no direct link with the service innovations.

Nature of Conclusions. The study does not shy away from the key questions concerning decentralization or from attempting to answer these questions. It concludes that decentralization has produced positive changes within the schools, taking into account staff, student, and parent activities and attitudes.

Study: Health Policy Advisory Center, "Evaluation of Community Involvement in Community Mental Health Centers," New York City, 1971.

Individual evaluations of six mental health service innovations, focusing on the amount and type of community involvement as outcomes, are the subject of this report. Each case was studied with a similar approach: site visits and the use of common questionnaires for interviewing service officials and members of the community. The study is typical of other field-based case studies, both in health services and in other urban services, in that the fieldwork does not follow a stringent research design and no attempt is made to present the questionnaire data in systematic fashion. The appendix contains a copy of the questionnaire and a full description of the field procedures.

The lack of emphasis on research design is typified by the study's description of its interview sample:

Interviews were conducted with center directors, their assistants and the Consultation and Education staff (when available). In each case the director was also requested to arrange interviews with Advisory Board members, as well as other people he deemed important to the case study . . . Appointments were also made with other concerned people by the Health-PAC staff, through its own contacts in the regions and through contact made during the site visits. On occasion, these interviews include center staff or former staff. Usually, however, individuals with consumer affiliations were seen—union leaders, Community Corporation staff, local civil rights leaders.

Similarly, the six centers were not chosen as a rigorous sample of all centers.

The report itself is easy to read and includes a considerable discussion of the history of each case, including descriptions of the demographic and political characteristics of the surrounding community. The descriptions do not include, however, any budget or patient utilization data. The report also contains a critique of the study by a member of the federal agency that sponsored both the service innovations and the evaluation study. The critique offers a further insight into the nature of the study by noting three of its most prominent characteristics: (1) the study provides insufficient documentation for its conclusions, (2) the choice of cases may be strongly biasing the results, but (3) most of the conclusions appear nevertheless to have a face validity.

This report thus poses a dilemma often associated with field-based studies: Even though documentation and research design are poor, the conclusions may nevertheless be the same as those that might be reached with entirely different methods. Without actual replication, however, it is difficult to determine how much confidence is to be put into the conclusions. The conclusions themselves separately cover each service innovation and the innovations as a group. In general, the study found adequate participation in the planning and operation of the services by *provider* groups but inadequate participation by *user* groups.

Validity of Methods. This study relies solely on nonrigorous field methods, with the results reported only in narrative form. Although a uniform questionnaire was used to interview various officials and community members, the questionnaires were not applied to a previously designed sample nor is there any report on the aggregate results. The field procedures and original questionnare are given in an appendix, but in general it is difficult to regard the study as having a research methodology.

Author Bias. This is one of the few cases in health services where the authors are not associated with the service innovation. The text of the study reveals no strong biases, but the report makes no attempt at self-criticism. The strongest element of author bias must be derived from knowledge outside the study itself: The authors' organization is known not as a research organization but as an advocacy organization, which thus raises some question about the "objectivity" of the inquiry.

Nature of Conclusions. The study was commissioned as a formal evaluation and thus reaches specific conclusions for each of the innovations and for all as a group. In spite of the lack of rigorous research methods, the study's conclusions appear to be corroborated in the critique by a program-related staff official, whose remarks are formally incorporated as part of the final report.

Study: Bruce Hillman and Evan Charney, "A Neighborhood Health Center: What the Patients Know and Think of Its Operation," *Medical Care* 10 (July-August 1972), pp. 336-44.

This study is a fairly typical representative of the health case studies. It uses empirical data—in this case a survey of a randomly selected group of 100 users of a neighborhood health center—but has a poor research design and incomplete reporting of the results.

The survey involved 56 questions administered to users two years after the opening of the health center. The response rate was low: just under 60 percent. The questions focused on patients' use of the facility (how convenient is it, how do you get to the center, do you know its phone number, do you know the name of your internist or pediatrician), and patients' satisfaction with the services (are you satisfied with your physician, have you had any problems with the center). The format of the questions is not explicitly given, and the study presents only a few tables with the responses to the questions. One of the tables attempts to present comparisons on a few questions between the patients' responses and a sample group of nurses providing the service, but no description is given of the nature of the nurse sample. Other tables present some cross-tabulations—for example, comparing characteristics of satisfied versus dissatisfied patients—but in no instance are the data reported in any but descriptive fashion.

The main shortcoming of the research design is the lack of any control group, either of the cross-sectional type or of a pre-post nature. This, in addition to the low response rate and the incomplete reporting of results, raises questions about the study's major conclusion: "These data support the idea that comprehensive Health Center care is accepted with enthusiasm by a large majority of urban indigent patients, many of whom have complicating social problems." The findings simply do not give any description of the potential health care without the center or of the results of any alternative sources of care.

The study does attempt to address the community control issue directly by inquiring about the patients' knowledge of who controlled the center (only 8 percent could name any of the institutions affiliated with the center) and about whether the patients preferred community control (only 9 percent replied affirmatively). The authors conclude from these results that community control has simply not yet become an issue among the patients.

The study presents a typically brief description of the service innovation and demographic characteristics of the general community. The demographic characteristics are given in a few sentences that do not attempt to be careful about precise characterization of the data or their sources (one statistic is cited as having come from a 1964 census, but no mention is made of the nature of that census). The description of the service innovation is just as brief and somewhat more unsatisfactory, since the operation of a center can involve a wide variety and range of activities. The study, like many others in the health field, simply does not cover in any detail the center's staffing, types of services, facility location or hours of service, or the relationship between the center and other institutions—for example, the medical school affiliation. This deficiency in describing what are in essence the "independent" variables makes difficult any generalization about the effect of service innovation, even where the dependent variables of patient health, utilization, and satisfaction are satisfactorily measured.

Validity of Methods. The study reports the results of a poorly designed and poorly presented interview survey. The design contains no control groups, a low response rate, and no systematic reporting of even the nature of the questionnaire instrument. Nevertheless, it does base its conclusions on specifically cited empirical data and thus is more explicit about the nature of the evidence than other field-oriented studies.

Author Bias. Like so many health studies, the authors present only their academic affiliations, but it is probable that they were also part of the staff of the service innovation, since their university jointly administered the innovation. The relationships should be made clearer, especially since the survey covers such questions as "Have you had any problems with the center?" How the survey was carried out as well as the nature of the interviewers—if identified directly with the providers of the service —would clearly bias the results.

Nature of the Conclusions. The study does reach conclusions on the two major issues: Health centers can successfully serve the urban poor, and community control is not yet an important issue among the patients.

Study: Rita M. Kelly et al., *The Pilot Project: A Description and Assessment of a Police-Community Relations Experiment in Washington, D.C.,* American Institutes for Research, Kensington, Maryland, January 1972.

This study is the most thorough of all the studies on police innovations. Its very thoroughness and length (345 single spaced typewritten pages, with 114 figures and tables each generally occupying a fraction of a page), however, call into question the basic strategy of evaluation research when applied to program innovations. An apparently massive research effort was undertaken to report on an innovation that clearly failed to produce any significant changes other than the formation of a highly politicized community board.

The research itself is well designed and its methods clearly discussed. The study was based on several sets of interviews, which included a partial experimental design (pre- and post-assessments for two experimental groups of residents and police, and post-assessments for two control groups of residents and police), interviews of apprehended citizens, and interviews of a stratified sample of all police in the city. The scale of the research effort is reflected in the total numbers of respondents:

Residents' experimental group, pre-test:	n = 546, response rate = 55%
Residents' experimental group, post-test:	n = 973, response rate = 80%
Residents' control group, post-test:	n = 342, response rate = 61%
Police experimental group, pre-test:	n = 181, response rate = all police in program were interviewed
Police experimental group post-test:	n = 165, response rate = 85%
Police control group, post-test:	n = 145, response rate = 88%
Apprehended citizens:	n = 50, response rate = 39%
Stratified citywide sample of police:	n = 196, response rate = 90%, 85%, and 87% in each stratum.

The bulk of the findings is based on elaborate analysis of survey results, with statistical (chi-square) tests used as well as such procedures as a factor analysis of semantic differential data.

The study covers the historical evolution of the innovation in considerable detail, following a comprehensive review of the literature. Two elements are notably lacking: systematic presentation of the innovation's budget and any attempt to interview the important early personnel in the project. Consequently, the reasons for certain turns of events (for example, neither OEO nor the original project director pressed very much for citizen participation at the outset) remain difficult to understand.

The study concludes that the development of an elected citizens' board constituted the major success of the project, but that the project failed in several other respects: police-citizen tension was not substantially reduced, the police failed to increase citizen employment to any extent, and police and citizens were not appreciably more understanding or cooperative toward each other. The authors then give a careful discussion of the general lessons to be learned, but several of these—for example, a service innovation is not likely to succeed if the police department fails to get involved—are not very surprising.

The main question raised by this study is not the validity of its conclusions, but rather whether similar conclusions would have been reached by a much more modest effort. Our impression is that, with the magnitude of the project's service failure, and with the study's failure to reveal any subtle or unexpected findings, the same conclusions might have been reached with less than one-fourth the effort.

In terms of the three methodological concerns, the study may be described in the following manner:

Validity of Methods. This study provides the most elaborate research design (pre- and post-tests with experimental groups, post-tests with control groups) found among our studies in public safety. The conclusions are based on comparisons among these groups and survey coverage of residents, policemen, and apprehended citizens. The "control" group may be subject to challenge in that it consists of another precinct that has census characteristics similar to the precinct in which the program innovation took place. However, all major conclusions are based not merely on experimental versus control group comparisons, but also on pre- versus post-test comparisons for the experimental group. In general, then, the research design is quite adequate.

One extension that might have improved the research would have been the analysis of other data besides survey data. The investigators neither interviewed several key persons on the project nor analyzed municipal records such as crime data or police service statistics.

Author Bias. The authors were part of an outside consultant group asked to evaluate the project. The authors openly state that an interim version of the report had an important role in the decision to fund the innovation for its third year. It is unclear whether this feedback role had untoward effects on the evaluation design or schedule. The report is generally self-critical and otherwise has no apparent biases.

Nature of Conclusions. The report is quite clear in providing two sets of conclusions, one dealing with the actual outcome of the specific program innovation and the other dealing with general lessons to be learned. Such general lessons are rarely discussed in other studies. Since the results show no substantial changes due to the innovation, there is little possibility that the conclusions reflect an overinterpretation of the results. However, it is unfortunate that pre-tests of research instruments do not include the questioning of their analytic appropriateness. It is not clear, for instance, that a program innovation calling for changes in police operations in one precinct will necessarily change the general attitudes of the precinct's residents toward police within a year's time. Costly surveys should be avoided unless there is some prior indication that a few changes in attitudes can be expected.

Study: George LaNoue and Bruce L.R. Smith, *The Politics of School Decentralization*, D.C. Heath, Lexington, Massachusetts, 1973.

This study contains case studies of school decentralization in five different cities. The study is one of the few in the education area that covers more than a single case study, but it is in many respects like multicase studies found in the other service areas.

The general approach of the study was to identify decentralization attempts in all large cities (over 500,000 population) through a questionnaire and then to select five cities for intensive site visiting, interviewing, and analysis of official records. The five cities were chosen on the basis of the diversity of decentralization experiences, geographical balance, and accessibility and cooperativeness for research purposes. The study's main concern was with the occurrence of decentralization and the political correlates of cities that attempt decentralization; it was not heavily concerned with an assessment of the decentralization experience.

The beginning of the study presents a brief analysis of the questionnaire responses, followed by individual chapters on the five different cities. The questionnaire analysis attempts to address general hypotheses—for example, the larger the city, the more likely the decentralization—through simple correlation analysis, with statistical results reported. The case studies then individually review the political climate, pressures for decentralization, and nature of citizen participation and describe the actual service innovation. Little is given in terms of evaluation or recommendations for each case. For these cases, the authors do not attempt to describe their methodology, but make rich use of official but unpublished data: voter turnout statistics for special elections, special analysis of turnover data, local attitudinal surveys conducted by special organizations like the League of Women Voters, and empirical results from other studies generally sponsored by the school boards. These data are used eclectically for each case but are reported adequately in over 50 tables.

Following the case studies, the authors provide a general discussion of decentralization, primarily based on a theoretical concern for various models of decentralization, as opposed to a policy-oriented or evaluative concern. Not surprisingly, the authors conclude that no single theoretical model is appropriate for all cases. Other conclusions are that local school boards are potentially more resistant to union pressures than are citywide school boards, that advocates of decentralization often misunderstood the political context and organization of school systems, and that decentralization might have been made easier by more explicit charters laying out specific authorities and responsibilities. The study is somewhat deficient in relating these general conclusions to the case study materials, as there is no systematic attempt to aggregate the case study lessons before arriving at the general conclusions.

As background information, the study provides more than adequate discussions of the broader context for decentralization, as well as the specific histories of decentralization in each of the five cities. The discussions of individual innovations do not, however, include budget or staffing trends. The whole study was generally very easy to read and included an extensive bibliography on school decentralization.

Validity of Methods. This study follows the standard nonexperimental research approach: intensive interviewing and use of official documents and records for five cities in which school decentralization occurred. The five cities were selected on the basis of responses to a questionnaire about decentralization addressed to all large cities. The results of the case studies are thus presented primarily in a descriptive manner, with the goal of the study being to record the decentralization process and the degree of citizen participation through voter turnouts for school board elections. Since the study makes no attempt to assess the effects of decentralization, the lack of an experimental design does not appear to be a great shortcoming. Because of the authors' reliance on the results of other (unpublished) studies, the cost of conducting the study was not high. Indeed, the authors report that the bulk of the study was carried out without outside financial support.

Author Bias. The authors conducted the study from a university setting and were in no way affiliated with any of the decentralizations. The authors appear suitably self-critical by clearly presenting their own academic and non-policy orientation, noting the shortcomings of any comparative analysis, and expressing concern about the difficulty in thoroughly describing the changes over time within a specific case study.

Nature of Conclusions. The authors' conclusions primarily deal with decentralization as a political process and are not tightly related to the findings in the individual case studies. The conclusions do not emphasize an assessment of the decentralization experiment.

Study: Donald F. Norris, *Police-Community Relations: A Program that Failed*, D.C. Heath, Lexington, Massachusetts, 1973.

This study is typical of the evaluations of police-community relations programs. The author spent considerable time in field work and in informally and formally interviewing officials involved in a police-community relations program in a small city (Richmond, Virginia). The reporting is in narrative form and makes no attempt to specify discrete observations or hypotheses. This form of research is common to other studies of police-community relations programs as well as to team police programs.

The formal interviews were of supervisory officials in the whole police department, other top police officials, members (past and present) of the police-community relations unit, and "selected persons in Richmond governmental and private life." Fewer than 100 persons were interviewed. Although the samples of persons interviewed do not purport to represent larger populations in a small city and with a fairly small program innovation (the initial police-community relations grant was for about $15,000 in a city with a police force of about 450 men), the sample can include the whole universe. The study focuses on the attitudes of police officers and community leaders (as opposed to average residents) toward the program.

The study is highly readable and includes a basic review of the literature, a detailed account of the initiation and implementation of the program, and the results of the field work and interviews. The lack of emphasis on research methodology is reflected in the omission of any discussion of the author's methods and research, the lack of any use of statistical inference techniques, and the omission, even in an appendix form, of the questionnaire instrument. However, responses to specific questions are fully covered in 35 tabular presentations.

The study lacks a rigorous research methodology and may be judged in the following manner for each of the three methodological concerns:

Validity of Methods. The Richmond program, as suggested by the title of the study, did not succeed in achieving any substantive change in police-community relations. Since the major failure was the inability to focus on community relations rather than on public relations, and since the program involved only a small effort, more rigorous research methods would probably have unnecessarily increased the costs of the study without changing the conclusions.

Author Bias. The author was not associated with the program in any way, yet he appeared to have appreciable access to records and officials within the police department. His only possible bias was in hoping that the program innovation would change more fundamental police-community relations and thus in judging the program to be a failure by that criterion.

Nature of Conclusions. The author presents his study in an evaluative manner and does not shirk from drawing conclusions about the program innovation. His major conclusion is that the program innovation resulted only in an attempt to improve the public relations of the police department. This conclusion is based on the field work and on the responses to the interviews, and it seems valid.

In summary, the study represents a modest research effort applied quite appropriately to a modest program innovation. Its only major flaw is the publication lag. For such a modest effort, the study should have been published right after it was carried out. (The innovation began in 1967; the field work was carried out during 1969-70; but the book was not published until 1973.)

Study: Barry Stein, *United Durham, Inc.: A Case Study in Community Control,* Center for Community Economic Development, Cambridge, Massachusetts, 1972.

This study illustrates the purely journalistic approach to case studies. Such an approach is common to the literature on community development corporations and infrequent in the other service areas. The main characteristics of the journalistic approach are: (1) a lack of any criteria, hypotheses, theoretical concerns, and so forth to quide data collection or allow the reader to understand the basis for final conclusions; (2) omission of any description of the field work procedures, such as the persons interviewed, the level of effort, or the logic for searching for documents or attending meetings; (3) no presentation of any evidence other than occasional quotations from respondents; and (4) no analytic connection between the findings and the conclusions. Unfortunately, the author fails to capitalize on the potential strengths of the journalistic approach. He does not describe the service innovation in much detail, does not give insight into the community or political circumstances surrounding the innovation, and does not provide any understanding of the personalities of the main actors.

The study's main concern is with the process of citizen participation in the organization of a community development corporation. The greatest amount of attention is given to the mechanisms for facilitating the participation of low-income residents in meaningful decisionmaking. The author describes some of the problems in gaining such participation, but his conclusion is optimistic and exemplifies the nonanalytic nature of the study:

Overall it [the CDC] must be judged a success insofar as the control of the organization is solidly in the hands of its low-income constituents.

Nowhere is this conclusion spelled out in operational terms.

Validity of Methods. This study exemplifies the journalistic approach to case studies. There is no analytic framework even resembling the scientific method. This approach should be distinguished somewhat from more systematic participant-observation, where the investigator does describe his procedures, number and type of people interviewed, and even the interview instrument. In this case, all of these elements are absent.

Author Bias. The author has no direct affiliation with the service innovation but is affiliated with a nonprofit organization clearly identified as an advocacy organization for CDCs. The nature of the advocacy organization is described in a short paragraph at the end of the study, which thus gives the reader some warning about the nature of the study. Nevertheless, the author is not very self-critical, and he provides no criteria or reference points for his judgments.

Nature of Conclusions. The conclusions in no way attempt to evaluate the general activity of the CDC but focus only on the citizen participation aspect. Here, in spite of several notations about the increasing problems that the CDC is having with citizen participation, the author concludes that participation has been a success. The author gives no operational definitions for any of his terms, so the reader cannot really understand what is meant by such crucial items as "participation," "success," or "control over the organization."

Study: George J. Washnis, *Municipal Decentralization and Neighborhood Resources: Case Studies of Twelve Cities*, Praeger, New York, 1972.

The most common approach to cases of citizen participation and decentralization is captured by this study. The case studies are descriptive accounts of the experiences in each of 12 cities, based on personal site visits to each city. The author's methodology is not elaborate. His observations are drawn from discussions with officials as well as other observers of the scene (e.g., the local reporter). Although the case studies lack any analytic rigor, the study as a whole does provide a good account of specific events in each city as well as a general discussion of the important issues about decentralization.

Each case follows a similar outline: background information about the city and the relevant neighborhoods, descriptions of the service innovations that occurred, discussion of related programs such as Model Cities, review of citizen participation activities, and recommendations for program improvements. Wherever possible, the case also presents municipal records reflecting activities in the decentralized facilities. The author's recommendations address specific improvements that each city can make, but there is no attempt to evaluate each city's program, or to compare the 12 cities systematically. In addition to the case studies, the book does present a summary discussion of major issues common to all decentralization innovations, such as administrative coordination, central management techniques, and citizen participation.

In terms of the three methodological concerns, the study can be summarized as follows:

Validity of Methods. The case studies are presented as descriptive accounts of progress in 12 different cities. The study has no analytic framework, and the cases are based on the author's own field work and interviews (though few field data as such are reported). This type of reporting is typical of the participation and decentralization literature; a potential refinement would not be the use of any quasi-experimental techniques but corroboration of the findings by a second or even third observer. The main virtue of this type of approach to case studies is that it provides information about many service innovations at fairly low cost.

Author Bias. The author carried out the study as a member of an independent consultant organization. There is no attempt at self-criticism in relation to methods or sources of information, but there appear to be no consistent biases in the reporting of each case.

Nature of the Conclusions. Aside from the specific recommendations concerning improvements for each service innovation, the study contains no assessment or evaluation either for individual cases or for the cases as a whole. This lack of any evaluative remarks is perhaps the most disappointing aspect of the entire study, since the author has clearly established a good comparative perspective.

Study: Melvin Zimet, *Decentralization and School Effectiveness: A Case Study of the 1969 Decentralization Law in New York City,* Teachers College Press, Teachers College, Columbia University, New York, 1973.

Of all the case studies of school decentralization, the present study exhibits the best use of research design and data. The study focuses on the effects of decentralization in one school district of 24 schools by analyzing official records of events before, during, and after decentralization occurred. The author makes explicit reservations about the possible shortcomings of the data, since they derive from records maintained by the school system, but the data he uses represent a comprehensive effort at assessing school effectiveness. To complement the analysis of school records, the author also carried out extensive interviews of school staffs and made firsthand observations of school conditions. The interview and observational results, however, are not reported in an explicit fashion.

The study examines seven potential measures of school effectiveness: reading scores, student absenteeism, student suspensions, school vandalism, teacher absenteeism, teacher requests for transfers out of the district, and principal requests for transfers. For each measure, data are presented for all schools in the district for every year from 1965 to 1972, with analysis focusing on 1970-72, the period in which decentralization was implemented. These measures not only appear to cover every current means of objectively assessing school effectiveness, but they include measures previously cited in the plans for decentralization as important decentralization goals: improvement of reading levels, reduction of student suspensions, and reduction of teacher absenteeism.

In addition to the study's explicit attempt to assess school effectiveness, the study also includes a review of the literature, a detailed historical account of the decentralization innovation, an elaborate chapter on the characteristics of the school district, including profiles of the prominent school officials and school board members, and actual breakdowns of the school district's budget and programs.

The author's conclusions derive primarily from his analysis of the school records. The data are presented separately for every school in the district. Trends within the district are compared with citywide trends (though without actual statistical comparisons), and the general result is that there is little evidence of change in either a negative or positive direction. The author makes no attempt to overinterpret these results; he merely notes that the evidence will not support either advocates or opponents of decentralization, except to the extent that either side can make a case based on "no change" results.

The author draws other conclusions regarding community participation that appear to be based on his field work. Here, he recommends ways in which community participation can be increased, although there is no systematic presentation of current participation rates or any evidence offered that there is any relationship between participation and school effectiveness.

In general, the study is well written and appears not to have required a massive level of effort. This latter factor seems to be important since the analysis of existing municipal records, if not precluded because of internal biases, can be done quite cheaply and is not a dominant theme in the other case studies in education or other services. In terms of the three methodological concerns, the study can be summarized as follows:

Validity of Methods. The study combines traditional field work with an analysis of municipal records on 24 schools in one decentralized school district (enrollment of about 30,000). The research design lacks any control group, but a control group would have been inappropriate because decentralization occurred in all districts of the city. The major analysis is thus a pre-decentralization versus post-decentralization comparison of several measures: reading scores, student absenteeism, student suspensions, school vandalism, teacher absenteeism, teacher requests for transfers, and principal requests for transfers. None of these measures alone adequately assesses school effectiveness, but they serve in the aggregate as a satisfactory set of indicators. Certainly, the effort made by this study to gather a variety of indicators has not been matched by other studies. The data are reported for every school in the district, for every year from 1965 to 1972, and for citywide totals, so that the basic analysis consists of the observation of long-term trends as well as a focus on potential breaks in trends from 1970 to 1971 (the year that decentralization began). The field work is not reported as systematically, but it does provide a rich source of descriptive evidence about key individuals and the district as a whole.

Author Bias. The author held an academic position during the course of the study and was not involved in the decentralization program. The study contains some attempt at self-criticism but in general seems to follow the pattern of an academic-based study, and the author displays little favoritism either in favor of or against decentralization.

Nature of Conclusions. The author allows the analytic results to speak for themselves: The trends showed no clear evidence of positive or negative changes, with some indicators improving and others deteriorating. The author does make some recommendations on the desirable nature of community participation, however, that draw more from the field work than from the analysis of municipal records.

Index

Index

Abt Associates, 245-247

Ackerson, Nels, 141n

Administrative decentralization, 27, 28, 74, 93, 97, 111, 126, 129

Aiken, Michael, 175n

Alinksy, Saul, 21, 145

Allied Services Bill (1972), 119

Ambulatory health-care services, case study, 247-248

Anacostia school district (Washington, D.C.), 128

Antioch College, 128

Antipoverty program, 21, 22-23, 143-144, 155

Banfield, Edward C., 7, 8, 24n, 175n

Bargaining for services, 4-7, 189

Barss, Reitzel and Associates, Inc., 22n

Bawden, D. Lee, 183n

Bedford-Stuyvesant Restoration Corporation, 142, 145, 155

Bell, Daniel, 126n

Bellan, Ruben C., 3n, 8

Bellin, Seymour S., 247-248

Benefit-to-cost calculus, 176

Blacks: and community development corporations, 142, 144, 155; and education, 124, 128; and health services, 92; and police, 70-71; and quality of urban life, 177, 180

Blankenship, L. Vaughan, 185n

Boards of education, 126, 134, 137

Booz, Allen Public Administration Services, Inc., 24n

Borough system (London), 112n

Boston, 97, 110, 138n

Bridenbaugh, Carl, 3n, 8

British Citizens' Advice Bureau, 110

Brown v. *Board of Education of Topeka*, 124

Brown, Claude, 177

Brown, DeForest, 144

Brown, Lee P., 72n

Bundy Report (1967), 125, 127

Bureaucratic control, 9-10, 66, 76, 80, 159-162, 189. *See also* Server-served relationship; Social symmetry

Busing, 125

Buskin, Martin, 126n

CAP. *See* Community Action Program

CDC. *See* Community development corporations

Campbell, Donald T., 39, 41, 183n

Capacity building, 28-29, 141, 144, 153

Caporaso, James A., 181n

Case survey method of research review, 33-34; decentralization sutdies, 37-44; list of case studies, 197-209; list of cities, 229-231; percent responses, 211-229; sources, 195-197; techniques, 34-37

Catholics, 127

Center for Criminal Justice Systems, 85

Centralization, 9-12, 15, 123

Challenge of Crime in a Free Society (Katzenbach Commission), 72n

Charney, Evan, 252-254

Checklist, 34-35, 37, 49

Chicago, 90n, 108n, 110, 112, 142

Cities, case study, listed, 229-231

Citizen boards, 30, 75, 117, 151-152, 162-164; and health services, 93-96, 99-101, 102

Citizen participation, 21-22, 24-25, 29-30, 117, 134, 188; case study, 260-261; and community development corporations, 151-152; and health services, 99-101; and police, 82-83; and service area differences, 162-166

Civil disorders, 69, 109. *See also* Crisis of the 1960s

Clark, Kenneth, 136

Cleveland, 144, 145-148

Client attitudes, 31, 51-53, 57, 61

Client control, 31, 54-56, 57, 61, 160, 161-163, 168, 170, 174-176; and community development corporations, 149, 150, 153; and education, 132, 133, 136; and health services, 101, 102; and police, 77-81. *See also* Community control

Client dimension, 24-26. *See also* Citizen participation

Cluster method of research review, 33

Coleman Report, 124

Columbia University, Bureau of Applied Social Research, 118n

Columbus, Ohio, 145

Community Action Agency, 23

Community Action Program (CAP), 21-23, 24, 30, 108, 113, 119, 143, 144, 166

Community aides, 97

Community control, 22, 23-24, 29, 75; and community development corporations, 153-154; and education, 124-126, 134-136. *See also* Client control

Community development corporations (CDC), 119n, 141-155; and blacks, 142, 144, 155; and capacity building,

267

About the Authors

Robert K. Yin is a senior research psychologist at The Rand Corporation's office in Washington, D.C. and has worked at the New York City-Rand Institute. He received the B.A. in history from Harvard University and the Ph.D. in psychology from the Massachusetts Institute of Technology, where he is also a part-time faculty member in urban studies. Dr. Yin is the editor of *The City in the Seventies*, has published many research articles, and is currently finishing a study on technological innovations in local services, *Tinkering with the System*.

Douglas Yates is an assistant professor of political science at Yale University. He is also Assistant Director of Yale's Institution for Social and Policy Studies. Dr. Yates attended Balliol College Oxford as a Rhodes Scholar and received the Ph.D. from Yale University in 1972. He is the author of *Neighborhood Democracy* which received the 1973 Leonard White Award of the American Political Science Association and is completing a book on urban decision-making entitled *The Ungovernable City*.

Selected List of Rand Books

Averch, Harvey A., et al. *How Effective is Schooling? A Critical Review of Research*. Englewood Cliffs, N.J.: Educational Technology Publications, 1974.

Bagdikian, Ben H. *The Information Machines: Their Impact on Men and the Media*. New York: Harper and Row, 1971.

Bretz, Rudy. *A Taxonomy of Communication Media*. Englewood Cliffs, N.J.: Educational Technology Publications, 1971.

Carpenter-Huffman, P., R.C. Kletter, and R.K. Yin. *Cable Television: Developing Community Services*. New York: Crane, Russak and Company, 1975.

Cohen, Bernard and Jan M. Chaiken. *Police Background Characteristics and Performance*. Lexington, Mass.: Lexington Books, D.C. Heath and Company, 1972.

Dalkey, Norman (ed.) *Studies in the Quality of Life: Delphi and Decision-making*. Lexington, Mass.: Lexington Books, D.C. Heath and Company, 1973.

DeSalvo, Joseph S. (ed.) *Perspectives on Regional Transportation Planning*. Lexington, Mass.: Lexington Books, D.C. Heath and Company, 1973.

Downs, Anthony. *Inside Bureaucracy*. Boston, Mass.: Little, Brown and Company, 1967.

Fisher, Gene H. *Cost Considerations in Systems Analysis*. New York: American Elsevier Publishing Company, 1971.

Jackson, Larry R., and William A. Johnson. *Protest by the Poor: The Welfare Rights Movement in New York City*. Lexington, Mass.: Lexington Books, D.C. Heath and Company, 1974.

Levien, Roger E. (ed.) *The Emerging Technology: Instructional Uses of the Computer in Higher Education*. New York: McGraw-Hill Book Company, 1972.

McKean, Roland N. *Efficiency in Government through Systems Analysis: With Emphasis on Water Resource Development*. New York: John Wiley & Sons, Inc., 1958.

Meyer, John R., Martin Wohl, and John F. Kain. *The Urban Transportation Problem*. Cambridge, Mass.: Harvard University Press, 1965.

Novick, David (ed.) *Program Budgeting: Program Analysis and the Federal Budget*. Cambridge, Mass.: Harvard University Press, 1965.

Pascal, Anthony H. (ed.) *Racial Discrimination in Economic Life*. Lexington, Mass.: Lexington Books, D.C. Heath and Company, 1972.

Pascal, Anthony H. *Thinking about Cities: New Perspectives on Urban Problems*. Belmont, California: Dickenson Publishing Company, 1970.

Pincus, John (ed.) *School Finance in Transition: The Courts and Educational Reform*. Cambridge, Mass.: Ballinger Publishing Company, 1974.

Quade, Edward S., and Wayne I. Boucher. *Systems Analysis and Policy Planning: Applications in Defense*. New York: American Elsevier Publishing Company, 1968.

Sackman, Harold. *Delphi Critique: Expert Opinion, Forecasting, and Group Process*. Lexington, Mass.: Lexington Books, D.C. Heath and Company, 1975.

Sharpe, William F. *The Economics of Computers*. New York: Columbia University Press, 1969.

Williams, John D. *The Compleat Strategyst: Being a Primer on the Theory of Games of Strategy*. New York: McGraw-Hill Book Company, 1954.

Wirt, John G., Arnold J. Lieberman, and Roger E. Levien. *R&D Management*. Lexington, Mass.: Lexington Books, D.C. Heath and Company, 1975.

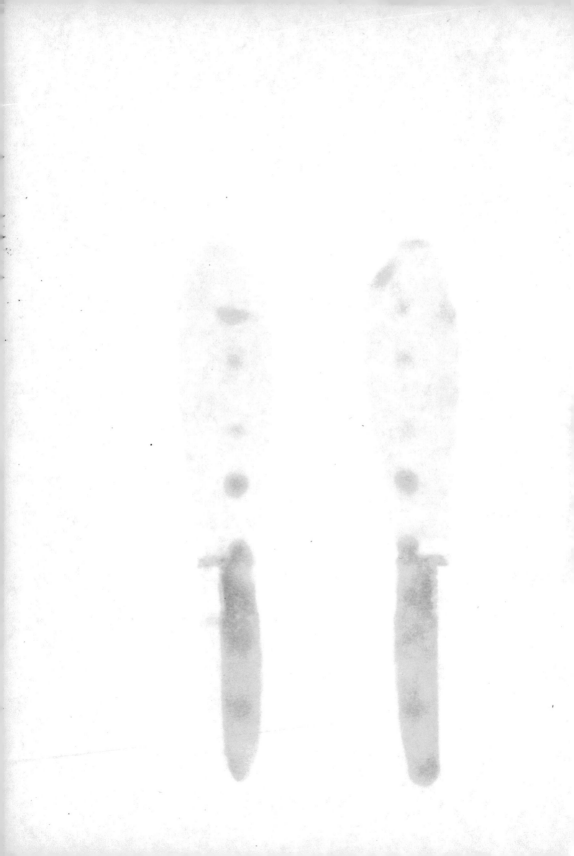